W9-BYV-054

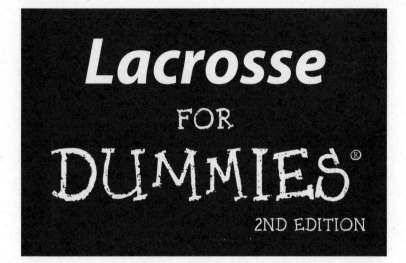

# Lacrosse
## FOR
# DUMMIES®
### 2ND EDITION

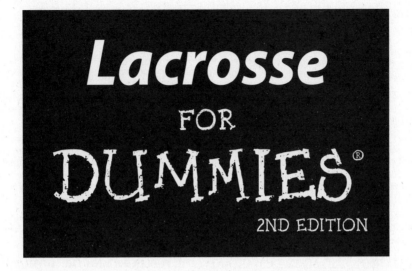

# Lacrosse
## FOR
# DUMMIES®
### 2ND EDITION

**by Jim Hinkson and Joe Lombardi**

John Wiley & Sons Canada, Ltd.

**Lacrosse For Dummies®, 2nd Edition**

Published by
John Wiley & Sons Canada, Ltd.
6045 Freemont Blvd.
Mississauga, ON L5R 4J3
www.wiley.com

For general information on John Wiley & Sons Canada, Ltd., including all books published by Wiley Publishing, Inc., please call our distribution centre at 1-800-567-4797. For reseller information, including discounts and premium sales, please call our sales department at 416-646-7992. For press review copies, author interviews, or other publicity information, please contact our publicity department, Tel. 416-646-4582, Fax 416-236-4448.

Wiley also publishes its books in a variety of electronic formats. Some content that appears in print may not be available in electronic books.

Library and Archives Canada Cataloguing in Publication Data

Hinkson, Jim

Lacrosse for dummies / Jim Hinkson. -- 2nd ed.

ISBN 978-0-470-73855-9

1. Lacrosse. I. Title.

GV989.H55 2010      796.34'7      C2010-900179-6

Printed in the United States

10 9 8 7 6 5 BRR 15

WILEY

# *About the Authors*

**Jim Hinkson:** Jim has been involved in the game of lacrosse since he was 19. He played lacrosse for 11 years and was a member of six Canadian national minor championship teams. He has coached at every level of lacrosse, from house league to professional, participating in two Canadian junior championships, and winning one. He also coached teams in Toronto, Whitby, and St. Catharines, Ontario, as well as the New York Saints and New Jersey Storms, who competed in the National Lacrosse League. Hinkson, who grew up on a farm in Oshawa, Ontario, has authored five books on lacrosse and coaching. Hinkson was the primary author of the first edition of *Lacrosse For Dummies,* which focused mainly on box lacrosse.

**Joe Lombardi:** Joe is one of the most established, respected, and versatile multimedia journalists in the New York/New Jersey/Connecticut tri-state area. He has worked as an editor and reporter for daily and weekly newspapers; as a writer for national magazines; as a host, announcer, and analyst on television and radio; and as associate publisher and contributor for several sports-related Web sites, including Rivals.com, CBS MaxPreps (www.maxpreps.com), and LaxLessons.com.

One constant throughout Joe's career has been his work on the lacrosse scene. He was a fixture on the scene during the sport's rapid growth. A New York City native, Joe grew up in historic Irvington in New York's Hudson Valley region. In 2008, he was named Man of the Year by the Lacrosse Coaches Association of Section 1 (Westchester, Rockland, Putnam, and Dutchess counties in New York). A graduate of the University of Dayton in Ohio, Joe is the primary author of *Lacrosse For Dummies,* 2nd Edition.

# Dedication

For Chuck Howard, a sports broadcasting pioneer, who taught me about lacrosse and broadcasting, and who would've loved to have seen the popularity the sport he loved now enjoys.

—Joe Lombardi

# Authors' Acknowledgments

**Jim Hinkson:** Thanks to my former teammates, players, and friends in lacrosse who have touched my life as I journeyed along my whirlwind lacrosse path. From Oshawa to Brooklin to Detroit to Peterborough to Windsor to Philadelphia to Rexdale to Whitby to St. Catharines to New York to Toronto to New Jersey, it has been a great ride with lots of ups and downs.

**Joe Lombardi:** I've watched and covered hundreds of men's and women's lacrosse games, but writing this book allowed me to enjoy a true first: I became a student of the game. Many thanks to the countless coaches and players for all their invaluable insights and for their eagerness and openness to help. I am especially grateful to Joe Alberici, Ric Beardsley, Kristen Carano Bulkley, Paul Carcaterra, Roy Colsey, Tom Interlicchio, and Brian Logue for going above and beyond in sharing their knowledge with me. Special thanks to two former Loyola University (Maryland) standouts, Jordan and Ryan Rabidou, for allowing me access to the valuable drills, practice plans, and plays that are now on display at LaxLessons.com. And finally, I'm indebted to my friend and colleague, Jim Stout, of CBS MaxPreps for generously providing photographs (taken by Stout and Ray Nelson) that are published in this new edition of *Lacrosse For Dummies*.

## Publisher's Acknowledgments

We're proud of this book; please send us your comments through our online registration form located at http://dummies.custhelp.com. For other comments, please contact our Customer Care Department within the U.S. at 877-762-2974, outside the U.S. at 317-572-3993, or fax 317-572-4002.

Some of the people who helped bring this book to market include the following:

*Acquisitions and Editorial*

**Vice-President Publishing Services:** Karen Bryan

**Editor:** Robert Hickey

**Project Manager:** Alison MacLean

**Senior Project Coordinator:** Elizabeth McCurdy

**Project Editor:** Elizabeth Kuball

**Copy Editor:** Elizabeth Kuball

**Technical Editors:** Joe Alberici, Kristen Carano Bulkley, and Brian Logue

**Editorial Assistant:** Katey Wolsley

**Cartoons:** Rich Tennant (www.the5thwave.com)

**Cover Photo:** iStock/kmlsphotos

*Composition Services*

**Senior Project Coordinator, U.S.:** Lynsey Stanford

**Layout and Graphics:** Joyce Haughey, Ronald G. Terry, Timothy C. Detrick

**Proofreaders:** John Greenough, Lisa Stiers

**Indexer:** Ty Koontz

---

**John Wiley & Sons Canada, Ltd.**

    **Bill Zerter,** Chief Operating Officer

    **Jennifer Smith,** Vice-President and Publisher, Professional & Trade Division

**Publishing and Editorial for Consumer Dummies**

    **Diane Graves Steele,** Vice President and Publisher, Consumer Dummies

    **Kristin Ferguson-Wagstaffe,** Product Development Director, Consumer Dummies

    **Ensley Eikenburg,** Associate Publisher, Travel

    **Kelly Regan,** Editorial Director, Travel

**Composition Services**

    **Debbie Stailey,** Director of Composition Services

# Contents at a Glance

*Foreword* ..................................................... *xxv*

*Introduction* ................................................. 1

*Part I: Getting Started* ..................................... 7

Chapter 1: Lacrosse and You ............................................. 9
Chapter 2: Suiting Up: Buying the Right Equipment ............... 17
Chapter 3: Meeting the Team .......................................... 27
Chapter 4: Laying Down the (Lacrosse) Law ....................... 43

*Part II: Playing Lacrosse* .................................. 63

Chapter 5: Getting the Ball into the Goal: Developing Offensive Skills .... 65
Chapter 6: Putting the Ball in the Goal: Shooting Fundamentals ........... 89
Chapter 7: Keeping the Ball out of the Goal: Developing Defensive Skills ... 101
Chapter 8: Goaltending ................................................ 115
Chapter 9: The Possession Game ..................................... 125
Chapter 10: Practicing Team Offense and Defense ................ 139
Chapter 11: Calling on the Special Forces: Specialty Teams ..... 157
Chapter 12: Becoming a Better Lacrosse Player — Physically and Mentally ... 171

*Part III: Coaching Lacrosse* .............................. 195

Chapter 13: Fundamentals of Coaching Lacrosse ................. 197
Chapter 14: Developing Your Coaching Philosophy for the Offense .... 207
Chapter 15: Coaching Defensively .................................. 231

*Part IV: Following Lacrosse: The Fan's Point of View* .... 247

Chapter 16: How to Watch Lacrosse ................................ 249
Chapter 17: Getting in the Game .................................... 263
Chapter 18: Keeping Up with the Pros ............................. 271

*Part V: The Part of Tens* ................................. 283

Chapter 19: Ten of the Greatest Men's and Women's Lacrosse Players .... 285
Chapter 20: Ten Reasons to Get Excited about Lacrosse .......... 289
Chapter 21: Ten Interesting Facts about Lacrosse ................ 293
Glossary ............................................................... 297
Appendix: Resources .................................................. 307

*Index* ....................................................... 313

# Table of Contents

Foreword.................................................................xxv

Introduction ............................................... 1

About This Book...........................................................1
Conventions Used in This Book......................................1
What You're Not to Read................................................2
Foolish Assumptions......................................................3
How This Book Is Organized ..........................................3
    Part I: Getting Started...........................................3
    Part II: Playing Lacrosse.......................................4
    Part III: Coaching Lacrosse ..................................4
    Part IV: Following Lacrosse: The Fan's Point of View .....4
    Part V: The Part of Tens.......................................4
Icons Used in This Book ................................................5
Where to Go from Here..................................................6

Part 1: Getting Started........................................ 7

Chapter 1: Lacrosse and You . . . . . . . . . . . . . . . . . . . . . . . . .9

Understanding the Game of Lacrosse..............................9
    The two forms of lacrosse: Field and box...............10
    Mars and Venus: How the men's and women's games differ .........11
Lacrosse: A Player's Game............................................12
    Playing offense: Stick skills and shooting..............13
    Defending: The do's and don'ts .............................13
    The goalie's goal: Keeping the ball out of the net...........14
    Possession is nine-tenths of the (lacrosse) law.............14
    Using specialty teams to your advantage................14
    Getting physical ................................................15
Coaches' Corner ........................................................15
From a Fan's Perspective..............................................16

Chapter 2: Suiting Up: Buying the Right Equipment. . . . . . . . . . . . . . .17

The Tools of the Trade: The Ball and the Stick .............17
    The ball..............................................................18
    The stick............................................................18
        Stick head...............................................19
        Stick length ............................................20
        Stick handle............................................20

From Head to Toe: Putting on the Equipment ..................................21
    Gloves ......................................................................................23
    Shoulder pads, arm guards, and elbow pads ...................................23
    Rib or kidney pads ....................................................................23
    Helmets ....................................................................................24
    Mouth guards ............................................................................24
    Running shoes ..........................................................................24
Supporting Your Kid's Body ....................................................24

**Chapter 3: Meeting the Team . . . . . . . . . . . . . . . . . . . . . . . . . . . . . . . .27**

Introducing the Field Lacrosse Players ...........................................27
    Putting the ball in the net: The attackmen ..................................29
        Feeders ................................................................................29
        Finishers ..............................................................................29
    Playing offense and defense: The midfielders ..............................29
    The first line of defense: Close defensemen ................................30
    Saving the day and keeping the ball in play: Goaltenders ............31
Introducing the Box Lacrosse Players ...............................................32
    Hanging out with the goalie: The creasemen ................................33
    Cutting corners: The cornermen ................................................34
    Directing floor activity: The pointman ........................................36
    Defending the net: The goaltender ..............................................36
    Defending the floor: The defensive players ................................37
Carrying the Offense: Keys for the Offensive Player ..........................37
    Practicing efficient stick handling ............................................38
        Catching ..............................................................................38
        Cradling ..............................................................................38
        Passing ................................................................................39
        Shooting ..............................................................................39
    Moving — with and without the ball ..........................................39
    Knowing where the ball is at all times ........................................40
Focusing on Defense: Keys for the Defensive Player ..........................40
    Establishing your position ........................................................40
    Using (or not using) the stick ....................................................41
Defending the Goal: Keys for the Goaltender ....................................41
    Taking your optimum goal position ............................................42
    Building up your save repertoire ................................................42
    Starting the offense ..................................................................42

**Chapter 4: Laying Down the (Lacrosse) Law . . . . . . . . . . . . . . . . . . . . . .43**

Field of Dreams: Playing Field Lacrosse ..........................................43
    Examining the field ....................................................................44
    Keeping the field game moving ..................................................45
    Substituting players ..................................................................46
    Unraveling penalties and physical play ......................................46
Box of Dreams? Inside the Boards in a Lacrosse Arena ....................48

Understanding the Game's Participants and Their Roles ........................50
    Introducing tonight's players ...............................................50
    Leading the team: The coach's role ........................................52
    Officials: The men in black...................................................52
Starting and Stopping Play and Everything in Between .......................53
Officiating Lacrosse...............................................................54
    Knowing what it takes to be a good official..............................54
    Looking at the different types of officials ................................55
    Managing the games within the game .....................................55
The Fine Print: All the Rules You Need to Know ...............................56
    Playing the game...............................................................57
    Losing possession on game violations......................................58
    Paying for penalties ...........................................................58

*Part II: Playing Lacrosse* .................................... *63*

**Chapter 5: Getting the Ball into the Goal:**
**Developing Offensive Skills. . . . . . . . . . . . . . . . . . . . . . . . . . . . .65**
Grasping Basic Stick-Handling Skills ...........................................65
    Getting a grip....................................................................66
    Cradling the ball................................................................66
Beyond Handling: Catching the Ball.............................................69
    How to position your body for the catch ..................................69
    Give and you shall receive the catch ......................................70
What's the Catch? Building Your Passing Skills ...............................70
    Positioning your body for the pass ........................................72
    Gripping the stick for the pass..............................................72
    Moving the stick forward with the pass....................................72
    Remembering the keys to good passing ...................................73
Working on Passing and Catching Drills.........................................74
    Individual passing drills ......................................................75
        1-on-0 form passing.......................................................75
        1-on-0 stationary passing ...............................................75
    Partner passing drills .........................................................76
        2-on-0 stationary passing drills .........................................76
        2-on-0 stationary timed passing ........................................77
        2-on-0 stationary passing with two balls...............................77
        2-on-1 "monkey in the middle" ..........................................77
        2-on-0 passing on the run................................................77
    Team passing drills.............................................................77
        Knockout drill...............................................................77
        Pepper drill ..................................................................78
        Zigzag drill...................................................................78

Beating the Defender: Moving with the Ball..................................................78
  Protecting the ball in the stick.........................................................78
  Taking a check.......................................................................78
  Dodging .............................................................................79
    Face dodge .......................................................................80
    Split dodge ......................................................................80
    Roll dodge .......................................................................80
    Bull dodge .......................................................................81
    Question-mark dodge ..............................................................81
Cutting: Moving without the Ball.......................................................81
Practicing Individual Offensive Drills.................................................83
  Individual cradling drills...........................................................83
    1-on-0 stationary cradling .......................................................83
    1-on-0 fake shot..................................................................83
  Stick-handling drills with a partner ...............................................83
  Protecting-the-ball-in-the-stick drills ............................................84
    1-on-1 circle drill...............................................................84
    1-on-2 circle drill...............................................................84
  Taking-a-check drills...............................................................84
    Shoot-through drill...............................................................84
    1-on-1 bump drill.................................................................84
    1-on-1 charging defender drill ...................................................85
    1-on-1 equalize pressure .........................................................85
    1-on-1 man-in-the-middle drill....................................................85
  Beating-a-defender drills...........................................................86
    1-on-1 offensive-move progression ................................................86
    Gauntlet drill....................................................................86
    1-on-1 offense from a stationary start with
      a cross-field pass .............................................................86
    1-on-1 live half-field drill......................................................86
    1-on-1 off the bench .............................................................87
    1-on-1 game ......................................................................87
  Taking shots after beating a defender..............................................88

**Chapter 6: Putting the Ball in the Goal: Shooting Fundamentals ....89**
Becoming a Great Shooter...............................................................89
  Acquiring a shooter's stick.........................................................90
  Getting the ball past the goalie ...................................................90
  Focusing on form ...................................................................91
  Resolving shooting problems.........................................................91
Shooting from a Long Distance..........................................................92
  Knowing the two best areas to shoot long............................................95
  Nailing the overhand shot ..........................................................95
Shooting Closer to the Goal ...........................................................96
  Developing a great fake.............................................................96
  Becoming a good close-in shooter....................................................97

Practicing Shooting Drills ............................................................. 97
    Focusing on long-ball shooting drills ................................................ 98
        Single-line drill .............................................................................. 98
        Semicircle long-ball shooting drill ............................................ 98
        Two-line shooting drills ................................................................ 98
    Working on close-in shooting drills .................................................. 99
        Single-line drill ............................................................................ 100
        2-on-0 shooting drill .................................................................... 100
        2-on-0 passing drill ...................................................................... 100

**Chapter 7: Keeping the Ball out of the Goal:**
**Developing Defensive Skills** . . . . . . . . . . . . . . . . . . . . . . . . . . . .**101**
    Stopping the Ball: Taking On the Stick Handler ............................ 101
        Communicating with your teammates ...................................... 101
        Playing with your feet .................................................................. 102
        Playing with your head ................................................................ 103
        Establishing effective defensive positioning ............................ 104
        Playing hard and with heart ...................................................... 105
        Defending the field of play .......................................................... 105
    Stopping the Player: Defending Offensive Players without the Ball ..... 107
        Off-ball-side defending ................................................................ 107
        Ball-side defending ...................................................................... 108
        Moving before the ball ................................................................ 108
    Drills to Build Your Defensive Skills ............................................ 109
        Developing defensive agility ...................................................... 109
        Drills for defending the stick handler ...................................... 110
            1-on-1 defensive progression .................................................. 110
            1-on-1 closing-out drill .............................................................. 111
            1-on-1 steal-the-ball drill .......................................................... 111
            2-on-1 fight-through-pick drill .................................................. 111
        Drills for defending other offensive players .......................... 112
            2-on-1 denying man on ball side or off-ball side ................ 112
            1-on-1 multiple defensive teaching drill ................................ 112

**Chapter 8: Goaltending** . . . . . . . . . . . . . . . . . . . . . . . . . . . . . . . . . .**115**
    Recognizing What It Takes to Play in Goal .................................... 116
        Focus ................................................................................................ 116
        Desire ................................................................................................ 117
        Stick-to-itiveness .......................................................................... 117
        Communication .............................................................................. 117
    The Basics of Goaltending ................................................................ 118
        Where it all starts: The ready stance ...................................... 118
        Staying centered ............................................................................ 119
        Following the ball .......................................................................... 119

Challenging the shooter................................................120
Communicating with the defense .............................122
Anticipating what's going to happen next ......................123
Making the Reflex Save ..................................................123
The Goalie on Offense....................................................123

## Chapter 9: The Possession Game ...........................125

The Art of the Faceoff ....................................................126
X marks the spot.........................................................126
Techniques of the trade............................................128
Faceoff fundamentals ...............................................129
Ground-Ball Wars.............................................................132
When ground balls happen.......................................133
How to make a ground ball yours ...........................133
What to do after you gain possession ...................135
Riding High .......................................................................135
Why rides matter .......................................................136
The most effective ride techniques........................136
Clearing Things Up ..........................................................137
Understanding why clears are crucial ....................137
Starting with the goalie ...........................................138

## Chapter 10: Practicing Team Offense and Defense ...............139

How the Players Fit In: Roles and Positions in Team
Offenses and Defenses ...............................................139
The attackman's role..................................................140
The midfielder's role .................................................140
Practicing a Team Offensive Philosophy.......................142
Keep it simple.............................................................143
Balance freedom and structure ..............................143
Attack! Attack! ...........................................................144
Focus on good shot selection...................................145
Building the Team Offense through Drills.....................146
Zero passing ...............................................................146
Quarterback drill........................................................146
Ball perimeter work...................................................147
X shooting drill...........................................................147
Practicing a Team Defensive Philosophy ......................148
Communicating on the field .....................................149
Pressuring the stick handler ....................................150
Forcing the ball ..........................................................152
When the ball is at the top side...............................152
When the ball is in the corner .................................152
Defending picks: To switch or not to switch.................153
Defending screens on the ball side: To switch
or not to switch, part 2.........................................154

Building the Team Defense through Drills ..............................................155
2-on-1 defending the pick-and-roll on the ball..............................155
4-on-4 shell drill to practice defensive positioning .....................156
3-on-2 help-side defense.....................................................................156

**Chapter 11: Calling on the Special Forces: Specialty Teams ......157**
Operating When You Have a Player Advantage ......................................158
Practicing patience on the man-up/power play...........................158
Aligning your players on the man-up/power play ........................159
Singling out good man-up/power-play players ............................159
Running set plays in the man-up/power-play offense.................160
Crease pass and shoot ...............................................................161
3-3 set with a screen ..................................................................162
1-4-1 ................................................................................................162
Roll with the rotation..................................................................163
Wide 2-2-2 set................................................................................164
3-3 camouflage .............................................................................164
Playing defense on the man-up/power play ...............................167
Defending at a Disadvantage: The Man-Down/Man-Short Defense .......168
Building your man-down/man-short defense...............................168
Playing offense on the man-down/man-short..............................170
Running man-down/man-short drills.............................................170
Rotation drill...............................................................................170
Delay drill ....................................................................................170

**Chapter 12: Becoming a Better Lacrosse Player —**
**Physically and Mentally ...................................171**
Understanding the Benefits of Being in Condition ..............................172
Stretching to Be Your Best .....................................................................173
How to stretch....................................................................................173
Stretching exercises for lacrosse....................................................174
Back stretches .............................................................................174
Leg stretches ...............................................................................175
Hamstring and quad stretches .................................................175
Abdomen and groin stretches ..................................................176
Stretching your neck and shoulders.......................................177
Running for Top Physical Conditioning.................................................178
Off-season and pre-season conditioning.......................................178
Long-distance and endurance conditioning ..........................178
Sprint conditioning .....................................................................179
In-season conditioning ......................................................................179
Conditioning drills without a ball ...........................................181
Conditioning drills with a ball .................................................182

Improving Your Quickness and Agility ........................................ 183

Offensive drills .......................................................................... 183

Defensive drills............................................................................ 184

Footwork drills ...................................................................... 184

The wave drill ........................................................................ 184

The shadow drill ................................................................... 184

Defensive square drills ........................................................ 184

Getting into Shape with Weights ................................................. 185

Mentally Preparing for Lacrosse ................................................ 188

Setting goals ............................................................................... 189

Practicing relaxation ................................................................. 189

Relaxing with a proper attitude........................................... 190

Relaxing by tightening and relaxing your muscles ............ 190

Relaxing with deep breathing............................................... 190

Visualizing your way to success ............................................... 191

Paying attention to self-talk ..................................................... 191

Controlling your emotions......................................................... 192

Focusing on the game................................................................. 192

Focusing on what you're doing ........................................... 193

Trying not to force concentration ....................................... 193

Focusing on the positive ...................................................... 193

Blocking out distractions..................................................... 193

Energizing yourself going into a game .................................... 194

## *Part III: Coaching Lacrosse* ........................................ *195*

### **Chapter 13: Fundamentals of Coaching Lacrosse** ............... 197

Determining Your Team's Style of Play ...................................... 197

Building Your Team....................................................................... 199

Developing a Game Plan .............................................................. 200

Understanding your opponent................................................... 200

Concentrating on defense........................................................... 201

Focusing on offense..................................................................... 201

Coaching Lacrosse to Kids: What You Need to Succeed........... 201

Being a good teacher ................................................................... 202

Instilling confidence .................................................................... 202

Practicing patience ..................................................................... 203

Fostering commitment ................................................................ 203

Building Team Unity: All for One, and One for All...................... 203

Recognizing What Gives Your Team the Edge............................ 204

### **Chapter 14: Developing Your Coaching Philosophy for the Offense** .... 207

Understanding the General Principles of Lacrosse Playing Systems ...... 208

Looking at offensive playing systems....................................... 208

Fast-break offense ................................................................. 208

Slow-down offense ................................................................ 208

Keeping the system simple......................................................... 209

Setting Up the Offense ...................................................... 211
Playing to your strengths on offense ......................... 211
Establishing your offensive formation ........................ 212
Executing your offensive system .............................. 213
Attacking the Zone Defense with a Zone Offense ............... 214
Understanding why teams play zone defense ............... 215
Recognizing the weaknesses of zone defenses ............. 216
Grasping zone-offense principles .............................. 216
Moving the ball ......................................... 217
Aligning in the gaps .................................. 217
Moving the players .................................... 217
Making sure the stick handler penetrates ......... 218
Attacking from the side of the offense ............ 218
Being ready to shoot ................................. 218
Being aggressive ...................................... 218
Defending the defenders ............................. 218
Running a Penetration Man-to-Man Offense ..................... 219
Knowing when to go one-on-one .............................. 219
Opening up penetration with outside shots ................. 220
Running set plays for a penetration offense ................ 220
Mastering the Motion Man-to-Man Offense ...................... 221
Passing to keep the offense (and defense) in motion ...... 221
Moving without the ball ......................................... 222
Cutting through the middle .......................... 222
Getting open for a pass .............................. 223
Setting picks: Forcing the defense to create openings ........ 223
Running the give-and-go play .................................. 224
Running the pick-and-roll play ................................ 224
Running Set Plays in Your Man-to-Man Offense ................ 225
Breaking Out on the Quick: The Fast-Break Offense ........... 227
Offensive Principles for the Women's Game ..................... 228

**Chapter 15: Coaching Defensively** ...................... **231**
Choosing Your Defensive Playing System ....................... 231
Going Head to Head: Playing a Man-to-Man Defense .......... 233
Recognizing the types of man-to-man defenses .............. 233
Ball-oriented man-to-man defense ................... 233
Man-oriented man-to-man defense .................. 234
Combination man-to-man ............................. 234
Playing both ways in the man-to-man defense .............. 235
Applying pressure in the man-to-man defense .............. 236
Forcing defensive action to get an offensive reaction ...... 236
Concentrating on getting the job done ....................... 237
Helping: Slides and rotations .................................. 238
Using the man-to-man defense in game situations .......... 238
Defending the off-ball pick-and-roll ................ 238
Defending a player standing in the middle of the field ....... 239
Defending the give-and-go play ..................... 239
Defending the odd-man break situation ............ 240

Defending the Zone .................................................................... 241
    Understanding the zone defense philosophy ........................ 241
    Containing the stick handler with a double-team ................. 243
Defense in the Women's Game ................................................... 244
    Emphasizing body positioning
        and footwork .................................................................. 244
    Everyone's a defender ......................................................... 246

## Part IV: Following Lacrosse: The Fan's Point of View .......... 247

### Chapter 16: How to Watch Lacrosse ..................................... 249

It All Looks a Little Familiar . . . ............................................... 249
    Recognizing the game's similarities to hockey ..................... 250
    Recognizing the game's similarities to basketball ................ 251
Knowing What to Watch For ....................................................... 253
    Watching the offense .......................................................... 254
        Getting open .................................................................. 254
        Executing plays ............................................................. 254
        Controlling the tempo .................................................... 254
        Pressing on the man-up .................................................. 255
    Watching the defense .......................................................... 255
        Forcing turnovers .......................................................... 255
        Forcing missed shots ..................................................... 256
        Going after ground balls ................................................ 256
    Watching the goalie ............................................................ 256
        Playing the angles ......................................................... 257
        Relying on reflexes ....................................................... 257
        Releasing the ball .......................................................... 257
    Watching the game action ................................................... 257
        Winning the faceoff ....................................................... 257
        Noting substitution patterns .......................................... 258
        Monitoring injuries ........................................................ 258
        Spying on the fans ......................................................... 258
    Closing out the game ........................................................... 258
Following Lacrosse on Television ............................................... 259
    Professional lacrosse .......................................................... 260
    NCAA lacrosse ................................................................... 260
    High school lacrosse ........................................................... 261

### Chapter 17: Getting in the Game ......................................... 263

High School Highlights .............................................................. 263
College Corner ......................................................................... 265
Introducing Minor-Level Box Lacrosse in Canada ........................ 267

### Chapter 18: Keeping Up with the Pros . . . . . . . . . . . . . . . . . . . . . .271

Everything You Need to Know about Major League Lacrosse ............271
  League basics ....................................................................................272
  The top players .................................................................................273
Everything You Need to Know about the National Lacrosse League......276
  League basics ....................................................................................276
  The top players .................................................................................280

## Part V: The Part of Tens . . . . . . . . . . . . . . . . . . . . . . . . . . . . 283

### Chapter 19: Ten of the Greatest Men's and Women's
### Lacrosse Players . . . . . . . . . . . . . . . . . . . . . . . . . . . . . . . . . . . .285

Jen Adams...............................................................................................285
Kelly Amonte Hiller ..............................................................................285
Jim Brown ...............................................................................................286
Roy Colsey .............................................................................................286
Gary Gait ................................................................................................286
Paul Gait..................................................................................................287
Tom Marechek ........................................................................................287
Dave Pietramala.....................................................................................287
Casey Powell ..........................................................................................288
Mikey Powell ..........................................................................................288
More Lacrosse Greats ...........................................................................288

### Chapter 20: Ten Reasons to Get Excited about Lacrosse . . . . . . . . .289

Lacrosse Is a Magical Game to Watch.................................................289
Lacrosse Is Simple to Play but Hard to Learn....................................290
Lacrosse Is Fast Paced...........................................................................290
Lacrosse Is High Scoring........................................................................290
Lacrosse Has a Great Feel — Literally .................................................291
Lacrosse Is a Fair-Weather Friend .......................................................291
Lacrosse Is a Community Game.............................................................291
Lacrosse Welcomes New Players ..........................................................292
Lacrosse Breeds Respect .......................................................................292
Lacrosse Creates Atmosphere...............................................................292

### Chapter 21: Ten Interesting Facts about Lacrosse . . . . . . . . . . . . . .293

Lacrosse Is the Oldest Team Sport in North America ........................293
"The Father of Lacrosse" Was a Dentist ..............................................294
The First Women to Play Lacrosse Were Scottish ..............................294
New York University Fielded the First College Lacrosse Team............294
Lacrosse Made Its Olympic Debut in 1904 ..........................................295

Body Contact Wasn't Allowed in Men's Lacrosse until the 1930s......... 295
The Mann Cup Was Originally Awarded to Field Lacrosse Teams ....... 295
Lacrosse Didn't Go Pro until the 1980s..................................................... 295
A Super Bowl Coach Has Roots in Lacrosse ........................................... 296
Lacrosse Is a Hit in Movies and on TV..................................................... 296

**Glossary** . . . . . . . . . . . . . . . . . . . . . . . . . . . . . . . . . . . . . . . . . . . . . . **.297**

**Appendix: Resources** . . . . . . . . . . . . . . . . . . . . . . . . . . . . . . . . . **.307**
Magazines ....................................................................................................... 307
Web Sites ......................................................................................................... 308
Television ........................................................................................................ 309
Organizations ................................................................................................. 310

*Index* . . . . . . . . . . . . . . . . . . . . . . . . . . . . . . . . . . . . . . . . . . . . . . . . . *313*

# Foreword

. . . . . . . . . . . . . . . . . . . . . . . . . . . . . . . . . . . . . . . . . . . . . . . . . . . . .

*M*y first memory of lacrosse is from when I was an 11-year-old boy. My father and I walked down to the local high school to practice pitching on the baseball diamond. Before long, my attention wandered to the football field, where a game I had never seen before was being played. At first, I had trouble following the game. But soon I began to appreciate how the ball was passed from player to player with great speed and accuracy. Over and over, this same process was repeated until, finally, a player was close enough to the goal to take a shot.

That is the game of lacrosse, my father told me. Well, needless to say, baseball practice was over for me — not for the day, not for the summer, but forever. I had to play this game. And so it began — my love affair with North America's greatest and fastest game. I was hooked by the speed, the contact, the strategy. And I'm sure that a million lacrosse players the world over have experienced something similar. To see this game is to love it.

With its unique style, rules, and following, lacrosse is a truly amazing sport. It's a combination of many sports: You can see bits and pieces of football, hockey, soccer, and basketball in a lacrosse game — hard, physical contact; shooting on goal; running up and down the field at high speed; and offensive and defensive strategy.

Lacrosse is an amazing combination of some of the greatest team games in the world, and, as such, it has quickly become one of the fastest growing sports around. When I started playing, a handful of lacrosse hotbeds existed in the United States: Maryland, upstate New York, and New York's Hudson Valley, where I'm from. Those hotbeds were where the game was played at its highest level among high school and youth teams. Today, lacrosse has exploded into a national phenomenon. Teams from Texas, Florida, California, and Colorado are among the many competing at the high school and youth level. Colleges are adding both men's and women's teams. Why has lacrosse grown so quickly? Watch one game, my friend — just watch one game. You'll be hooked, too.

Roy Colsey

Three-time first-team All-American and Division I Midfielder of the Year and member of two national championship teams at Syracuse University; four-time Major League Lacrosse All-Star, National Lacrosse League All-Star

# Introduction

· · · · · · · · · · · · · · · · · · · · · · · · · · · · · · · · · · · · · · · · ·

*L*acrosse is the fastest growing sport in North America, with the record number of players and fans in field lacrosse now spearheading that growth. In this book, we explore the reasons for this surge in participation and fan interest, but if you've ever been to a game — or better yet, if you play or coach lacrosse — you already know the reasons.

In a nutshell, lacrosse features the physicality of football, the speed and quickness of hockey, and the passing and transitions of basketball. Anyone can play this sport — from shorter people with speed and quickness to bigger people with strength and power. And after you start, it's very tough to stop. Lacrosse is habit forming.

## About This Book

The first edition of *Lacrosse For Dummies* emphasized box lacrosse. In this edition, we shift the focus to field lacrosse, but we still offer plenty of information and insights on box as well. Both editions have one important thing in common: Like the first edition, this book is for players, coaches, and fans at all levels of lacrosse.

The beauty of *For Dummies* books is that you can use them to find what you need to know, without having to wade through a bunch of stuff you don't care about. Just pick up the book and start reading anywhere you want. Sure, you can read it from front to back, but you don't have to — you can read each chapter on its own, without feeling like you're in the dark.

## Conventions Used in This Book

We don't use many special conventions in this book, but be aware of the following:

- ✔ When we introduce a new term, we put it in *italics* and define it shortly thereafter (often in parentheses).

✔ When we give you a list of steps to take in a particular order, we put the actionable part of the step in **bold** so you can easily find what you're supposed to do.

✔ When we mention Web addresses and e-mail addresses, we put those in `monofont` so they stand out from the surrounding text.

When this book was printed, some Web addresses may have needed to break across two lines of text. If that happened, rest assured that we haven't put in any extra characters (such as hyphens) to indicate the break. So, when using one of these Web addresses, just type in exactly what you see in this book, pretending as though the line break doesn't exist.

Throughout the book, when we refer to *box lacrosse,* we're talking about the version of the game that is most popular in Canada and that is played exclusively indoors — with fewer players per team and a reduced playing surface. Field lacrosse can be played either outdoors or indoors, so, for that reason, we don't use the terms *indoor lacrosse* or *outdoor lacrosse.*

Finally, despite the male-oriented names of positions — such as attackman and defenseman — most of the information found in this book applies to all lacrosse players, male and female. When distinct differences exist between men's lacrosse and women's lacrosse, we make sure to note them.

# What You're Not to Read

If you're short on time, you'll be glad to know that you don't have to read everything to get the information you need. You can safely skip sidebars (text in gray boxes); they're interesting, but not essential to your understanding of the topic at hand. You can also skip anything marked with the Technical Stuff icon (see "Icons Used in This Book," later, for more information).

# Foolish Assumptions

When we wrote this book, we made a few assumptions about who you are. You probably fall into one of the following categories:

- ✔ You know nothing about lacrosse, but you saw it being played somewhere and it piqued your interest. You want to know more.

- ✔ You already play lacrosse, but you want to improve. You're looking for techniques and strategies you can use to up your game.

- ✔ You're a parent whose son or daughter has started playing lacrosse. You want to know what to expect from your kid's coach, and what exactly those kids are doing when they're out on the field.

- ✔ You're a coach who wants to read about drills that other coaches run to improve their teams.

# How This Book Is Organized

*Lacrosse For Dummies,* 2nd Edition, is presented in five parts, starting with the basics of the game — such as the ball and stick, the number of players, the equipment used, and the way the game is played. The rest of the book moves through how to watch the game, how to become a player, how to coach lacrosse, and how to follow the game. So this book can be whatever you want it to be — simple and basic or in depth.

## Part 1: Getting Started

This part gives you a good idea of what the basic game of lacrosse is all about, breaking the game down into simple terms and discussing the different player roles and positions, as well as some particulars about how the game is played. This part also discusses lacrosse equipment and how to get dressed so that you're well protected — a necessity in this sport. Finally, it gives you an overview of officiating, so you know what those guys in black-and-white stripes mean when they wave their arms around.

# Part II: Playing Lacrosse

How do you score goals and prevent them from being scored? Those are the two most simple, yet most critical, aspects of lacrosse. In this part, we take an in-depth look at both — providing information that helps you develop offensive and defensive skills. We also take an up-close-and-personal look at what it takes to play goalie. We break down all the key components of two of the most important parts of lacrosse — the possession game and specialty teams. Finally, we tell you what you need to know to become a better player — both mentally and physically.

# Part III: Coaching Lacrosse

Here, you discover the fundamentals of coaching lacrosse, including building a team and preparing for games and practices. We also tell you how a coach *game coaches,* from setting up an offensive system to establishing a defensive system and then applying these systems to certain situations in a game. We also look at specific offensive formations, as well as specific defensive sets.

# Part IV: Following Lacrosse: The Fan's Point of View

Are you new to the game? In this part, we tell you what you should look for when watching lacrosse — offense, defense, you name it. We also cover how and where you can follow all levels of lacrosse on TV. Then we take an in-depth look at "the surge," which in this case, refers to the continuing growth in the popularity of the game. At many colleges and high schools, lacrosse's popularity is hardly a new phenomenon, so we fill you in on the most tradition-rich high school and college programs. Finally, we tell you everything you need to know about the two pro leagues — Major League Lacrosse and the National Lacrosse League.

# Part V: The Part of Tens

This essential part of every *For Dummies* book is fun because it includes our list of the top lacrosse players of all time. Now, considering the fact that this list includes men and women, field lacrosse players and box lacrosse players, you can look at this chapter as the starting point of discussions — and arguments. We also give you ten reasons to get excited about lacrosse (as if you needed them!), as well as ten interesting facts about the game.

In the back of this book, we include a couple of resources to share some of the nuts and bolts of lacrosse with you. To understand the game, you have to understand the language of lacrosse, so we include a glossary of lacrosse vocabulary. And the appendix offers some resources for more information on lacrosse, including magazines, Web sites, and organizations.

# Icons Used in This Book

Every *For Dummies* book has icons in the margins, to draw attention to important tidbits and valuable advice. *Lacrosse For Dummies* uses the following icons:

The Tip icon points you to what some of the best players and coaches have to say about the game and how they play and coach it. Anytime you see this icon, you're sure to find suggestions that will help improve your play.

The Remember icon points out important information that you want to remember.

The Warning icon offers some cautionary words about potential safety concerns and other dangers that you may face when playing or coaching lacrosse.

Need to know why something happens the way it does in lacrosse? The Technical Stuff icon alerts you to information that you can choose to read or skip. It's not necessary to your understanding of the material, but it sure is interesting!

Whenever we give you information specific to the women's game, we flag it with this icon.

Plenty of differences exist between the game of box lacrosse (which is played indoors) and the game of field lacrosse (which is typically played outdoors, but can also be played inside). This icon helps you sort out the details.

# *Where to Go from Here*

If you're a beginner or a fan, you may want to turn to the glossary of lacrosse terms and their definitions at the back of this book. Or start with Chapters 3 and 4, where we cover the fundamentals of the game. If you're a parent and new to the sport, turn to Chapter 13 and read about youth lacrosse and coaching. If you're a spectator, Chapter 16 is a great introduction to watching lacrosse. No matter who you are, Chapter 4 can help you understand the rules of the game. If you're a coach, you may want to start with Part III. Or if you've already played for a few years and want to pick up some new tips, start with Part II. Finally, the Part of Tens appeals to just about everybody. Use the index and table of contents to find the information you're looking for, or dive right in with Chapter 1!

# Part I
# Getting Started

The 5th Wave                    By Rich Tennant

"Who's ready for another burger?"

# In this part . . .

*E*very lacrosse game starts with a faceoff — or, in the women's game, a draw. This part begins this book's play for you. Here, you discover the basics of the game — everything you need to get a head start in understanding how the game is played. You find out the game's most fundamental elements, including the roles of each player on the field or on the floor and the rules of play.

# Chapter 1

# Lacrosse and You

................................................

## In This Chapter

▶ Taking a big-picture look at lacrosse

▶ Playing lacrosse

▶ Coaching lacrosse

▶ Watching lacrosse as a fan

................................................

The popularity of lacrosse is at an all-time high. Why? Because more people in more places have been exposed to lacrosse. It really is that simple. As anyone who watches the sport for the first time quickly discovers, lacrosse is habit forming — some may even say addictive. It combines the best attributes of several of the most popular sports around — football, basketball, hockey, and more. It's fast moving, challenging, and never dull. Plus, you don't have to have superhuman strength or size to succeed at lacrosse.

In this chapter, we provide a quick overview of the differences between field lacrosse (which is typically played outdoors) and box lacrosse (which is played indoors), as well as between the men's and women's games. Then we look at lacrosse from three perspectives — that of the player, the coach, and the fan.

Whether you're playing lacrosse for the first time or looking to improve your game, whether you're coaching a team or you're a parent or fan, lacrosse — and this book — has something to offer you. This chapter gets the ball rolling.

# Understanding the Game of Lacrosse

Someone watching a lacrosse game for the first time may be surprised, intimidated, or just plain confused — after all, there's a lot going on. Players are running on and off the field or floor rapidly, possession is often up for grabs, and the hits just keep on coming (except in the women's game, where contact is not allowed). Lacrosse is a game of running, dodging, spinning, cutting, and faking. It offers plenty of excitement — from sprinting all out on a fast break to outrunning an opponent for a goal.

Lacrosse is a high-scoring game, which makes it especially exciting for fans. If you ever see a shutout in a lacrosse game, mark it on your calendar, because chances are, you'll watch thousands more games and never see another.

With lacrosse, throwing a ball — accurately — is the name of the game. The difference between lacrosse and most other sports is that you have to throw the ball using a stick, not with your hand.

A lacrosse ball is about 8 inches in circumference and about 2½ inches in diameter. It weighs a bit more than 5 ounces.

Although it's not easy, with good instruction and lots of practice, in a short time, almost anyone can master the basic skills needed to play the fastest game on two feet. In fact, unlike many other team sports where size and strength are essential, lacrosse rewards the small and the speedy. Sure, it helps to be big (especially if you're also fast), but small players can excel in lacrosse if they're quick, intelligent, aggressive, and skilled with a stick.

In the following sections, we fill you in on the two forms of lacrosse and the ways in which the men's and women's games differ.

## The two forms of lacrosse: Field and box

Lacrosse comes in two main forms:

- ✔ **Field lacrosse:** Today, field lacrosse (which got its start with Native Americans — see the nearby sidebar "The origins of lacrosse") is the most popular form in the United States. There are 10 or 12 players on the field (depending on whether the players are men or women — see "Mars and Venus: How the men's and women's games differ"). The playing surface is 110 yards long and 60 yards wide for men, a little bigger for women. The goals are 6 feet high and 6 feet wide.

- ✔ **Box lacrosse:** Box, which is most popular in Canada, is played on the equivalent of an ice hockey rink, in which the ice has been replaced with artificial turf. Box lacrosse has fewer players than field lacrosse — only 6. The players are assigned different roles — offense, transition, or defense — depending on their position. The playing surface is smaller (180 to 200 feet long and 80 to 90 feet wide), the goals are smaller (4 feet high and 4 feet wide), the goalies wear more protection, and there is more scoring than there is in field lacrosse.

Box lacrosse has been strictly a male domain for most of its history. But lately, some upstart women's leagues have formed in Canada.

For more on the rules of lacrosse, and the differences between field and box lacrosse, check out Chapter 4.

## Mars and Venus: How the men's and women's games differ

Men's lacrosse is one of the oldest sports in North America — possibly dating back to the 12th century (see the nearby sidebar "The origins of lacrosse"). But the first women's lacrosse game wasn't played until 1890 in Scotland; it wasn't played in the United States until 1926 in Baltimore, Maryland. And women's lacrosse wasn't played at the Division I level in the National Collegiate Athletic Association until 1982.

The field lacrosse game for women has grown and evolved over the years. For example, formal boundaries weren't instituted until 2006 (before that, no hard boundaries existed), and you can count on more changes in the women's game in the years to come.

### The origins of lacrosse

Lacrosse was first played by Native Americans, usually as a way to settle disputes between tribes or to celebrate and honor religious rituals. The Cherokee Indians referred to the sport as *Tewaaraton* (which means "little brother of war") and actually used it to train for battle.

In these early contests, the field of play could stretch for hundreds and hundreds of yards with no boundaries to speak of, teams could number well into the hundreds, and a game could last for several days. The small, speedy, and healthy players would've been the earliest stars of the game.

The sport was called *baggataway* by the Six Nations of the Iroquois in the area that is now western New York and southern Ontario. *Baggataway* is an Algonquian verb meaning "to hit with something." The Iroquois narrowed the number of participants significantly (to around 15 per team), set up goals, and established boundaries.

The name *lacrosse* was born when French explorers first witnessed the sport. The French thought that the stick looked like the staff of a bishop — which was known in France as *la crosse.*

One thing is for sure, though: The game has caught on. Today, there are three times as many women's collegiate lacrosse programs as there were in 1990. In fact, the sport is so popular that colleges are having trouble finding enough qualified officials and coaches, especially outside the sport's traditional East Coast hotbeds.

Some key differences do exist between the men's and women's game:

- ✔ **Physical contact:** The main difference between men's and women's lacrosse comes down to contact. In the men's game, physical contact is legal — and encouraged (especially by coaches) — while in the women's game, it is not. As a result, there is far less protective equipment in the women's game: Men wear helmets, mouth guards, gloves, shoulder pads, elbow pads, and often ribs pads, whereas women wear mouth guards and protective eyewear, but (with the exception of goalies) no helmets or padding. (For more on lacrosse equipment, see Chapter 2.)

- ✔ **Number of players:** In the men's game, ten players are on the field — three attackmen, three midfielders, three defensemen, and a goaltender. In the women's game, there are 12 players on the field — offensive attack players (first home, second home, third home, and two attack wings) and the defense (center, two defensive wings, point, cover point, third man, and goalie). (Turn to Chapter 3 for more on all these positions.)

- ✔ **Sticks:** Unlike men's lacrosse, mesh is not permitted for the pockets of women's sticks; the pockets must be strung in the traditional way. Also, the top of the ball must be above the sidewall when it's in the pocket.

- ✔ **Field size:** In men's lacrosse, the field measures 110 yards long and 60 yards wide. In women's lacrosse, the field is a bit bigger: 120 yards long and 70 yards wide.

# Lacrosse: A Player's Game

Although you can get a ton of enjoyment from lacrosse by coaching or watching the sport, the most thrilling way to participate is by playing the game yourself. If you're not shooting and scoring, you're hustling for ground balls, checking the opposing stick handler, or making big saves. If you're a lacrosse player, there's *never* a dull moment.

Each position in lacrosse requires different skills — for example, attackmen need shooting ability, midfielders need speed, and defensemen need toughness — but every lacrosse player needs strong stick skills and good hand-eye coordination.

Whether you're an attackman or a long-stick midfielder, the main attribute you need to play lacrosse is not really a skill at all: You need to work hard and hustle all the time. So many good things in lacrosse — getting a ground ball, making a big check — are a direct byproduct of doing just that.

## Playing offense: Stick skills and shooting

Good offensive skills start with the stick. You won't be able to shoot the ball hard and with accuracy if you aren't an adept stick handler. As we cover in Chapter 5, the best way to improve those skills is through practice.

We all like to work on things we're already good at. In lacrosse, you need to do the opposite. If you're dominant with one hand, you should strive to improve your other hand. Being able to pass, catch, and shoot with either hand is essential in beating your defender and, ultimately, the goalie.

Dodging is also crucial. Think of dodging like ball fakes in basketball. They're moves that allow you to get past a defender, often including faking one way and going another. Dodges are crucial — especially for midfielders, who have more of the field to operate on offensively.

In Chapter 6, we offer some shooting drills and exercises you can use to take your skills up a notch. In addition, we examine the differences in shooting techniques from close range to the goal, as well as from the perimeter.

## Defending: The do's and don'ts

Hard hits and checks often garner the most attention, but effective defense includes many things that rarely — if ever — draw oohs and aahs from the crowd.

Specifically, we're referring to assets such as communicating with your teammates, using good footwork, and playing with your head. Granted, these attributes aren't exactly glamorous, but they are the keys that make for a strong defender. We break down all this — and more— in Chapter 7.

In addition, we take a look at specific ways to defend offensive players — both when they have the ball and when they don't. We also give you some drills that will help you develop your defensive agility, as well as other key defensive skills.

## *The goalie's goal: Keeping the ball out of the net*

Keeping the ball *out* of the net is the goalie's job — and it's a tough one. In fact, there's no position quite like the goalie on the field. After all, who else is willing to stand in the line of fire of shots coming directly at him — from all angles — often at speeds as high as 100 miles per hour? Yes, indeed, goaltenders are a breed apart.

In addition to needing mental strength, goaltenders need plenty of other attributes to stop the ball from crossing the goal line. We examine the basics of goaltending — from proper stance to following the ball — in Chapter 8.

## *Possession is nine-tenths of the (lacrosse) law*

Offense, defense, goaltending, specialty teams . . . these are all critical to winning lacrosse. But the possession game is the most important of them all. Period. That's because you can't score if you don't have the ball.

From faceoffs and ground balls to rides and clears, the possession game is complex. We take a look at all it in Chapter 9, starting with the faceoff. Lacrosse is one of the few sports where you can score and then get the ball right back again — that's why faceoffs are so crucial.

## *Using specialty teams to your advantage*

When one team has a player advantage for a period of time following a penalty, that's known as a *man-up opportunity.* Whenever this situation occurs, there are two specialty teams on the field — the man-up team (the offensive team that has the advantage) and the man-down team (the defensive team that is shorthanded).

In box lacrosse, man-up opportunities are known as *power plays,* the same term used in ice hockey.

In Chapter 11, we talk about what makes for effective players on specialty teams — both when you're a man-up and when you're a man-down. We also take a look at the best kind of shots to take when you have a player advantage. Finally, we outline some especially effective man-up plays.

## Getting physical

Being the best lacrosse player you can be starts with being in the best possible physical condition, so that you're in a position to succeed when game time comes. In Chapter 12, we pinpoint specific steps you can take to ensure that you're at your best physically, including ways to improve quickness, agility, and strength, with some weight-training pointers as well.

Being the best player you can be also involves being mentally ready. In Chapter 12, we cover goal setting, relaxation, visualization, self-talk, focus, and getting energized.

# Coaches' Corner

When a team executes its game plan effectively, coaching looks easy. But the reality is, coaching is hard work — and if you've coached for more than a few minutes, you already know that.

The best way to get your team to succeed is to put it in position to do so. That means putting players at the right spots at the right times. It also means finding the right style of play to match your team's strengths and weaknesses. (See Part III for more on the fundamentals of coaching lacrosse.)

You also need to develop your coaching style for both the offense and the defense. We tell you the most effective offensive and defensive schemes to employ in Chapters 14 and 15, respectively.

Your players have to be physically prepared before the start of each game, but they have to be just as prepared mentally. To help your players play intelligent lacrosse, scouting is critical at the higher levels of the sport — usually starting at the varsity level in high school and becoming more intense at the collegiate and professional levels. For example, is the opposing goalie stronger on high shots or low ones? Is the opposing team's best attackman adept at shooting with his off hand? This kind of knowledge is vital. In fact, effective scouting can make the difference between a win and a loss. (We give you tips on scouting in Chapter 13.)

Another key part of coaching is making sure your players are ready to play. Are they confident? Are they motivated? Are they focused? These are just some of the questions you need to ask yourself before each and every game. (Turn to Chapter 13 for more on motivating your players to succeed.)

# From a Fan's Perspective

If you're a fan of lacrosse, you're in good company: There are more lacrosse fans today than ever before, and that number is only growing.

In lacrosse, the action is constant, which means that you have to keep track of many different elements simultaneously — from offense and defense to specialty teams and goaltending. (We tell you specifically what to look for in Chapter 16.) There's never a dull moment in a lacrosse game.

If you're almost anywhere in North America these days, there should be a lacrosse game near you, whether at the youth, collegiate, pro, or recreational level. In Chapter 17, we take a look at the premier high school and collegiate programs playing the game today. We also cover tradition-rich minor-league box lacrosse in Canada, and we touch on the spread and growth of the international game. We tell you where — and when — you can follow the action, from the youth level to the pros.

Pro lacrosse now has both box and field versions. We tell you what you need to know about both those leagues in Chapter 18, as well as provide online sources for news and information.

So go out and catch the action! That's especially good advice if you're relatively new to the game. There's no substitute for watching as much lacrosse as possible to familiarize yourself with the rules and the unique aspects of the game. And you have plenty of opportunities to do just that: There are more outlets providing coverage of the game than ever before. Turn to the appendix for more on where you can watch some of the action on TV.

# Chapter 2

# Suiting Up: Buying the Right Equipment

*In This Chapter*

▶ Following the rules on stick length, head width, and pocket width

▶ Protecting yourself with padding, mouth guard, and more

▶ Equipping your kid for lacrosse

Some players are known for their exceptional stick skills or shooting ability. Others are recognized for their speed, aggression, quickness, or size. Lacrosse players have many different physical attributes, but they're all outfitted the same. In this chapter, we take a look at the equipment you need to play the game, whether it's field or box lacrosse, men's or women's, adult or youth. We also provide some pointers for parents on buying equipment.

## The Tools of the Trade: The Ball and the Stick

When you get right down to it, you can enjoy a good lacrosse workout — whether it be shooting off the wall by yourself or throwing and catching with a friend — with just two tools: a ball and a stick. In this section, we take at the two basic tools with which it all starts.

## The ball

In the early playing days of lacrosse, the ball had no standard size, although most were about the size of a tennis ball. Most lacrosse balls had an outside cover of rawhide or deerskin and were stuffed with deer hair. Or they were just plain round wood wrapped with rawhide. In 1867, Dr. George Beers, a Canadian dentist considered by many to be the "father of lacrosse" because he created the first set of rules, replaced the hair-stuffed deerskin ball with a hard rubber ball.

Today, this so-called Indian rubber ball is standard for all lacrosse play. The ball, which can be white, yellow, or orange, generally measures just less than 8 inches in circumference and about 2½ inches in diameter, and it weighs a little over 5 ounces.

The National Collegiate Athletic Association (NCAA), the governing body of U.S. collegiate sports, approved the use of a lime-green-colored ball, though you're not likely to see it in wide use anytime soon. There's no truth to the rumor that the NCAA is considering applying a lime dye to the lacrosse field grass to really spice up the game.

## The stick

The stick first used by Native players was about 3 feet long with a circular net at one end, laced with thongs to hold the ball in place. This netted pocket at the end of the stick was very deep in order to carry the ball. The deep pocket of the stick made it difficult to throw the ball, though, so the early game had little passing — it was more a game of strength and endurance than a game of skill.

In the 1880s, the stick changed: Its handle (or *shaft*) was curved at the end, and a large, flat, triangular surface of webbing extended from the top down about two-thirds the length of the handle. The deep-pocket stick used by the Native players required less skill, but this new flat stick increased dodging and led to more passing, which sped up the game.

Today, men's lacrosse players play with aluminum- or titanium-handled sticks with plastic heads. The stick, or the *crosse,* still has a net pocket at the end, but the depth is much shallower than it was in the game's beginnings — about the diameter of one ball or slightly less.

Sticks in women's lacrosse are usually made of wood, laminated wood, or synthetic material.

In the following sections, we cover the various parts of the stick, and tell you what the rules say about sticks, as well as what to look for when you shop.

Try out a few sticks before you buy. As you play more, you'll get a better idea of the kind of stick you like by playing with your own stick, as well as by trying out other players' sticks.

### Stick head

The stick head (see Figure 2-1) for all men's field lacrosse players *except* the goalie must measure 6½ to 10 inches wide. The goalie's stick head must measure 10 to 12 inches wide.

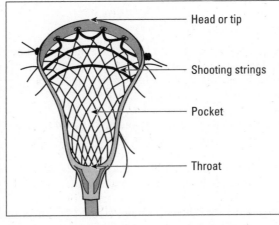

**Figure 2-1:** The head is the part of the lacrosse stick that is used for handling the ball.

- Head or tip
- Shooting strings
- Pocket
- Throat

For all women's field lacrosse players *except* the goalie, the stick head must measure 7 to 9 inches wide. The goalie's stick head can be up to 12 inches wide.

The width of the pocket in a field lacrosse stick should be 6½ to 10 inches. By rule, the pocket must be shallow enough to see a portion of the ball over the sidewall.

In box lacrosse, the width of the pocket should be 4½ to 8 inches; for the goaltender in box lacrosse, the pocket can be no more than 15 inches wide.

The biggest difference between men's and women's field lacrosse sticks is in the pocket: In the women's game, there is no mesh, except for on the goalie's stick.

Most lacrosse stick heads come flat when you buy them — that is, they have no pockets. You have to create (and then re-string) the pocket yourself. Try not to make your pocket right at the throat of the stick. You want it more toward the center of the mesh.

You may be able to ask your local sporting goods store to create the pocket for you before you take your new stick home.

Introduced in the mid-1990s, *offset heads* (with the head set back from the shaft) are tremendously popular with players of all levels in both forms of lacrosse. An offset head allows the pocket to be deeper while still releasing the ball with a high trajectory, enabling the shooter to increase the velocity of the shot while still adding torque to the cradle and making it harder for the ball to come out.

### Stick length

Standard length for sticks in men's field lacrosse is 40 to 42 inches from the end of the head to the end of the handle. Sticks for defensive players (as well as one midfielder) can measure 52 to 72 inches in length. The goalie's stick can be 40 to 72 inches long.

In women's lacrosse, the stick must be between 35½ and 43¼ inches in length. The goalie's stick must be between 35½ and 48 inches in length.

In box lacrosse, the stick's length should be between 42 and 46 inches. The goaltender's stick has no minimum or maximum length.

Longer sticks are designed for defense. They make it harder for opposing offensive players to score, but they also limit field defensemen from getting involved offensively because of the decreased stick-handling ability that comes from carrying around 10 to 20 additional inches of stick.

Use a legal length that feels comfortable to you. If you're choking up on the grip, the stick is too long for you. If you're handling the stick properly, there's no need to cut it off to make it shorter. If you cut your stick off short and you're still growing, you may have to have to buy a new handle or another stick before another season begins.

Don't cut your stick too short. Officials will check for legal stick length and may assess a minor penalty to a player with an illegal stick. In the 2002 World Lacrosse Championship, for example, a U.S. player received this penalty during the championship game against Canada.

### Stick handle

Unlike hockey players, lacrosse players don't use left-handed or right-handed sticks. Sticks are made neutral, which means that the middle of the tip of the head is lined up exactly in line with the handle.

# From Head to Toe: Putting on the Equipment

With the advent and use of the plastic stick and aluminum handle, lacrosse has moved in a new direction. Players used to pad up along their arms to prevent any unnecessary injuries from wooden sticks. In today's game, however, the philosophy about equipment seems to be "less is more." Players are dressing light, with equipment that gives them more flexibility and less bulkiness.

Wearing the proper lacrosse attire (shown in Figure 2-2) is about more than just having the right look with the latest cool jersey. Equipping yourself for lacrosse is really more about making sure that you have all the accessories that will help keep you safe and healthy, as well as suiting yourself up to play the best possible lacrosse.

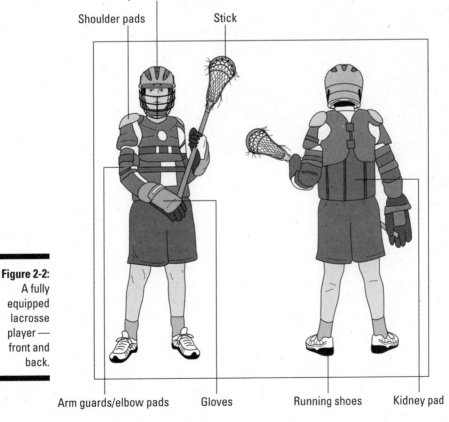

Hockey helmet with mask

Shoulder pads

Stick

**Figure 2-2:**
A fully equipped lacrosse player — front and back.

Arm guards/elbow pads     Gloves     Running shoes     Kidney pad

Other than the goaltender, women's players don't wear helmets (see Figure 2-3). But they must wear protective eyewear, mouth guards, and gloves. Some players also wear soft headgear and nose guards. (In addition to a helmet, face mask, mouth guard, and throat and chest protectors, the goalies may also wear padding on their shoulders, arms, hands, and legs.)

**Figure 2-3:**
Women's lacrosse position players wear protective eyewear and mouthpieces, but no helmets.

Photo by Raymond J. Nelson/MaxPreps.com

In field lacrosse, goalies use helmets, throat guards, chest protectors, and gloves.

Goalies in box lacrosse are much more protected, with all the same equipment as field goalies wear, plus shoulder pads, leg pads, and shin guards. In addition, unlike the field lacrosse chest protectors, the chest protectors of box lacrosse goalies include arm guards, because more shots are taken from close range to the goalie in box than in field.

## Gloves

Lacrosse gloves are similar to hockey gloves, but they have a lot more flexibility, which allows you to handle the stick properly.

If you're a hockey player, and you're just trying your hand at lacrosse, you can save a little money by using your hockey gloves. If you don't play hockey, the differences between lacrosse and hockey gloves are big enough to warrant buying lacrosse gloves.

What do you look for in a lacrosse glove? Basically, you want a good fit. Some less expensive gloves have a little more nylon on the top; the more expensive ones have leather tops. Both styles give adequate protection, but leather tends to last longer. Manufacturers put mesh in the palms so that the gloves can breathe a lot more, last a lot longer, and give you a better feel of the handle.

Breathability is especially critical for box lacrosse played in hot arenas.

## Shoulder pads, arm guards, and elbow pads

Most lacrosse shoulder pads are fairly skimpy, but that helps players move more freely. Besides, the biggest function of lacrosse shoulder pads is to hold your arm guards on so that your arms don't get banged up. A three-piece pad comes all connected, with curved fiberglass to protect forearms, elbows, and biceps. With a properly fitted three-piece pad, you don't need extra elbow pads.

## Rib or kidney pads

The rib or kidney pad (it's the same piece of equipment but it's referred to by both names) is a one-piece unit that typically fits over the shoulders like suspenders and wraps around your stomach and lower and middle back for protection.

Rib or kidney pads are not mandatory to wear, but they are recommended. This is especially true for youth players, who tend to get hit in that area of the body more frequently.

## Helmets

In a sport as hard hitting and physical as lacrosse, head protection is vital. (Believe it or not, in the early days of lacrosse, men didn't wear helmets at all.) The lacrosse helmet should fit properly and not move or flop around. Helmets are also equipped with a set of grills in the front. Some have face-masks, though this is not nearly as common.

## Mouth guards

The mouth guard not only protects your teeth from getting chipped and cracked but also helps prevent concussions by keeping your teeth from jamming together.

You can get your dentist to make you a guard, or you can buy a premade one that's a bit cheaper but will do the job effectively. The biggest difference between the two is that the dental mouth guard is built from a mold taken of your teeth, so it tends to stay on your teeth a little more comfortably and leads to less gagging.

## Running shoes

Look for three-quarter-cut or high-top shoes rather than low-cut shoes. The higher-cut shoes are better at absorbing all the cutting and picking and rolling of lacrosse. Also, keep your lacrosse shoes separate from your everyday shoes. Wearing your lacrosse shoes daily will break down the soles, causing you to slip and slide in a game.

Make sure your shoes are a good fit; shoes that are too big will cause blisters. Some players wear two pairs of thick socks for absorption and protection of their feet. Others wear ankle socks for looks and comfort. Just make sure your socks are smooth when you put them on, because any wrinkle can cause blisters.

# Supporting Your Kid's Body

The single most important thing a youth player can wear is the kidney pad (see "Rib or kidney pads," earlier in this chapter).

The equipment used for youngsters is the same as the big boys — and girls — use for both field and box lacrosse. However, youth lacrosse players use their own specially made sticks, sometimes known as *junior sticks*. Junior sticks have thin aluminum handles. These sticks are fine for smaller players (ages 4 to 8), but kids ages 9 to 12 have to start getting into full-size handles because they're too strong for junior sticks. Between ages 9 and 12, they can still use aluminum, but most players use titanium, titanium alloy, or even wooden handles, which are the cheapest.

The rule for the length of the stick, from the end of the head to the end of the handle, is 36 inches or less for players up to 12 years of age in youth lacrosse.

Table 2-1 is a rundown of equipment kids need to play the game. ***Remember:*** Be sure to check with your local league for its unique requirements before making a purchase.

| Table 2-1 | A Youth Lacrosse Equipment Shopping List |
|---|---|
| *Boys* | *Girls* |
| Stick | Stick |
| Gloves | Protective eyewear |
| Helmet with faceguard | Mouth guard |
| Mouth guard | Running shoes or cleats |
| Rib or kidney pads | Helmet (for goalies) |
| Shoulder pads | Throat protector (for goalies) |
| Arm pads | Chest protector (for goalies) |
| Athletic supporter and cup | Shoulder pads (for goalies, optional) |
| Elbow pads | Arm pads (for goalies, optional) |
| Running shoes or cleats | |
| Throat protector (for goalies) | |
| Chest protector (for goalies) | |

If you're buying equipment for the first time, talk to parents of older players about equipment and the best places in your area to buy it.

If you're coaching youth lacrosse, make sure that parents know what equipment they need to provide before the first practice. You don't want kids showing up to practice without mouth guards, for example, and having to watch from the sideline because their parents thought mouth guards would be provided.

# Chapter 3

# Meeting the Team

. . . . . . . . . . . . . . . . . . . . . . . . . . . . . . . . . . . . . . . . . . . . . . . . . . . . . . . . . . .

### In This Chapter

▶ Looking at the lacrosse positions

▶ Scoring on offense

▶ Dominating on defense

▶ Tending the goal

. . . . . . . . . . . . . . . . . . . . . . . . . . . . . . . . . . . . . . . . . . . . . . . . . . . . . . . . . . .

*I*n this chapter, we introduce the players on the field and floor. In addition to breaking down each position, and talking about the number of players needed and what their responsibilities are, we also look at what it takes to be an effective player on offense and a dominating player on defense. This chapter covers the basics — giving you a leg up in understanding and playing lacrosse with success.

## Introducing the Field Lacrosse Players

A men's field lacrosse team includes nine players, plus the goaltender. A women's team has 11 players, plus the goaltender.

Each field lacrosse team is allowed a maximum of six players (plus the goalie) on half the field at any one time. When a men's field team is in its offensive zone, it must keep three players (plus the goalie) behind the midfield line. Of course, it's not six on ten, because its opponent can only have six players (plus the goalie) defending the zone at the same time. This so-called *split field* in field lacrosse forces more specialization in playing positions.

In women's field lacrosse, a maximum of seven players (plus the goalie) are allowed on half the field at any one time. When a women's field team is in its offensive zone, it must keep three players (plus the goalie) behind its midfield line.

# A look at women's field lacrosse

Women's field lacrosse at the U.S. collegiate level is the fastest growing sector of the sport, aside from the overall growth in popularity of the sport, beginning with the youth level. In part, this growth is thanks to Title IX, a federal regulation specifying that the athletic participation of every National Collegiate Athletic Association (NCAA) institution must mirror the gender ratio of its student body.

Major universities outside the Northeast, such as Florida, Northwestern, and Oregon, have established varsity women's lacrosse programs over the past decade. Following this trend, youth programs and club teams have dramatically expanded and advanced, introducing more young girls to the sport.

Although women's lacrosse is similar to the men's game in overall excitement and appearance, the two games have some significant differences:

✔ With the exception of goalies, women do not wear padding or helmets, because body checking is not allowed.

✔ Women's sticks can't enter an imaginary 7-inch bubble around any player's head, and stick checks must be made away from the offensive player's body. The result is that the women's game places much more emphasis on defensive footwork and positioning than the men's game does.

✔ Women's stick shafts are narrower and the pockets are much shallower, which makes passing and catching vastly different from the men's game. In the men's games, passes are more frequent and unleashed at higher velocities.

✔ Women's teams have 12 players on the field (including a goalie), as opposed to 10 for men.

✔ Field sizes are recommended to be 120 yards long and 70 yards wide for women, which is 10 yards longer and 10 yards wider than it is for men.

✔ The offensive end of the field, which can hold only seven offensive players and seven defensive players (plus the goalie), is set off by a restraining line located 30 yards from the end line.

✔ Penalties for fouls are free position shots, taken from either an 8-meter arc around the goal (for a major penalty) or a 12-meter arc around the goal (for a minor penalty). Offending players must stand 4 meters behind (for a major foul) or to the side (for a minor foul), while the offensive player takes a free position shot.

✔ Faceoffs, which are called *draws* in the women's game, begin with the ball pinched between the backs of the opposing players' stick heads, which are held waist-high.

The four main men's field lacrosse positions are attackman, midfielder, defenseman, and goalie, though each position includes even more specific roles. Men's teams employ three attackmen, three midfielders, and three defensemen.

The main women's field lacrosse positions are attack and defense (which includes the goaltender). Here's a look at the positions on the field:

✔ **Attack:** The attack positions are made up of first, second, and third homes, all of whom are responsible, in differing degrees, for delivering goals. In addition, the two attack wings move the ball from defense to offense.

✔ **Defense:** The defensive assignments are broken down into the following areas: center, two defensive wings, point, cover point, third man, and goalie. The center handles draws. The wings are similar to midfielders in the men's field games — with offensive and defensive responsibilities. The point covers the opposing team's first home; the cover point, the opposing team's second home; and the third man, the third home. The goaltender is the last line of defense.

This section introduces you to field participants and the roles they play. In addition, we take a look at offensive and defensive concepts that are applicable to both the men's and women's games.

# Putting the ball in the net: The attackmen

The attackmen are the primary offensive weapons looking to feed and score. They create most of the offense and generally don't play defense. Attackmen are the three players kept on the opposite side of the midline while the ball is at the other end.

Attackmen often stay on the field the whole game. Many attackmen have the ability to both feed and score, but some of them focus on one of those offensive elements and become specialists in that area.

## Feeders

Feeders are the attackmen who set up scoring players. They're obviously adept passers, but they also have outstanding field vision. Feeders often operate from the *X position* (the area behind the net).

## Finishers

Finishers are the attackmen who deliver the goals. They generally have strong stick skills, quick releases, and hard, accurate shots. The trend in recent years is for finishers to have good strength and size — normally traits you would see in midfielders — so that defensemen have trouble moving them out of the *crease area* (the area just outside the crease, which surrounds the goal).

# Playing offense and defense: The midfielders

Midfielders play offense and defense, following the flow of the game and getting involved at both ends of the field. Midfielders, or "middies," are crucial to a team's transition offense and defense.

Teams generally run three lines consisting of three midfielders each. For example, some midfielders may be defensive specialists, coming on the field only in certain situations, while others may play only faceoffs and then run off the field. However, many midfielders also run regular midfield shifts, and a select few are dangerous offensive weapons.

Although the three field players with longer sticks play defense, a fourth long stick can be used in the midfield. This player is known as a *long-stick midfielder*.

To be an effective two-way midfielder, you need size, speed, strength, stamina, and aggression. Midfielders must have it all in order to be effective both offensively and defensively. No position on the lacrosse field requires such a myriad of skills.

Midfielders must play both ends of the field. Doing that requires athleticism and endurance.

## The first line of defense: Close defensemen

The three close defensemen generally stay on their half of the field while their team is on offense, though they are allowed to cross the midline in transition as long as an equal number of midfielders stays back.

The role of the defensemen is generally to stop the opposing attackmen from scoring or creating offense. Occasionally, a defenseman will be dispatched to cover a dominant opposing midfielder (as shown in Figure 3-1).

Here are some traits that are common among the best defensive players in the game:

- **Communication:** Communication is a critical component of the defenseman position. Because the ball moves frequently when the opposing team is on attack, defensemen must react accordingly — that means making quick slides and switches. In order to effectively executive these slides and switches, defensemen must communicate with their teammates frequently and effectively.

- **Agility:** Because offensive players make quick cuts and are effective dodgers, defenders must have the agility to stay with them.

- **Footwork:** Good technical defense starts with footwork. In fact, footwork is even more important than quickness — although being quick certainly helps.

**Figure 3-1:**
A
defenseman
guards an
attackman.

*Photo by Jim Stout/MaxPreps.com*

## Saving the day and keeping the ball in play: Goaltenders

Goalies in field lacrosse have to be more athletic than those in box lacrosse because of the larger goal: It's 6 feet high and 6 feet wide in field lacrosse. Field lacrosse goalies play with their sticks held upright and the head of the stick pointing skyward, as shown in Figure 3-2.

In box lacrosse, goalies use the hockey style, where the stick is held on the ground.

In addition to stopping shots and getting the ball out of the defensive end, goalies are also responsible for directing the defense.

Photo by Jim Stout/MaxPreps.com

**Figure 3-2:**
A goaltender
gets in
position
to make a
save.

TIP

Goaltenders need the following attributes:

- **Good reflexes:** Shots on net come hard and fast, so if a goaltender doesn't have good reflexes, it's a problem. A big problem.

- **Fearlessness:** A field lacrosse goalie is protected by relatively little equipment — just a helmet, chest protector, throat guard, and gloves — and faces shots that routinely come in at over 90 miles per hour.

# Introducing the Box Lacrosse Players

To make up a *line* (a group of five players who go on the floor together) you need two creasemen (right and left), two cornermen (also right and left), and a pointman. When transitioning from defense to offense, the pointman can come up either side of the floor or up the middle of the floor. And don't forget the most important player on the team, the goaltender.

BOX LACROSSE

# Which side of the floor do you play on?

At the youth level of box lacrosse, inexperienced players sometimes play both sides of the floor, because they don't know what they should do except run around, go after every loose ball (youth lacrosse has a lot of those), and try to hit anybody who moves.

But where players position themselves on the floor is important for both offensive and defensive strategy. For example, the cross-check is a defensive maneuver to stop or slow down the stick handler; with the cross-check, players are getting hit on the side of the arm while carrying the ball.

If the stick handler goes down the wrong side of the floor — in other words, a left-shot creaseman

goes down the left side of the floor — an incoming cross-check would force him to turn his body *away* from the cross-check to protect the ball, thereby turning his back to the play.

But if that same stick handler goes down the proper side of the floor — in other words, a left-shot creaseman goes down the right side of the floor — he can still turn sideways to protect the ball from an incoming cross-check, but he won't be forced to turn completely away from the play. He can continue to face the play to see who's open or to see the net.

Players need to know their position on the floor. They also need to be aware of the role they've been assigned to carry out in the position.

# *Hanging out with the goalie: The creasemen*

The two creasemen are generally good goal scorers and usually play at the front of any fast break. A *fast break* is an offensive situation in which players move quickly up the floor from the defensive to the offensive end, often as a result of forcing a turnover on defense (such as stealing the ball) and usually with at least one more offensive player than defenders.

After they get into the offensive end, and the fast break or odd-man situation has been successfully defended, the creasemen have a number of offensive options:

- **Cut to the ball.** From their floor position, which is usually in the area around the crease of the goal area (from center left or right out to the sideboards), creasemen can move toward the stick handler in anticipation of a pass.

- **Pop out in the crease area.** By stepping out to receive a ball in the crease area of the floor, a creaseman can look for a one-on-one opportunity against the goalie or against a defender to get to the goalie.

✔ **Set a pick.** A creaseman can assist a teammate, either the stick handler or another offensive player, by *setting a pick* — that is, stepping in the path of his teammate's defender. A pick may allow the stick handler to work away from his defender to get an open look to the goal for a shot, or it may allow an offensive teammate to work away from his defender to get open for a pass.

In fact, the best creasemen are great at setting picks; the pick may often lead to a pass to the creaseman for a possible short shot on goal, an offensive set play known as the *pick and roll*.

Creasemen are very adept at going one-on-one against their defenders when close around the goal. They should also be good loose-ball players, because one of their primary roles is to go after every loose ball in the near-goal corner on a missed shot at the goal or on an errant pass to a teammate.

The critical qualities required in a good creaseman include stick skill, intelligence, mobility, quickness, and vision of the floor.

On defense, creasemen are usually not the bigger (and better) defenders who would play against the better offensive players on the opposition, but they still should play good defense, usually defending the offensive players nearest the centerline. This defensive positioning allows the creasemen to get a quick start on any fast-break opportunity.

## Cutting corners: The cornermen

When transitioning from defense to offense, the two cornermen run up the floor behind the creasemen, often carrying the ball to try to create a fast-break opportunity.

In an offensive set — that is, after a fast break or odd-man situation is over — cornermen have the following options:

✔ **Shoot long.** With their typical positioning around the center of the offensive zone, cornermen look for most of their shots from long range.

✔ **Look to go one-on-one.** With the ball, a quick-footed cornerman can look for opportunities to take on his defender, trying to shake him free for either an open shot on goal or a pass to a teammate. Also, taking advantage of a defender's slip, cornermen can quickly move toward the goal and take on another defender one-on-one. More often than not, this situation leads to a quick pass to a creaseman or other cornerman, whose defender has moved to help out his beaten teammate.

✔ **Look for a cutter.** When carrying the ball, a cornerman faces the play, waiting for a teammate (usually a creaseman) to shake free a bit from his defender and cut toward the ball. A good pass from the cornerman to a cutter can then set up an open shot on goal.

✔ **Wait for a pick.** On a pick-and-roll play, the cornerman's defender is usually the recipient of the pick. With his defender knocked off by his teammate's pick, a cornerman can look to score or look to pass to the creaseman who set the pick.

On offense, the cornermen help create action by passing the ball, either across the floor or down into the crease area. This skill is especially critical when the defense is preventing a lot of player movement on the offensive end of the floor.

On defense, cornermen are usually the better defenders on a team, the players through whom the opposing offense must go.

# Where does the winger play?

Many Canadian box lacrosse coaches also coach hockey and, of course, many young lacrosse players also play hockey. This overlap is natural — after all, hockey and box lacrosse are very similar — but it can cause some problems.

First, in hockey, a right winger is usually a *right shot* — a player who shoots from the right side of the body — who plays on the right side of the ice. But in lacrosse, the right-shot players play on the left side of the floor and are called left creasemen or left cornermen. And the right creasemen or right cornermen play on the right side of the floor, but are left-shot players. It all comes down to getting the best angle on the shot and protecting the stick with your body.

In addition, box lacrosse coaches who come out of hockey often call their offensive players *wingers* or *centers* — using these terms

isn't ideal (because they're not accurate), but it isn't a major problem. On the other hand, it *is* a problem when coaches call the backcourt players (or the last players to come up the floor on offense) defensemen. If you call these players defensemen, they may develop a tendency to stay out of the regular flow of the offense, as they would in hockey. Defensemen in hockey stay at the blue line and very seldom leave that area. If a lacrosse defender stays near the centerline without getting into the regular flow of the offense, the team ends up with three offensive players against five defenders.

To avoid this tendency, try thinking more like a basketball coach. When your team has the ball, every player is an offensive player, and when your team doesn't have the ball, every player is a defensive player.

## Directing floor activity: The pointman

The pointman's responsibilities are similar to the cornermen's responsibilities. He can move up the floor behind a cornerman or run up the middle of the floor.

The pointman needs all the qualities of a cornerman. He needs to be

- ✔ **A good long-ball shooter:** The pointman's primary position in the offensive zone is in the top area of the floor, closest to the centerline.

- ✔ **Good at going one-on-one:** If he can create some distance between himself and his defender, the pointman can more easily look to pass to a teammate closer to the goal.

- ✔ **Smart with the ball:** The pointman should develop the ability to read his own teammates' energy level so that he can determine which side of the floor to pass to in order to create the best scoring opportunity.

The pointman's biggest asset is his ability to make good plays — that is, to initiate the action on an offensive set play and still be a threat to score.

A pointman can be a bigger, slower player who isn't usually a great scorer. A pointman should, however, make up for this lack of speed with a great sense of the action on the floor, the awareness to anticipate where the ball goes and when the ball doesn't go where it's supposed to, and the ability to get back quickly on defense.

## Defending the net: The goaltender

The goaltender's job is to stop the ball from going into the net. Sounds pretty simple, but it's the hardest position to play. Goalies are the backbone of the team — a team won't be successful without good goaltending. Goalies have to know how to play the angles, how to take away corner shots, and how to move around the crease area to get in good position to stop the ball.

But good goaltenders should be able to do more than just stop the ball; they also have to be able to initiate a fast break or breakout. A good goalie is a real threat if he can send a deep pass to a player breaking out down the floor or even an accurate short pass to a teammate to run the ball up the floor.

The better the goalie, the better the team.

Goalies tend to be a little different — as the saying goes, they walk to the beat of a different drummer — and that's probably one of the reasons why so many of them are so good.

## Defending the floor: The defensive players

All offensive players — creasemen, cornermen, and pointmen — are also defensive players. Lacrosse is similar to basketball in this sense — when the player or one of his teammates has the ball, they're on offense, and when they don't have the ball, they're on defense.

In the National Lacrosse League, most positions are now specialized. Offensive players play strictly on offense, and defensive players play defense.

Unlike on offense, defensive players have no set positions. Usually, a line sent out to the floor includes two or three players whose strength is playing defense rather than scoring. These players pick up the better offensive players on the opposing team to defend. The players on a line whose skills are primarily offensive usually end up defending the weaker offensive opponents when on defense.

Having several players on a line who can play both offense and defense well is usually a luxury. But many lacrosse teams today tend to go with a so-called *offense-defense system,* which allows players who excel on one end of the floor or the other to run on and off the floor, depending on which team has possession of the ball. A solid defender, for example, is on the floor to play defense when his team doesn't have the ball. When his team takes possession, he heads for his team's bench to be replaced by a more offensive-minded player.

# Carrying the Offense: Keys for the Offensive Player

The ability to handle the ball — that is to pass, catch, cradle, and shoot with great skill — gives you and your team a tremendous advantage in a lacrosse game. But you also need to use certain offensive skills when you aren't carrying the ball.

On offense, you have to be able to beat a defender, whether you're with the ball or without the ball. And you should never take your eyes *off* the ball — you have to know where the ball is at all times.

This section offers the basics that you need to be successful on the offensive end of the field or floor.

## *Practicing efficient stick handling*

Stick handling (also called ball handling) isn't really true handling — you don't use your hand at all. Instead, efficient stick handling requires great skill with handling the lacrosse stick. And the best stick handlers can work wonders with the ball and stick, whether catching, cradling, passing, or scoring.

To become a great stick handler — or at least to master the fundamentals of stick handling — you have to practice. Walk to school while cradling a ball, spend Saturday mornings in the off season throwing and catching off an outdoor wall (preferably one without windows), or set up a goal-shaped target to practice shooting against.

Take the time to become comfortable with the basics of each of the stick-handling skills in the following sections.

### Catching

Your best chance for catching a pass in your direction is to make sure that you're facing the passer and you can see the path that the ball is taking toward your stick. After the ball reaches your stick, drop the stick back slightly as the ball hits the pocket to minimize the risk of the ball popping back out.

Make sure that you're facing the direction that the pass is coming from, and allow your stick to give a little as it receives the ball. If you follow these two tips, you should have little trouble with any pass sent your way.

### Cradling

Efficiency at *cradling* (holding the ball in your stick's pocket while you decide whether to shoot or pass) allows you to scan your options on the playing surface without having to look constantly at your stick to make sure you still have the ball. You can use different styles of cradling depending on the game situation. For example, if you're being tightly defended, you should cradle with both hands, and the stick should be positioned closer to your body so it's more difficult for the defender to strip the ball away from you.

Your goal is to

- ✔ Protect the ball from a defender.
- ✔ Hold onto the ball while you watch for a teammate to cut for a pass or for an opening for a shot on goal.
- ✔ Always be ready to release the ball.

### Passing

Just as you need to be in the proper position to catch a pass, positioning is critical for making a pass. However, facing the receiver directly is not usually the best bet. Instead, you want to have a slightly sideways stance because you're also likely to be keeping the ball away from a defender at the same time that you're passing it. Also, make sure that you've made eye contact with the receiver before you send a crisp, two-handed pass her way.

### Shooting

Shooting is just like passing, except to a smaller target that doesn't move but has a large, padded object in the way trying to "catch" your pass. The four most effective shot styles to work on are the overhand long shot, the underhand long shot, the sidearm long shot, and the backhand shot that's usually from close in.

# Moving — with and without the ball

Lacrosse is a game of constant movement. If you have the ball, you're working around the offensive zone trying to find an open teammate or trying to find an opening through which you can take a shot. If you don't have the ball, you're moving and running and picking and shifting and trying to shake free an opponent so that you can be in position to take a pass or pick up a ground ball.

Moving with the ball takes a combination of quickness, anticipation, and vision. Quick, darting moves may help you get past a defender so that you can break for the goal or pass to an open teammate. Anticipating when and from where a check is coming may create yet another opening for a scoring opportunity.

Keep your eyes on the activity in the rest of the offensive zone while also looking out for defenders — this takes particularly sharp concentration while you're also moving around the playing surface. (Some of the best playmakers in the game — or in any game, for that matter — do seem to have eyes in the backs of their heads.)

Moving without the ball helps you beat a defender and get open for a pass. The most basic play and most effective move without the ball is just to speed past your defender on the off-ball side. You can use quickness and deception, you can slash at your defender's stick to knock it down and go, or you can just check your defender and push off.

## Knowing where the ball is at all times

*Field vision* — the ability to see what's happening on the playing surface at all times — is a tremendous asset to successful lacrosse. The best players can see what their teammates are doing, anticipate where their teammates are going, know where the defensive players are and what they're likely to do, and still be able to keep an eye on where the ball is in the zone.

You need some time and practice to be able to have the kind of field vision that the best players have, so for now, work on making sure you know where the ball is. If you know which of your teammates has the ball, you can then quickly look around the field for an opening, for an opportunity to set a pick, or to anticipate a shot on goal and a possible ground ball.

# Focusing on Defense: Keys for the Defensive Player

Half the battle of playing defense is good position. Of course, you need to know how to stop an opponent with the ball and without the ball, but good position saves you a lot of unnecessary work. How you use your stick on defense is also important, whether you use it as a slash, poke-check, or check. And sometimes you have to use your body to compensate for making wrong decisions.

This section offers the basics that you need to gain success on the defensive end.

## Establishing your position

Defensive positioning is a matter of how you play your opponent in relation to the rest of the defensive zone. Depending on game situations, you may choose to defend an offensive player by forcing him toward the sidelines or by trying to get him to go higher up in the zone. Making the correct decision — knowing where on the field you'll be in the right place at the right time defensively — is half the battle of playing solid defense.

Positioning also requires some understanding of how your teammates defend. By keeping yourself in a positive defensive position — such as between your opponent and the goal or between your opponent and the middle of the zone — you can be in a more ideal position to help out a team-mate who has been beaten or to double-team a cutting offensive player.

## Using (or not using) the stick

Stick-checking is more of an integral part of playing defense in field lacrosse than it is in box lacrosse. In the field game, where sticks can be up to 72 inches long, stick checks make up roughly 85 percent of the defensive tactics.

Footwork is crucial for a stick check in order to keep yourself in good position to make a check or use the body. Stick checks are effective in causing turnovers — deflecting passes or shots, stripping the ball from the opponent's crosse, and forcing a player into throwing an errant pass or shot. If an offensive player loses the ball, a defensive player's stick check likely caused it. Field defenders use physical pressure with the body to keep an offensive player from dodging and putting herself in a good spot to shoot or pass.

In box lacrosse, stick checking is a legal defensive tactic. At one time, the thinking was that you should use your stick on defense only as an emergency measure or as an accessory to a cross-check. In the National Lacrosse League today, however, stick-checking on the stick handler's gloves is one of the main tactics for stopping a stick handler. But this tactic remains illegal in minor lacrosse.

When you try to stick-check a player, you're trying to stop the momentum of a usually running, often rather large, opponent with a piece of aluminum or wood. It's a bit like trying to block a 300-pound defensive lineman in football with a 170-pound place kicker.

What you should be stopping your opponent's momentum with is your body and a legal cross-check. In this better scenario, you hold the stick with both hands across your body as additional leverage for the check. In this position, you're also keeping your hands on the stick so that you can quickly move to pick up a loose ball or intercept a pass.

# Defending the Goal: Keys for the Goaltender

Goaltender is a unique position on the field. After all, in men's lacrosse, at any given time, there are three attackmen, three midfielders, and three defensemen . . . but only one goaltender. As a result, most of what you need to know about this position is unique from all others. Here's a look at few of the most important traits you can have as a goalie.

## Taking your optimum goal position

The so-called *ready stance* is a balanced and relaxed position in the crease, ready to react forward, backward, or sideways, depending on the location of the ball. With your knees bent, your back straight, and your positioning square to the ball, this body positioning in front of the goal puts you in the best shape to take on any and all comers.

## Building up your save repertoire

Field goalies have to defend a larger net than box goalies do. About 90 percent of a field goalie's saves are stick saves. Generally, field goalies use their bodies to save only when the ball gets by the stick and hits them in the chest.

Lacrosse goaltending comes down to two basic styles of saves:

- ✔ **Reflex saves:** Reflex saves are the kind of saves that you make as a response to a shot — for example, a save that kicks away a low-flying shot, a body save that deflects a high shot, or a stick save that knocks away a bounce shot.

- ✔ **Angle saves:** Angle saves are about positioning your body in the goal in anticipation of a shot. With good body positioning, you're effectively reducing the number of potential angles that an offensive player has for a shot.

## Starting the offense

Possibly the most underappreciated skill that a lacrosse goalie can have is her ability to jump-start the offense with a well-timed and perfectly executed outlet pass. After stopping a shot, a goalie's quick-release pass to a teammate streaking toward the offensive zone can lead to a fast-break, two-on-one (or three-on-two) scoring opportunity.

Passing quickly and accurately is a highly specialized skill, especially with the bulky equipment that goalies wear today. Use your team's practice time to work on your passing. It's a good exercise when your coach has the rest of the team running drills at the other end of the field or floor.

# Chapter 4

# Laying Down the (Lacrosse) Law

*In This Chapter*

▶ Recognizing the playing field (or box)

▶ Following how the game is played

▶ Understanding the game's officials

▶ Playing by the rules

As with any team or individual sport, lacrosse is played by a set of rules. Rules are there for a reason: They help dictate the flow of the game so that all players start on the same level playing field, so to speak. Rules also help the game's fans understand what's happening on that level playing field.

Of course, the primary objective of the game is to score more goals than the other team. And you do this by getting the ball past the other team's goalie and into the netting of the goal.

Whether you're curious about the slashing penalty or just need to know how long the playing field is, this chapter gives you the basic lacrosse rules and regulations.

## Field of Dreams: Playing Field Lacrosse

Field lacrosse is played primarily outdoors (though it can be played indoors on artificial turf) on a large playing surface. Men's teams have ten players per team — three attackmen, three midfielders, three defensemen, and the goalie.

Women's field lacrosse teams have 12 players — 5 attackers, 6 defenders, and the goalie.

Men's lacrosse games are played in quarters lasting 15 minutes for college (for a total of 60 minutes for the game), 12 minutes in most high schools (for a total of 48 minutes), and 8 minutes for most youth leagues (for a total of 32 minutes).

Women's lacrosse is played in two 30-minute halves at the collegiate level (for a total of 60 minutes for the game) and two 25-minute halves at the high school level (for a total of 50 minutes).

## Examining the field

Field lacrosse traverses a large space, which produces a wide-open game with specialized positions and an emphasis on team coordination on offense and defense.

The men's game is played on fields measuring 110 yards long and 60 yards wide.

The women's game is played on a field measuring 120 yards long and 70 yards wide.

Fields are divided by a midline and two restraining lines 35 yards from the end lines; the restraining lines signify the offensive and defensive zones surrounding each goal. A field's midline serves as the off-sides line. When the ball is in one end, seven defensive players (including a goalie) and six offensive players are allowed between the end line and midline.

In the women's game, a defender cannot remain in the *arc* (the 8-meter semicircular area in front of the goal in which major fouls are called) for over 3 seconds unless she's within a stick's length of the offensive player.

Figure 4-1 shows the field lacrosse layout.

Out of bounds is called as it is in soccer or basketball on all plays except shots. If a player throws an errant pass at midfield over the sideline, the possession is awarded to the other team. But if he unleashes a shot over the goal, whichever team has a player closest to where the ball crossed out of bounds gets possession. When a player takes a shot that clearly misses the goal, everyone generally sprints to the end line trying to gain or maintain possession.

Field lacrosse goals measure 6 feet wide by 6 feet high, and the crease is a full-circle 9-yard radius surrounding the goal area. Offensive players are not allowed inside the crease. Goals are waived off and/or possession is given to the defense if an offensive player steps inside the crease.

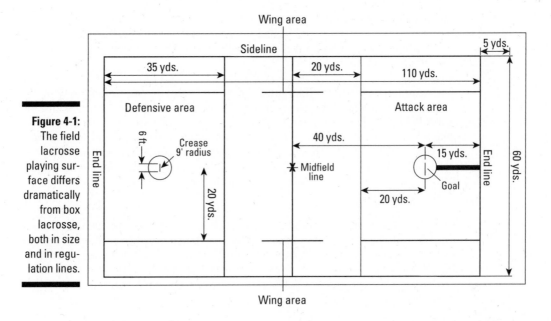

**Figure 4-1:** The field lacrosse playing surface differs dramatically from box lacrosse, both in size and in regulation lines.

The crease violation is a controversial call among some field lacrosse fans. The *dive* (trying for a closer shot by entering the crease by air — that is, not *stepping* in the crease area) was taken out of the NCAA game before the 1999 season in an effort to protect goalies from offensive players leaping into the crease. Although he didn't perform the straight-on dive that the NCAA was worried about, Syracuse's Gary Gait made an unforgettable move by jumping from outside the crease behind the goal and dunking a shot around front against Penn in the 1988 national semifinal game. He pulled the move, later coined the "Air Gait," twice in the 11-10 win.

## Keeping the field game moving

Youth, high school, and college field lacrosse games — for both men and women — have no shot clock for the offense. The men's game does have some rules to help the game keep up its fast-moving pace:

- **Defensive clear-out:** Defensive players have 20 seconds to clear the ball past the defensive area line, or a technical foul is called and possession is given to the opposing team.

- **Five-second count:** If any sort of stalling occurs between the defensive area line and midline, officials will give the player with the ball a 5-second count, during which he must cross midfield or advance within 5 yards of an opponent.

> ✔ **Ten-second count:** When they've moved over the midline, teams have 10 seconds to advance the ball into the attack area. If the offensive team moves the ball out of the attack area after it has entered, a new 10-second count is started.

The summertime professional outdoor lacrosse league, Major League Lacrosse, has a 60-second (formerly a 45-second) shot clock. Coaches and officials have talked about experimenting with a shot clock in the college game. Without a shot clock, officials can keep teams from stalling by issuing a "keep it in" warning if the teams are obviously holding the ball from play in the attack area and not advancing toward the goal. In the last 2 minutes of games, the team with the lead must keep the ball in after it enters the attack area.

Faceoffs begin each quarter and follow each goal. Two players meet at the faceoff, with each team stationing a player on each *wing* (20-yard lines parallel to the sidelines placed 20 yards from the center circle). When the whistle blows, the wing players can converge on the ball, but no other players can cross over the restraining lines and into the middle of play until possession is gained by one team or the other.

Draws are the women's version of faceoffs. The ball is drawn upward after it's put between the sticks of two standing players.

## Substituting players

Attackmen and defensemen are substituted less frequently than midfielders, who generally come on and off in three-man lines. (See Chapter 3 for details about the roles of field lacrosse players.) Some teams have specialty defense units, but the first defensive line generally sees the most action. Faceoff specialists and wing players often run directly off the field as soon as their team gains possession.

A 10-yard special substitution box straddles the midline and serves as the exclusive entrance and exit for all players to the field — no limit is placed on the number of substitutes a team can make.

## Unraveling penalties and physical play

Penalties generally last 30 seconds or a minute, though some penalties last up to 3 minutes, depending on the severity of the violation. (For example, a penalty for using an illegal stick is three minutes.) After the team with the player advantage scores, the offending player is released from the penalty box, unless the foul was non-releasable, in which case the penalty is carried out for the duration, regardless of scoring. Only harsher penalties earn non-releasable calls.

If the team without the ball commits a technical foul, it has to play without a man for 30 seconds. Technical fouls committed by teams with the ball simply give possession to the opponent.

In women's lacrosse, minor and major penalties do not result in extra-player advantages. Instead, the team that receives the benefit of the ball, gets what is called a *free position shot,* which is similar to a foul shot in basketball. For major fouls, the player called for the foul must stand 4 yards behind the offensive player. For minor fouls, the player is placed 4 yards off and in the direction she was approaching the offensive player at the time of the foul.

Because man-up opportunities often last just 30 seconds, one errant pass or ill-advised shot can squander the advantage very quickly. The best NCAA man-up units generally achieve a 50 percent success rate, while the success rate for the best man-down units hovers in the mid-80s.

Any player accumulating five personal penalties is ejected from the game, though this is an extremely rare occurrence, and the player's team does not have to play short-handed after the expulsion. Fighting is almost nonexistent in field lacrosse, thanks in part to stiff penalties. Occasional heat-of-the-moment skirmishes break out during games, but actual one-on-one, gloves-off fisticuffs do not happen in field lacrosse. In the NCAA and at the high school level, fighting results in an automatic ejection, a three-minute non-releasable penalty, and suspension from the next game.

If a goalie commits a penalty, he must serve the time and is replaced with a backup. (For more information, see the nearby "Penalties and goalies" sidebar.)

A field lacrosse player can't *cross-check* (using the portion of the stick between his hands to check his opponent). Cross-checking is a personal foul, earning between one and three minutes of penalty time. In field lacrosse, no check is legal on a player without the ball. Players are allowed to push and use sticks to hold opponents' sticks, as long as they're within 5 yards of a loose ball.

Contact to the body — either with one's own body or with a stick — is not permitted in women's lacrosse, marking the biggest difference between it and the men's game. A defensive player marks an opponent by being within a stick's length of the offensive player.

Lacrosse sticks, or *crosses,* must conform to regulations. One stick is checked at random after each quarter in field lacrosse. Coaches can specifically request that an opposing player's stick be checked. Violation carries a three-minute non-releasable penalty.

### Penalties and goalies

It's not open season on the goalie, as long as he remains in the crease area. When a goalie is outside the crease, an opponent may chase or stick-check him. If the player tries to check the goalie too hard or take him out of the play, a penalty may be assessed. Goalies are aware of this rule and sometimes trick opponents into committing stupid penalties. Also, when a goalie has been taken out on a check illegally, it can lead to payback and additional penalties, because most teams stick up for their goalies.

When in the crease, goalies are not to be interfered with at all. Anything from a ball-possession violation to a major penalty may be assessed for messing with the goalie in the crease.

Goalies may be assessed penalties, particularly when they step outside the crease. When a goalie hits or illegally picks on a player outside the crease, he may be called for a major penalty. (All those pads to protect the goalie from flying balls can be painful to the unsuspecting opponent.)

In field lacrosse, the goalie serves the penalty (with the team getting a minute to warm up the backup goalie), except in some youth leagues in which a designated player (called an *in-home*) does the time. Goalie penalties in box lacrosse are served by a teammate who is on the floor at the time of the infraction.

## Box of Dreams? Inside the Boards in a Lacrosse Arena

You've entered an arena to watch a box lacrosse game. That in and of itself results in a different lacrosse experience for most field lacrosse players and fans, who may have never had the experience of watching a game indoors. As soon as you look at the floor, you notice different markings than you'd find on the ice for hockey or on a basketball court, sports that are also played in an arena. You'll probably also notice that the playing surface is artificial turf rather than cement, wood, or ice.

Although artificial turf is easier to run and fall on than cement, wood, or ice, it's not as easy on the legs as an outdoor grass field is.

The box lacrosse playing area must have boards around the sides and the ends of the playing surface with a minimum height of 3 feet. The fact that the playing area is surrounded by boards — making it "lacrosse with walls" — is another major difference from the field game.

Arenas vary in size, so playing surfaces are not always uniform in size, which also differs from field lacrosse. However, most box lacrosse playing surfaces are 180 to 200 feet long and 80 to 90 feet wide, and the features inside those playing surfaces are the same (see Figure 4-2):

✔ **Restraining lines:** The two lines that run across the width of the floor (from the team benches to the penalty boxes) have several functions:

- They restrain players. The eight players who are not involved in competing for the faceoff must line up behind the restraining lines until the ball comes out of the faceoff circle, at which time they can pursue a loose ball or defend the stick handler.

- They serve as the 10-second threshold. When a team takes possession in its own zone, it has 10 seconds to move the ball over the opposite restraining line. If 10 seconds pass before the ball crosses that line, the team forfeits possession.

- They serve as the over-and-back line. After the team on offense has crossed over the opposite restraining line, it can't allow the ball to go back over that line (toward the center faceoff circle) or it risks losing possession of the ball.

✔ **Change area:** The rectangular boxes that run parallel to the team benches are there for shifting players in and out of the game, similar to ice hockey. A player coming off the floor must have his foot in the box before the player replacing him can come on the floor. If an offensive player comes on the floor too early, the offensive team loses possession of the ball. If a defensive player goes onto the floor too early, the defensive team faces a two-minute penalty. These rules are similar to field lacrosse, except, of course, for the presence of the box in front of the bench, which in field lacrosse is the sideline.

✔ **Crease:** This semicircular marking around the goal is 9 feet in diameter and serves to protect the goalie. In field lacrosse, the crease is 18 feet in diameter. If an opposing offensive player enters the crease, the offense loses possession of the ball. If an opposing offensive player is stepping on the line of the crease or is in the crease and scores, the goal is disallowed. But if the ball goes into the net before he steps into the crease, the goal stands. These rules are the same in field lacrosse.

✔ **Nets:** Box lacrosse nets are smaller than field nets. Box nets are 4 feet wide and 4 feet high.

The playing surface isn't the only difference between box and field lacrosse. Pro, major, and junior box lacrosse games consist of three 20-minute periods (similar to hockey) for a total of 60 minutes, while some youth box games can be as short as 32 minutes.

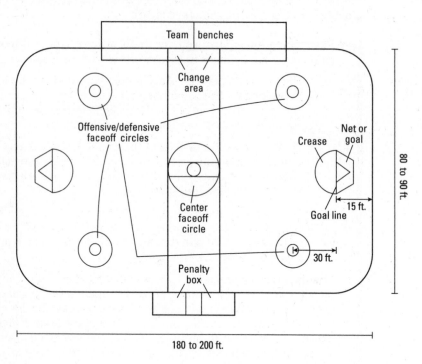

**Figure 4-2:**
The box lacrosse playing surface can measure 180 to 200 feet long and 80 to 90 feet wide.

# Understanding the Game's Participants and Their Roles

A lacrosse game is a match of skill and wits with three primary groups of participants: the players, their coaches, and the game officials. This section offers a brief rundown of what each group of participants does during a game. For more detailed information about some of these gamers, check out Part II of this book for players and Part III for coaches.

## Introducing tonight's players

With more and more skilled athletes playing lacrosse, the game has become more specialized, with players assigned specific roles to match their physical or mental attributes. But, to some degree, every player must be versatile, because in lacrosse, you can go from playing offense to defense and back to offense in a split second.

TECHNICAL STUFF

# Cheers to Beers: The first set of lacrosse rules

The first sign of lacrosse turning into a more organized game came in 1867, when Dr. George Beers, a Montreal dentist, presented a code of rules to a lacrosse convention in Kingston, Ontario. The rules adopted became the basis of the game that developed over the ensuing years, first for field lacrosse and later for box lacrosse:

✔ The object of the game was to send the ball, by means of the lacrosse stick, through the enemy's goalposts.

✔ The game was opened by the act of "facing off," in which two centers held their lacrosse sticks on the ground and the ball was placed between them.

✔ The major rule was that the ball could not be touched with the hands except by the goaltender. The goaltender could only block the ball with his hand; he couldn't throw it with his hand.

✔ The field was a minimum of 150 yards long.

✔ A goal umpire represented each team.

✔ Teams had 12 men on each side with no substitution except for injury.

✔ The positions were goal, point, cover point, center, third attack, second attack, first attack, out home, and in home.

✔ The hair-stuffed deerskin ball was replaced with a hard rubber ball.

✔ A new stick was introduced, with a shaft ending in a sort of crook and a large, flat, triangular surface of webbing extending as much as two-thirds the length of the stick. Because this new stick was large and flat and there was no pocket — unlike the short, narrow, bagged stick used by the Native Americans — the game became more of a catching-and-throwing game than a running-and-dodging game. The new lacrosse stick was held with two hands; players retained the ball in the pocket using a continuous rocking motion.

✔ Fouls included spearing, tripping, holding, slashing with the stick, throwing the stick, stopping the ball with the hands (the goaltender was exempt from this rule), and general rough play. Fouls were penalized either by suspension of the offender until a goal was scored or until the end of the game.

✔ No one could interfere with a player who wasn't in possession of the ball.

✔ The goals were 6-foot-tall poles placed 6-feet apart.

✔ The first side to score three goals won the match.

Because of his efforts in promoting and organizing lacrosse, Dr. George Beers is known as the "father of lacrosse."

The attack players are expected to provide the team with the majority of its scoring. The defensive players, including the goaltender, are expected to prevent the other team from scoring. Midfielders are expected to do it all — including the most amount of running.

Each men's field lacrosse team has 10 players on the field at any given time; for women's teams, it's 12 players.

Unless a player (or two) is in the penalty box, each box lacrosse team has six players on the floor at any one time, including the goalie, a pointman, two creasemen, and two cornermen.

Because most players these days have either offensive or defensive special-ties, you'll see a lot of *line changes* (running to and from the benches as players exchange positions, depending on who has possession of the ball). If a team gains control of the ball, some players run the ball up the field and others run to the bench so that the better offensive players can get on the field to score. If a team loses possession of the ball, some players run back on defense and others run to the bench to get the better defensive players on the field to stop the opposition from scoring. Some players can play both ways — offense and defense — which makes them very valuable.

## Leading the team: The coach's role

The coach's primary role during a game is to change the lines and put out special checking assignments against the opposition's best offensive player. When a penalty has been called, the coach calls for either the man-up offense, when the opposing team is penalized, or the man-down defense, if his team receives the penalty.

Most teams have three coaches:

- ✔ **Head coach:** The head coach oversees the whole operation of the game. The head coach also makes sure that the bench is organized and makes all final decisions on who should play at what time in the game.

- ✔ **Offensive coach:** The offensive coach changes the offensive players and gives feedback to the offensive players to make them better.

- ✔ **Defensive coach:** The defensive coach changes the defensive players and gives feedback to the defensive players to make them better. The defen-sive coach also makes sure that the players pick up the correct *checking assignment* (which tells each player which opposing player to defend).

## Officials: The men in black

In a lacrosse game, a minimum of two — and sometimes as many as four — officials are assigned to work each game. The official's job is to make sure that the rules of the game are enforced. Officials try to assure that the game is run smoothly and is played on as close to an even level as possible. If the players try to take advantage of the rules by doing something illegal, the offi-cial will call a penalty on the offender.

In addition to monitoring the play of the game, officials are responsible for ensuring that players are using the proper equipment, including the appropriate game wear, such as helmets and pads, that help prevent injuries, and the proper game equipment, such as the lacrosse stick.

For more on officials and the role they play, turn to "Officiating Lacrosse," later in this chapter.

# Starting and Stopping Play and Everything in Between

The basic elements of the game are pretty much the same no matter who's playing. To determine possession at the start of each quarter and after every goal, a faceoff occurs. Play is stopped when a goal is scored, when a penalty is called, and when the ball goes out of bounds.

The women's lacrosse version of the faceoff is called a *draw*. Here, the ball is positioned between the opposing players' sticks, which are held horizontally at the center of the field.

Just about every other event that starts or stops play of the game involves ball possession (see Chapter 9). You gain possession from chasing down loose balls and ground balls, from winning faceoffs, from intercepting bad passes, and from recovering shots at the net.

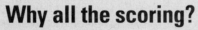

## Why all the scoring?

In 1954, the National Basketball Association (NBA) instituted a 24-second clock — each team had 24 seconds during an offensive possession to attempt a shot or turn the ball over. In its first year of use, the 24-second clock increased scoring in NBA games by more than 17 percent. NBA teams averaged more than 13 points per game over the previous season.

Many levels of lacrosse also play with a shot clock. In Major League Lacrosse (MLL), the shot clock is 60 seconds. In the National Lacrosse League (NLL), a 30-second shot clock begins when a team gets possession of the ball. The offensive team must get a shot on net during that time, or it loses possession of the ball. If the offensive team shoots the ball at the goal and doesn't score, it can recover the rebound or loose ball, after which the clock starts all over again. You can get off a lot of shots 30 seconds or 60 seconds at a time.

You can also lose possession of the ball, turning the ball over to your opponent when they may or may not have earned it. You can give up possession by taking more than 10 seconds to get the ball into the offensive zone, by setting illegal moving picks, by doing an illegal draw on the faceoff (for example, having a foot inside the small circle), by touching the ball in play with your hand, and by having too many offensive players on the field.

# Officiating Lacrosse

If you ask the question, "Who would want to be an official in any sport?" the likely answer would be, "Not too many." Officials are constantly plagued by that question, especially with all the verbal abuse from players, coaches, managers, and, of course, fans. Many fans take officials for granted. Others believe that officials are there to be abused and are convenient to blame when a game is lost. Well, the truth is, without fans, the game wouldn't be the same; but the game *needs* officials to interpret its rules fairly and accurately for both teams so that fans can get the most enjoyment out of the sport.

In field lacrosse, game officials are referred to as just that — "officials." They're known as "umpires" in the women's game and "referees" in box lacrosse.

## Knowing what it takes to be a good official

Working as a an official in any sport, you must gain respect from players, coaches, peers, and fans. And you gain this respect by developing a reputation for calling a good game and by being consistent in the calls that you make.

You have to enjoy the sport, you have to be physically and mentally fit, and, most important, you have to know the rules. Proper positioning — that is, being in the best position to see the most action — is an asset to an official. Conditioning and practice enable you to be in the right place at the right time. Proper positioning also assures players and coaches that you're up to the tempo of this very fast-paced game.

When you're a team player, you get to know your teammates and what to expect of them. The same is true with refereeing: When you work as an official, you often have different partners to cooperate with, so you have to get to know each other's styles.

The hardest and most difficult thing to do as an official is to let the players play the game while still keeping control of it. Officials must know what to call, when to call it, and when to let things go. Patience also plays a big part, because officials are constantly challenged by players who want to find out what they can get away with.

An official calls what he sees from where he's positioned. A good official keeps up with the pace of the game and quickly covers the play. Because youth lacrosse is generally played during the spring and summer, hot weather can add a lot of friction to the game, and tempers can easily flare when calls are missed.

## Looking at the different types of officials

Most high school field lacrosse games are officiated with two or three officials. A bench official is often added for playoff games. College officiating crews are often comprised of a head official and two other officials. A bench official and bench manager may also be used. An official scorer must be provided by the home team.

Two umpires officiate most women's field lacrosse games, though three umpires are used at the NCAA level. The home team must provide an official scorer.

The NLL uses a four-man refereeing system. Three referees — the crew chief, the referee, and the technical referee — are on the floor. The technical referee (or tech ref) watches the benches, determines when a team has too many players on the floor, and starts the faceoffs. The crew chief and the referee call the balance of the game as if they were working only a two-man system, with the crew chief having the final say when discrepancies occur or when something is missed. The fourth referee operates the shot clock, times the penalty situations, and monitors the game flow.

## Managing the games within the game

Throughout any game, officials keep their eyes on what they call *mini-games* (bursts of exciting action that take place over a short period of time, usually benefiting one team only). You may notice some mini-games after a team has been hit with several penalties in a row, after one team has scored several goals in quick succession, or after a team loses a once-commanding lead. All these events frustrate players and coaches, adding an extra challenge to the officials' roles. Good officials recognize these situations and know how to keep control of the game and make sure that all calls are legitimate and not overblown.

In box lacrosse, when referees lose control, fighting will erupt — and this could lead to bench-clearing brawls. Being an official in a brawl situation is tough, and when the crowd gets involved, it can be mind-boggling.

The best any official can do when a fight breaks out is to take a step back and make mental notes on what's happening, looking for the dirty stuff that leads to major penalties and match penalties. When the situation starts to wind down, then the official's "coaching" begins, with a lot of yelling at players and coaches. The players eventually come to grips and stop fighting, as they, too, become aware of the game misconduct and possible suspensions looming.

As for unruly fans, leave them to the public law enforcers who are often present. It's their job.

Here are a few guidelines that can help you become the best official you can be:

- ✔ **Be consistent.** Lacrosse is a fast-paced game with a lot of contact (in the men's game) and many borderline calls to make or not make. So, you have to be consistent in what you call a penalty and what you don't and set the tone early in the game.

- ✔ **Be fair.** Fairness is the most important attribute of any official. Officials are the only objective and neutral arbiters of the game. Act accordingly.

- ✔ **Communicate with coaches.** Talk to both head coaches throughout the game, but especially after calls they may dispute.

- ✔ **Admit mistakes.** We all make them — so will you. When it happens and you realize it, acknowledge it and correct it.

# The Fine Print: All the Rules You Need to Know

The sidebar "Cheers to Beers: The first set of lacrosse rules" earlier in this chapter offers an interesting look at how the game was played in its early years. This section looks at how lacrosse is played today, including the rules that dictate the game and the penalties that enforce those rules, from the perspective of how an official calls the game.

## Playing the game

Though the following game situations may seem clear, the official makes them all, well, official. The official signals you may see during a game for these situations are shown in Figure 4-3.

- ✔ **Delayed penalty:** When a penalty occurs during play and the non-offending team has possession of the ball, the referee signals a delayed penalty, meaning that a penalty is being called against the defensive team. The offensive team is allowed to continue play until the defensive team gets possession, at which time play is called and the penalty is assessed.

- ✔ **Faceoff:** The faceoff takes place after a goal, at the beginning of every quarter or period, or when the ball goes out of bounds or over the playing boards.

- ✔ **Goal disallowed:** If a team scores, but the goal is disallowed because someone was standing in the crease or for some other violation, the referee signals no goal.

- ✔ **Goal scored:** When the ball goes into the net, the referee signals a goal.

- ✔ **Shot on net:** When a shot on net is called, the team closest to the ball when it goes out of bounds gains possession when the ball is thrown in bounds.

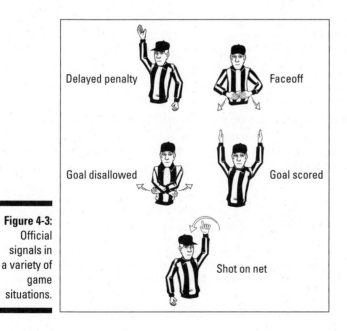

**Figure 4-3:**
Official
signals in
a variety of
game
situations.

Delayed penalty

Faceoff

Goal disallowed

Goal scored

Shot on net

# Losing possession on game violations

These infractions of the rules lead to the offensive team losing possession of the ball. When play is stopped because of these violations, the defensive team receives possession in its own zone. Figure 4-4 shows the official signals for these situations:

- **Five-second count:** After stopping the ball in the crease, the goaltender has 5 seconds to get the ball out and to a teammate or lose possession of the ball.

- **Twenty-second count:** When a defensive team takes possession of the ball in its own zone, it has 20 seconds to push the ball up into its offensive zone.

  In box lacrosse, this is a 10-second count, but the signal is the same.

- **Back over:** In box lacrosse, when an offensive team has the ball in its offensive zone, and the ball goes back over the offensive line into the neutral zone or into the defensive zone, for any reason other than a shot on net, the offending team loses possession of the ball.

- **Free-hand check:** If the stick handler pushes off a defending player, usually with his upper arm and forearm, possession is awarded to the non-offending team.

- **Goal-crease violation:** This violation is called when an offensive player reaches or leans into the crease (except for faking or attempting a shot). Minor and major penalties may also be assessed for illegal play around the net (see the next section).

- **Hand ball:** If a player other than the goalie touches the ball with his hand outside of the goal crease, possession is awarded to the non-offending team.

- **Shot-clock violation:** In the MLL, if the offensive team does not attempt a shot in 60 seconds (30 seconds in the NLL), it loses possession of the ball. (The official has no signal for this violation; instead, the shot clock buzzes to indicate that time has expired.)

# Paying for penalties

Men's lacrosse has timed penalties — 30 seconds, 1 minute, and 3 minutes in field, and 2-, 5- and 10-minute penalties as well as match penalties in box. Combinations of penalties can also be assessed depending on the infraction.

**Figure 4-4:**
Official
signals for
game
violations.

5-second
count

20-second
count

Back over

Free-hand check
(or warding off)

Goal-crease
violation

Hand ball

In women's lacrosse, teams receive free position shots after penalties, which are similar to foul shots in basketball in that the team that benefits from the call is awarded a free shot on goal (or pass if it so chooses).

Box lacrosse also has game and gross misconducts, which are not timed penalties but instead exclude the penalized player from the game (and possibly future games, depending on the severity of the penalty).

The team that is called for the penalty must serve it, resulting in the offending team playing one player short. The non-offending team goes on a man-up (field lacrosse) or power play (box lacrosse), which gives them an advantage for the time of the penalty. If the non-offending team scores during the penalty, the penalized player can leave the penalty area and return to play. For a major or match penalty, the man-up (or power play) can result in two potential goals before the penalty is wiped out. Depending on the league, the penalized player may or may not be released; if not, another player can play for the balance of the penalty time.

The most common personal fouls in men's field lacrosse are

✔ **Slashing:** No stick swing is allowed against the body of the opponent.

✔ **Tripping:** Any checking below the waist of an opponent, whether by a stick or by any part of a player's body, is tripping.

✓ **Unnecessary roughness:** This is called when excessive contact to the opposition, which can often be violent, occurs.

✓ **Cross-checking:** Cross-checking is usually delivered to the midsection of the arm or on the back area. Cross-checking is legal when the opposing player is in possession of the ball. When the cross-checked player doesn't have the ball, it's an infraction.

Other personal fouls include

✓ **Illegal stick:** Officials perform random stick checks at the end of each quarter to make sure stick length and pocket size conform to regulations. For example, if, when placed in the pocket on a stick check, the top of the ball is under the top of the sidewall, the stick is illegal. (For more on stick regulations, turn to Chapter 2.)

✓ **Unsportsmanlike conduct:** This penalty may be assessed when a player or someone on the bench conducts himself in an unsportsmanlike way.

✓ **Illegal body check:** This penalty occurs when a player checks an opponent below the waist, above the shoulders, or from the rear, or when he checks an opponent who is within 5 yards of a loose ball or who doesn't have possession.

Technical fouls include pushing, holding, off sides, illegal screens, stalling, and warding off.

## Penalties in the box

Here are some of the two-minute box lacrosse penalties, also referred to as minors:

✓ **Cross-checking:** See the "Paying for penalties" section for a description.

✓ **High-sticking:** No stick-check is allowed above the shoulders of an opposing player.

✓ **Holding:** When a player grabs hold of another player's body, sweater, and/or stick, thereby keeping him from the play, this penalty is called.

✓ **Checking from behind:** This penalty is called when a player cross-checks an opponent from behind. This penalty can be a 2-minute, a 5-minute, or even a match penalty, depending on the severity of the hit.

✓ **Hooking:** A player can't use the stick as a "hook" to slow down an opponent.

✓ **Interference:** This penalty applies to several situations. It's used when a player makes contact with an opposing player during a line change, or otherwise interferes with a player or goalie. Other examples include when a player loses his stick and an opponent redirects it so that it can't be retrieved, or when a player gets in the way of another player who doesn't have the ball but is executing a play.

✓ **Slashing:** See the "Paying for penalties" section for a description.

✓ **Tripping:** See the "Paying for penalties" section for a description.

✓ **Unsportsmanlike conduct:** See the "Paying for penalties" section for a description.

✓ **Too many players on the floor:** This infraction usually occurs when one player is a little too fast to get on the floor during a line change (or one player is a little too slow to get off the floor).

All the common minor penalties can lead to 5- or 10-minute penalties, depending on the severity of the infraction and the discretion of the referee. Here are some of the common 5-minute penalties:

✓ **Boarding:** Players may hold up opponents against the boards to try to slow down their momentum or steal the ball, but checking a player into the boards brings down a major penalty. If you bring down the player and he doesn't get back up, you may be up for some serious suspension time.

✓ **Butt-ending:** Jabbing an opponent with the butt end of the lacrosse stick (or sometimes even pretending to jab your opponent) will land your butt in the penalty box for 5 minutes.

✓ **Charging:** No credit card will get you out of this penalty. A 5-minute penalty is given for rushing and running into an opponent.

✓ **Fighting:** Drop your gloves and you may be finished for the game (and your team will likely spend the next 5 minutes of the game short-handed). Drop your gloves more than once, and you could risk missing several games or even the rest of the season.

✓ **Spearing:** Similar to butt-ending, this penalty involves jabbing an opponent with the mouth of your stick.

Unfortunately, extreme penalties do occasionally happen in box lacrosse. These infractions typically involve getting caught up in a fight between two other players (called *third man in*); severe unsportsmanlike conduct, usually directed toward a referee; and deliberate attempts to injure another player. Get hit with one of these penalties, and you'll be leaving the game earlier than you anticipated. You'll also likely be suspended. These penalties are the 10-minute penalties, game misconducts, and match penalties. For these penalties, you'll be removed from the game and a teammate will take your place in the penalty box.

# Part II
# Playing Lacrosse

The 5th Wave      By Rich Tennant

©RICHTENNANT

"Your passing's fine, but you're still scooping a little deep."

## In this part . . .

*H*ere you discover how to be the best lacrosse player possible. For offensive players, this part includes tips and tricks to improve your passing, catching, and shooting skills. Defenders find out about proper positioning, delivering legal checks, and defending the most popular offensive plays, among other topics. We also throw in a separate chapter just for goaltenders. This part covers the value and fundamentals of playing team offense and defense, as well as an overview of the possession game, including a look at the importance of faceoffs and ground balls. We fill you in on the important role of specialty teams. Finally, we help you take your game up a notch, mentally and physically.

# Chapter 5

# Getting the Ball into the Goal: Developing Offensive Skills

*In This Chapter*

▶ Creating magic with the stick: Stick-handling skills

▶ Cradling the ball

▶ Catching and passing the ball

▶ Moving — with and without the ball

**D**efense wins championships. Having possession of the ball is as important as it gets. So too is limiting turnovers and penalties. But, in the end, the name of the game is scoring. That's because the team with the most goals at the end of the game wins. You can't get much simpler than that. In order for your team to get to that point, however, players must have offensive skills that lead to numerous scoring opportunities. In this chapter, we show you how to develop your offensive skills — or the skills of the players on your team, if you're a coach — to help your team score big.

## Grasping Basic Stick-Handling Skills

Few players are great stick handlers, the kind you watch with awe from the stands. A backhand shot into the top corner of the net or an over-the-shoulder long bounce shot, a great stick fake on the goalie or on a defender, a great pass threaded through a crowd of players into the receiver's stick — you wonder how they saw any opening and how they could get that shot or pass off. All these moves, and more, make up stick handling. When a player has skills, the ball seems to be glued to his stick, and his stick has "eyes" on every pass and every shot.

Because lacrosse players don't actually touch the ball as they do in basketball, this skill is best labeled *stick handling,* rather than *ball handling.* But you'll hear people use the term *ball handling* in lacrosse. Just know that it means the same thing.

How do you become a great stick handler? Simple. You practice and practice and practice, on your own time. You pass at the wall, you play one-on-one with an imaginary defender, and you do crazy tricks with the ball in your stick. You practically sleep with the stick and ball — they're with you all the time, wherever you go. You do this until the ball and stick feel like they're an extension of your body and until you can do almost anything you want with the ball.

## Getting a grip

The key to handling the stick — whether you're cradling, catching, passing, or shooting — is the grip. You hold the stick with your fingers, snugly but loosely, so that your wrists can turn and rotate freely. You definitely don't want to grab the stick tight with your fingers wrapped around the shaft and the palms of your hands touching the shaft.

Where you place your thumbs is an individual preference — place them wherever they feel comfortable. Some players like to let them just gently wrap around the shaft; others like to place them along the shaft.

Where you place your *top-arm hand* (the hand that's attached to the arm that's closer to the top of the stick) also depends on where it feels comfortable. Your top-arm hand can be placed slightly below or slightly above the midpoint of the handle. (***Note:*** If you're a left-handed player — that is, if most of your passes and shots come with the stick on your left side of your body — your top-arm hand is your left hand. Right-handed players use the right hand as the top-arm hand.)

Your bottom hand is usually placed at the butt end of the stick. Some players like to make a bump with tape at the end of the handle so that their hands don't slip off the end of the handle, and for better support of the stick.

Your grip on the stick doesn't change much during a game. In other words, you keep the same grip whether you're passing or catching. When shooting, players typically slide their top-arm hand down closer to the bottom hand so that they can get more of a whip in their shot, which helps them get more power.

If you're a beginner, you may have trouble catching the ball, so try to grip the stick higher up on the shaft, even at the throat of the stick, to make catching the ball easier. Holding the stick this way is almost like holding a baseball glove, and you improve your chances of catching the ball. When you go to pass, you can always slide your top hand down the shaft to the midpoint area.

## Cradling the ball

*Cradling* is maintaining possession of the ball in the pocket of your stick without passing, catching, or shooting and without having to look at the ball. With practice, you'll know when the ball is in your stick by feeling its weight, not by looking at it. By cradling, you can look at the net, see your teammates cutting, and concentrate on beating your defender, all without worrying about whether you have the ball in your pocket.

The idea of cradling is to use both your wrists and arms to create the most amount of rotation possible. A cradler puts his dominant hand at the top of the stick and his other hand at the bottom. The dominant wrist and arm should curl toward the shoulder on the dominant side, while the other hand should simply guide. It has no purpose in the actual cradle.

Cradling is the key to ball handling in the women's game. Without a pocket to stabilize the ball, women's players must employ centrifugal force, using a sweeping yet controlled movement of the cradle to anchor the ball in the stick. Cradling is often taught to beginners as an ear-to-ear motion — the shaft of the stick is held vertically to either the left or right ear before it's slowly moved to the nose and then to the opposite ear, before repeating the process in the other direction and back. As players' skills advance, they modify their cradling so that it's done with minimal motion and on one side of the body only.

In field lacrosse, you have more room to run than you do in box lacrosse, so you have to be more versatile at using both hands with the cradle. But, because field players have more space to work with, they can sometimes employ a one-handed cradle, using the free arm to protect the arm in which they're carrying the ball and keeping the stick vertical.

A warding penalty can be called if you use your free arm in any way to hold, push, or control the defender.

Most box players have better stick skills and protection than their field lacrosse counterparts, because box players can't simply run away from defenders while cradling the ball. They're constantly under pressure from someone.

Players practice three basic styles of cradling, depending on the game situation:

- ✔ **Small cradle:** You use the small cradle (shown in Figure 5-1) when standing stationary, looking to pass to a teammate, or getting ready to shoot. You hold the stick in a horizontal position while rocking only the stick's head back and forth slightly by the wrist of the top-arm hand, getting ready to pass or shoot. The small cradle locks the ball into the middle of the pocket, setting it up for a quick shot, dodge, or pass.

- ✔ **Medium cradle:** You use the medium cradle (shown in Figure 5-2) when running up the field or floor with the ball in a passing or shooting position. Here, you hold the stick at a 45-degree angle to the field and the cradle is a little more vigorous. You use the top-arm hand to swing the stick and head forward and backward to keep the ball in the stick while you're looking to pass or shoot.

✔ **Large cradle:** You use the large cradle (shown in Figure 5-3) when taking a check. You hold the stick in a vertical position with large movement of the stick swinging in and out from your body, using the top-arm hand. When the stick is held in this position, your body protects the stick while you continue to cradle to feel the ball in your stick.

**Figure 5-1:**
The small cradle is great for when you're standing still, looking to pass, or preparing to shoot.

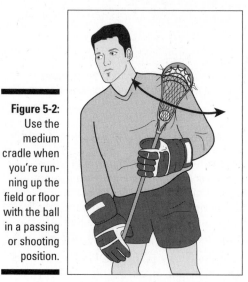

**Figure 5-2:**
Use the medium cradle when you're running up the field or floor with the ball in a passing or shooting position.

**Figure 5-3:**
The large cradle is useful when you're taking a check.

# Beyond Handling: Catching the Ball

Most players who first play the game have more difficulty catching the ball than passing it. It's amazing how the ball can fall right into an inexperienced player's stick and he can still wind up dropping it. A player who's new to the game will tend to tighten up on his grip as the ball approaches his stick instead of relaxing his grip and relaxing his top-hand arm. By tightening up, the stick acts like a tennis racquet and the ball ricochets off it. This section starts with the basics of catching, before we move on to passing.

## How to position your body for the catch

The first step in catching the ball is to make sure your body is in the right position. Face the stick handler and hold your stick up over your shoulder and in front of your body for a target. Hold the stick with your fingers — in other words, don't grab the stick hard — and place your thumbs along the shaft. Your top hand should be slightly below midpoint of the handle, while your bottom hand is placed at the butt end of the stick. For beginners, keep your eye on the ball all the way into the pocket of the stick.

## Give and you shall receive the catch

*Giving* is moving the stick back to absorb the ball into the pocket of the stick. To explain the importance of giving on the catch, consider whether you could catch a tennis ball with a tennis racquet. If you held the racquet out straight and didn't move it when the ball hit, the ball would bounce off the racquet. But if you tried to absorb the tennis ball onto the racquet by moving the racquet back as the ball moved toward it, the ball would drop onto the racquet without bouncing off.

Catching in lacrosse involves the same motion. Start with the stick beside your head. As the ball approaches the stick, relax your top arm backward and drop the stick back to gradually absorb the ball into the pocket of the stick. By the time you actually catch the ball, the stick should be behind your body (as shown in Figure 5-4). And now you're in a position to pass the ball back to your partner.

In women's lacrosse, the best technique to use is to both give and catch passes at ear level to develop correct habits as opposed to the bucket catch, in which the stick is dropped and the ball settles in place without much skill being necessary.

Always catch passes with two hands, and don't move your hands while catching. Then, after you catch the pass, swap hands quickly — move the head of the stick from one hand to the other. The defense will be forced to adjust and won't know which direction you're going.

These days, players don't *wind up* their sticks as much as they used to. Winding up is pulling a stick far behind your waist or below your shoulder before shooting. Instead, most of today's players hold the sticks beside their heads to catch and shoot all in one motion. This adjustment helps them get off their shots quickly, giving the goalie less of a chance to stop the shot.

# What's the Catch? Building Your Passing Skills

To play lacrosse successfully and with confidence, you have to know how to handle the ball and pass it. As with catching the ball, the most important place to begin is with your stance.

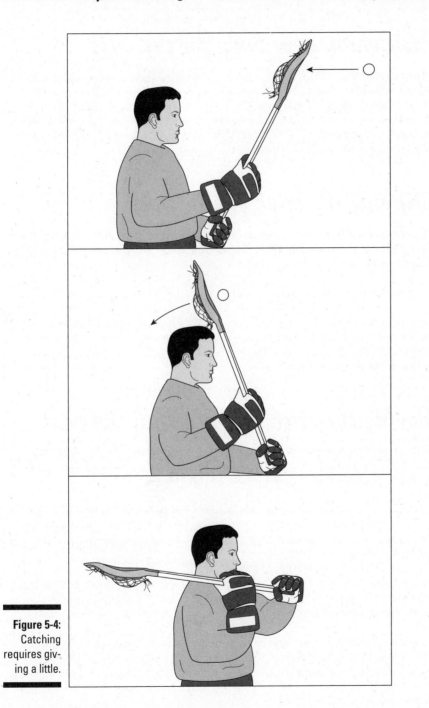

**Figure 5-4:**
Catching
requires giv-
ing a little.

## Positioning your body for the pass

A sideways stance is the best position for passing the ball because it also helps you protect the stick in a game. Before you pass, position yourself sideways from the player who will receive the pass. This position is more realistic in a game situation, because if you have the ball in your stick, you're probably being checked or bothered by a defender. Turning your body sideways protects the ball from the defender.

## Gripping the stick for the pass

The grip of the stick is the same as it is for stick handling and catching. Your top hand is at the midpoint of the shaft, and your bottom hand is at the end of the handle.

Always pass with two hands.

Some players like to move their hands closer for passing and farther apart for catching, but you want to make sure not to move your hands when passing. When you have the ball, hold the stick vertically at a 45-degree angle with your top hand beside your head.

## Moving the stick forward with the pass

To start your passing motion, move the top hand straight back, with the butt end of the stick pointing at your target. As you prepare to release the ball, step with your front foot to get power into your pass.

On the forward motion of the stick, transfer your weight from the back foot to the front foot — the foot opposite your stick. Be careful not to step with the foot on the same side as your stick because you'll not only lose power but look and feel awkward.

As you bring the stick forward, snap both your wrists and bring the stick's head straight ahead — not across your body — with your top arm fully extended and the butt of your stick touching your elbow (see Figure 5-5).

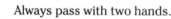

To make sure that you've thrown a perfect overhand pass, your stick should come close to touching your elbow. In reality, the butt of your stick doesn't usually end up touching your elbow — it misses your elbow by a few inches to the inside. What you want to avoid is the butt ending up in the stomach area, which creates a side-arm passing motion that isn't as accurate as the overhand passing motion.

**Figure 5-5:**
The passing
motion.

# *Remembering the keys to good passing*

Here are some other important passing points to keep in mind:

- ✔ **Don't hold onto the ball too long.** If you do, you'll open yourself up to drawing a check from the defense, or even drawing a double team.

- ✔ **Throw hard, crisp passes that are short and parallel to the field.** The shorter the pass, the less chance it has of being intercepted.

- ✔ **Don't stand still after catching the ball.** Make the defense work by moving around.

✔ **Try to pass after picking up a ground ball.** Because the ball was loose, a defender is probably behind you ready to check you or try to strip the ball away. So try to find the nearest open man (preferably with a short stick). This strategy is also crucial for igniting your team's transition game — a key component for just about any successful lacrosse team.

✔ **Stress accuracy over power.** Pass quickly but don't sacrifice accuracy.

✔ **Use the head of the receiver's stick as your target.**

✔ **Keep in mind that every pass thrown is the responsibility of the passer.** Make eye contact with your receiver to let him know that you're looking for him. When you do so, you become the eyes of your receiver. If your receiver is covered or turning his head for the pass, keep your eye on your teammate's defender to see if the defender is going to hit him.

✔ **Don't pass out of panic.** Even if you have a defender — or two — draped on you, keep moving and look to make a good pass instead of forcing a pass that could easily be intercepted.

If you drop passes regularly, you could be thinking too far ahead of yourself — that is, thinking of shooting or passing off the ball before you catch it. You drop the ball not because of poor technique, but because of poor concentration. Concentrate on catching the ball first, before you think of shooting or making a play.

In order for a team to pass successfully, the players must be adept at moving without the ball and moving well to the ball. Good movement without the ball allows you to get open so that you can catch a pass. Moving to the ball is especially effective when you aren't being watched by the defense.

# Working on Passing and Catching Drills

Passing and shooting on the run are among the most important elements of lacrosse. Being able to seamlessly pass, catch, and shoot on the run is much more important than any behind-the-back shots, bounce passes, or stick fakes.

Behind-the-back passes and bounce passes are more common in box lacrosse than they are in the field game. The playing surface is smaller in box, so players use behind-the-back passes to deceive the opposition because there is less reaction time. And bounce passes are a more reliable form of moving the ball in box lacrosse than they are on grass.

The drills in this section are designed to help you improve your catching and passing skills. You can work on these drills by yourself, with a partner, or with your teammates before or after practice. Or you can play a little pass-and-catch around the neighborhood with a group of friends.

Here are some key things to focus on during passing and catching drills:

- ✔ **Situate your body in a position so that you block the defender from the ball — similar to boxing out in basketball.**

- ✔ **Look at your partner's stick head.**

- ✔ **Relax the stick right before the ball arrives, and let the momentum of the ball carry it back a few inches.** Think about catching the ball as if it were an egg.

- ✔ **Don't stab at the ball when you're trying to make the catch.** If you do, the ball will likely pop out.

- ✔ **After catching the ball, drop your stick farther back.** This way, you can pass the ball from behind your body, with your stick level to the field.

- ✔ **Throw hard, level passes, and stay away from rainbow passes.** Rainbow passes are high-arcing passes that take forever to reach their destination. By the time the receiver catches the ball, he's being hit by the defender and he can't make a good play.

- ✔ **Snap your wrists forward on the release of the ball.**

- ✔ **Freeze your stick on the follow-through.** In other words, hold your stick for a second at your target so that you get more accuracy on your pass.

- ✔ **Take pride in hitting the receiver's stick.**

Make sure you're continually fixing or correcting your stick's head. Check where the pocket should be, how deep the pocket should be, and how many shooting strings there should be. (See Chapter 2 for more about the stick head.)

# Individual passing drills

Here are a couple of passing drills that you can practice on your own. These drills emphasize the progression of passing and catching — grip, catch, and pass.

### 1-on-0 form passing

In this drill you pretend to pass without a ball. It's a good idea to have a teammate or coach watch you — someone who can tell whether you're doing all the basics right. Good passers should be able to analyze themselves or other players and correct their mistakes.

### 1-on-0 stationary passing

Shoot and pass against a wall, the arena boards, or a target high on the Plexiglas. All the great players develop their passing skills with this drill.

# Partner passing drills

The following drills are ones that you can practice with a teammate or a parent or a coach. These drills are how great passers are made. Do a few of them every day to develop into a good passing player.

## 2-on-0 stationary passing drills

These drills will definitely help with your passing form. In these drills, just two players pass back and forth; it may help to have a third player around to watch and help correct any flaws.

- ✔ **Practice catching with one partner throwing the ball with her hand, not with her stick, to the other partner.** You can start with tennis balls so that you avoid the tendency to "cheat" by using the weight of the lacrosse ball to help you catch.

  This simple drill is important, because if you start to throw the ball back and forth with your sticks, the balls will be on the field or anywhere except near the receiver's body. By throwing the ball with the hand, at least you're throwing accurately and your partner will have a chance to practice catching.

- ✔ **Pass and catch with only one hand, usually the top hand.** This is a good drill for catching and developing wrist snap for passing.

- ✔ **Pass and catch from a passing distance you would normally throw from in a game, about 30 feet.**

- ✔ **Move closer together and pass from a short distance, about 10 feet apart.** Continue making hard and level passes, even at this distance.

- ✔ **Move to opposite sides of the field to practice passing from a far distance.** Again continue making hard and level passes from this longer distance. You may have a slight arc on the pass because of the distance, but not enough to slow the ball down.

- ✔ **Practice fake passes.** From a normal distance, fake a pass one way and then pass the other way to your partner.

- ✔ **From a normal distance, do "hot potato" or "quick stick" passing.** This is passing without any real catch — the ball goes in the stick and is thrown back, all in one motion.

- ✔ **Practice winding up for a long shot and then passing.** Take a wind-up position, stick level to the field, as if you're going to shoot. Then fake a shot by twisting your top wrist in before passing.

- ✔ **Practice fake shots.** Fake a shot by bringing the stick across the front of your body and then back as if shooting, but instead pass to your partner. Or you can fake a shot by turning your stick in with your wrists, freezing the defender, and then stepping across as if shooting, but instead passing to your partner.

### 2-on-0 stationary timed passing

In this drill, you and your partner count the number of passes you can catch in 30 seconds.

In a variation on this drill, if you're practicing with a number of teammates, you can race to see who's the first pair to catch 20 passes.

### 2-on-0 stationary passing with two balls

In this drill, one partner throws a ball in the air while the other partner throws bounce passes.

### 2-on-1 "monkey in the middle"

This defensive-pressure drill helps you avoid panicking with the ball when you're being pressured by a defender. Stand about 20 feet apart from your partner, with a defensive player between the two of you. The defensive player attacks the stick handler and tries to intercept his pass. The stick handler passes around the defender's stick to his partner. The stick handler can't pass until the defensive player is close to him.

For a variation on this drill, the passer can fake a pass and step around the defender to pass. The defender then goes after the other partner and plays that person's stick.

### 2-on-0 passing on the run

For this drill, you work with a number of teammates. Players form two lines beside the net — right-handed players in one line, and left-handed players in the other. Partners run down the field to the other end, passing back and forth.

## Team passing drills

Here are some passing drills that you can work on as a team, either at practice or before a game, in addition to the ones your coach gives you.

### Knockout drill

Line up six players — three sets of partners opposite each other. Start the drill with two balls. The players pass the balls back-and-forth in random order. If a player throws a bad pass or drops a good pass, she gets a point. When a player has three points, she's out of the drill. The drill continues until there are two players left passing two balls back and forth and, finally, one winner.

The only rule is that you can't pass to a player who already has a ball.

### Pepper drill

Line up four passers with one ball opposite one receiver who has a ball. The passers pass to the receiver quickly, and as soon as the receiver passes a ball, the next passer passes to him.

Make him pass quickly so that as soon as a ball is released, another one is coming at him.

### Zigzag drill

This drill improves stick handling because of its high repetition of passing.

Line the whole team up with everybody opposite a partner. Place a bucket of balls at both ends of the line. From one end, the players pass all the balls down to the other end of the line in a zigzag formation.

# Beating the Defender: Moving with the Ball

The great lacrosse players are great because they can easily beat a defender and score. You need to be able to pass or collect ground balls, but the biggest offensive asset that a player can have is to be able to beat your opponent one-on-one.

## Protecting the ball in the stick

You're going to handle the ball sometime during a game, so you need to know how to protect it from a defender. The key here is the ability to cradle, pass, and shoot the ball without looking at it. You need to know that the ball is in your stick by cradling and by feel — this gives you freedom to concentrate on protecting the ball from a defender by looking at her rather than trying to look at the ball and at the defender at the same time.

## Taking a check

Another step in the basics of beating a defender is learning how to take a check. The natural tendency when you get hit is to tighten up with your body, but this can cause you to become rigid with the stick. Plus, when you're hit, the ball will be jarred loose out of your stick. Instead, do the opposite when you receive a check: Relax and lean into the direction of the force of the hit.

When you see or feel a hit coming, take a wide stance to absorb the hit and cradle the stick, making sure the ball faces away from the force of the direction of the hit so that the ball doesn't pop out of the stick. As you approach your defender with the ball, hold the stick low and horizontal across the front of your body. Just before you get hit, bring your stick up in a vertical position and turn your body sideways to take the hit on the arm, protecting the ball in the stick. Keep your head up to look at the net; you may want to shoot or watch your checker over your shoulder to see what he's going to do next.

You can slide your top hand up to the throat of the stick to cradle the ball on a hit, or you can keep your top hand at the midpoint mark of the handle to be in a position to pass or shoot.

Unless you're an experienced player, don't try to pass when you're being checked. Instead, hold onto the ball until you're free to dish it off to a teammate.

## Dodging

One of the most important attributes of any player on offense is the ability to dodge. Dodging is the lacrosse equivalent of a basketball player driving to the basket past a defender and not just settling for catching and shooting from outside. In lacrosse, the purpose of a dodge is to free your hands to make a pass or take a shot.

These key elements all lead to effective dodging:

- ✔ **Use both hands.** This way, the defender won't know what direction you're heading. The easiest player to prevent from dodging is the player who isn't adept with his off hand. If you aren't adept with your off hand, the defender will overplay your strong hand, forcing you to pass off.

- ✔ **Keep your head up.** By keeping your head up, you'll have a good view of the entire field, which will help you see where to pass or shoot after you complete your dodge move.

- ✔ **Protect the stick.** If you don't protect your stick, the ball will probably be stripped by your defender. Protecting your stick is especially important when dodging because, by their very nature, dodges usually are made when within a stick check's reach of the defense.

- ✔ **Change direction and speed.** Doing one or both of these things is an effective way to set the defense up for a dodge.

In the following sections, we cover the five primary dodge moves.

# The keys to beating a defender

If you want to be a good one-on-one player, you need the following assets:

- The ability to hang onto the ball when being checked.

- The ability to move both ways — inside to the middle of the field and outside toward the sideline.

- First-step quickness to change direction.

- Balance to stay standing.

- Upper-body strength to receive a hit and overpower your defender.

- Intelligence to out-think the opponent.

- Deception to make the defender expect an action and then see something else.

- Instinct — great players have a knack for beating defenders without thinking about how they do so.

A great saying in lacrosse is to be quick, but don't hurry. When beating a defender, you should have control of your body. Keep your offensive moves simple — the less movement, the better. Stay relaxed and loose, with your knees bent. Slow down and do things with a purpose, using patience before you accelerate. When you hurry, you tend to appear unsettled, frantic, flustered, and confused.

Remember, however, that if you don't attack the defender, he'll attack you. So neutralize your defender by making him react to an offensive move.

### Face dodge

In a face dodge, you run at a defender, pulling the stick across your face to the opposite side of your body, and then continue around the defender using your body to shield the stick.

### Split dodge

A split dodge involves more of a fake than the face dodge does. You run right at the defender, stutter-stepping and switching the stick from one hand to the other. This move is very similar to the crossover dribble in basketball.

The key is to fake that you're going in one direction, and then change directions — and hands — after planting your outside foot. Changing speeds completes the move to perfection.

### Roll dodge

A roll dodge is a spin move, in which you slip around a defender using your body to shield your stick. Run at a defender with your stick in your right hand, plant with your left foot, and spin away from and around the defender. (Do the opposite if you're starting left-handed.)

### Bull dodge

A bull dodge is common in the box game and really can only be used effectively by an offensive player with size and power. It's simply leaning into a defender while cradling the stick away on the opposite side and using your size and strength to create enough room to pass or shoot.

### Question-mark dodge

The question-mark dodge is the most complicated of the dodge moves. Starting behind the goal, you can go left or right, curling around and in toward the goal, before sharply spinning back away from the cage and shooting, creating a question-mark path.

This move is not used to beat a defender as much as it is to create enough space to get off a shot.

# Cutting: Moving without the Ball

Moving without the ball helps you to beat a defender and get in the clear for a pass. The most basic play and effective move without the ball is the *go play*, where you just cut past your defender from the off-ball side. It can be a move of first-step quickness and deception; you knock your defender's stick down and go.

Another common move is the body fake, a deception in which you make your defender think you're going to do one thing and then you do something else. The body fake is a move more of quickness than of strength. Your quickness helps make the fake move look like the real thing, instead of looking like a fake. You make a body fake usually on the run to get your defender off balance by reacting to your fake. You can make one of two body fakes:

- ✔ The outside-fake move, where you fake a cut to the outside and then cut back inside
- ✔ The inside-fake move, where you fake a cut to the inside and then cut back outside

The other type of fake is the fake shot, which is an offensive move that has more to do with the stick than the body. A good fake shot freezes the defender for a split second to give you enough time to go around him. You can wind up to fake a shot and then pull your stick in front of your body and go around the outside of the defender.

## Cutting to the cage

So you want to know what the best box lacrosse players, the ones in the National Lacrosse League, use to beat the best defenders? Read on.

✔ **The inside-slide or bull move:** This is the most common one-on-one move used by players to cut across the top of the zone. All you do is lean into your defender and try to muscle your way past him across the top of the offense, a natural move. Usually, this move starts on the side of the floor so that, when you eventually get by your defender, you're in the middle of the floor in a good position to shoot.

You have to turn your body sideways to take the cross-check on your non-stick shoulder, remembering to take a wide stance for balance and support and to lean with your body and dip your shoulder into the cross-check. Swing or cradle your stick vertically so you know where the ball is. When you have the ball in your stick, it should never stop moving.

✔ **The outside-slide move:** In this move, the stick handler leans into his check and cuts outside toward the boards to slide back in toward the net. You need this move to counter the inside-slide move when defenders overplay you to force you to the boards. In the past, this move was used only periodically, but now it's executed as much as the inside-slide move.

When you approach the defender, turn your body outward facing the boards, while at the same time swinging your stick outside to protect it. Taking the cross-check on the stick side, or inside shoulder, lean your body weight on the defender as you move down the side of the floor, trying to weasel your way back in to get on the inside of the defender.

✔ **The inside and outside spins:** To execute the inside spin, you fake the outside-slide move (make it look real), lean on your defender who is cutting to the outside while receiving a cross-check, and then quickly roll back inside and cut across the top for the shot.

To execute the outside spin, you fake the inside-slide move (again, make it look real), lean on your defender cutting to the inside while receiving a check, and then quickly roll back and cut outside for the shot.

Relax on the hit. Resisting a check is counterproductive. Instead, you should relax your body to become dead weight and equalize pressure, which makes it harder to push you out of the way. And protect your stick after you go by the defender because the defender will go after your stick from behind you to dislodge the ball. In fact, some defenders even let you go by them on purpose — this is called the *matador defense* — and then try to stick-check you from behind. This is similar to the *trail check,* in which a defender checks the stick of an offensive player from behind out of necessity but not by design — because the offensive player is one or more strides ahead of the defender, often near the goal area.

# Practicing Individual Offensive Drills

Though lacrosse is a team game, you can play it by yourself to get better. The great players have always stressed how important it is to their games to go to a wall and practice on their own. They always have a stick in their hands. Instead of putting it away between practices, they constantly cradle or shoot. They play against imaginary defenders, practice stick faking or body faking, or shoot at a net or a wall. All this practice is never work to them, but fun, helping them in their drive to be the best.

You can practice many of the drills in this section on your own. But most important, take a tip from the game's great players and work with your stick whenever you have the chance, not just in practice or during a game.

## Individual cradling drills

The drills in this section help with both cradling and stick handling.

### 1-on-0 stationary cradling

Stand still and practice cradling the ball in your stick. This is one of the best drills that you can do at any time, anywhere, on your own.

For a little variety, try jogging while cradling.

### 1-on-0 fake shot

From all positions (overhand, sidearm, and underhand), just keep the ball in your stick and circle your body without dropping it. Or keep the ball in your stick and wave the stick out in front of your body.

## Stick-handling drills with a partner

Try your hand at these 2-on-0 catching and passing drills with a partner:

- **Pass two balls simultaneously.** You can try both players passing through the air, or one partner passing through the air and the other throwing a bounce pass.
- **Throw underhanded passes only.**
- **Throw sidearm passes only.**
- **Throw behind-the-back passes only.**

✔ **Pass and catch the ball with only one hand on your stick — first your left hand and then your right hand.**

✔ **Swing your stick to your opposite hand and then flip the ball underhand or overhand to your partner.**

# Protecting-the-ball-in-the-stick drills

Working with your teammates or a couple of friends, these drills help you with ways to keep defenders from poking the ball out of your stick.

### 1-on-1 circle drill

In this drill, the defender tries to check the stick handler's stick using the over-the-head check, wraparound check, or stick-check. The stick handler looks over his shoulder to protect the stick while constantly cradling. The stick handler can only move in a confined area. Start and stop on the whistle, or you can play it so that whoever hangs onto the ball the longest is the winner.

### 1-on-2 circle drill

This drill is similar to the drill in the preceding section, except the stick handler can move a little bit more because he now has two defenders trying to get the ball off of him.

# Taking-a-check drills

As a lacrosse player, you have to be ready to take a hit, even when you're practicing. Working on these drills will help you get your body ready to absorb a real hit during a real game.

### Shoot-through drill

Start with four lines — two down low just behind the goal and two above the restraining line. (Two players act as defensemen on either side of the goal.) The drill starts with the upper lines carrying the ball and passing off to the players down low, who catch the passes while moving toward the goal. The stick handlers then power through hard checks from the defensemen before unleashing their shots.

### 1-on-1 bump drill

The defensive player pushes the stick handler with his hands, and then he bumps the stick handler with his body. The key here is that the stick handler has to relax his body on any hit instead of tightening up.

# Making a game of drills

Running drills doesn't have to be all work and no play. Here are a couple of suggestions for turning your box lacrosse practice sessions into a competition:

✔ **Tag game:** Use five balls with six players in a confined area marked off by cones. The player without the ball is "it," and he must go after the stick handlers and try to steal a ball from one of them. If he's successful, the player whom he stole the ball from is now it.

✔ **British bulldog game:** In this game, there are two teams, one along the sideboards with balls, the other in the middle of the floor. On the call "British bulldog," players with the balls run across the floor to the other side, trying not to get checked off or lose the ball. If a player is checked and loses the ball, he now becomes part of the defensive team to check the stick handlers. Last man with a ball is the winner.

### 1-on-1 charging defender drill

In this drill, the stick handler is stationary while the defender runs at or charges the stick handler to hit him with his body and dislodge the ball.

The stick handler must relax on the hit.

### 1-on-1 equalize pressure

The stick handler leans on the defender and moves across the top of the field or floor, trying to slide off the check for a shot. If he runs out of territory, he rolls or spins back and still leans on the defender, but he tries to cut around the defender on the outside.

In a variation on this drill, the stick handler leans on the defender and moves outside, trying to slide off the check and back inside for a shot. If he runs out of territory, he rolls or spins back and still leans on the defender, but he tries to cut around the defender cutting across the top.

### 1-on-1 man-in-the-middle drill

The defender plays behind the offensive man who receives a pass from the pointman at the top of the offense. The defender can only push on the offensive player while the offensive player leans into him relaxed to catch the ball, turn, and shoot.

# Beating-a-defender drills

These drills are best practiced with teammates or friends. You need to have the experience of seeing a defender lose his balance or get fooled in some way so that you can anticipate when to blow past him.

### 1-on-1 offensive-move progression

This drill is a progression to practice offensive moves — first when neither player has a stick, then when only the offensive player has a stick, and finally when both players have sticks:

- ✔ One partner practices an offensive move to beat his partner. The defender plays token defense by just leaning on the stick handler with his stick.

- ✔ One partner practices an offensive move to beat his partner. The defender pushes and shoves with his stick.

- ✔ One partner practices an offensive move to beat his partner. The defender uses solid checks.

### Gauntlet drill

In this drill, stick handlers zigzag, or go in and out, around a straight line of stationary players. This drill helps players work on balance, quickness, protecting the stick, and relaxing when taking a hit.

The stationary players can't move, but they can check the stick handlers as they go through the line to force them to protect the balls in their sticks. They can try to stick-check the stick handlers to try to get the ball from them, either while the stick handler faces them or after the stick handler has passed them.

### 1-on-1 offense from a stationary start with a cross-field pass

Start with two lines with balls — left handed and right handed. The first offensive player in each line is covered by a defender. The first offensive player in one line doesn't have a ball, but he receives a cross-field pass and then goes one-on-one against the defender, just as in a real game.

The offensive player who just passed receives a pass from the next player in line and goes one-on-one. You rotate from the offensive line to a defender.

### 1-on-1 live half-field drill

Start these one-on-one drills with the stick handler having a ball, with the defender having the ball and passing it to the offensive player, from a ground-ball situation, or from a pick situation. Here are some variations:

- ✔ The stick handler tries to beat the defender by turning sideways to receive the cross-check.

- ✔ The stick handler tries to beat the defender by turning his back to the defender and rolling back and forth.

- ✔ The stick handler tries to beat the defender by working him (rolling back and forth, faking one way or the other) for as long as he can. With patience and continual movement, an offensive player can beat any defender.

- ✔ The stick handler tries to beat the defender when the defender tries to take the ball from him. The defender can use an over-the-head check or wraparound check.

- ✔ The stick handler tries to beat the defender facing him in just 5 seconds.

The offensive player should keep his stick cocked as much as possible, always look to shoot, and not shoot from the wrong side of the field, but go back to his proper side to shoot (that is, the left-shot side or right-shot side).

### 1-on-1 off the bench

A right-shot player rolls the ball to the goalie and breaks for a return pass around midfield. When he catches the ball, a left-shot defender comes off the bench to play defense. They go one-on-one.

### 1-on-1 game

Make up two teams — right shots and left shots. The defender has the ball and passes to the offensive player in front of him. The offensive right shot gets one point if he beats his defender and another point for a score. You can play to 15 points.

Here are some variations on this drill:

- ✔ The stick handler on the run attacks the defender.

- ✔ The stick handler, from a stationary position, attacks the defender.

- ✔ The stationary offensive player receives a cross-field pass and then goes one-on-one.

- ✔ The offensive player cuts to the ball on the run for a pass and shot.

- ✔ The offensive player receives a down pass in the corner area or pops out and goes one-on-one.

# *Taking shots after beating a defender*

The section "Practicing individual offensive drills," earlier in this chapter, offers suggestions for some of the most basic offensive moves that you can make to try to get in position for an open shot. You can use the following drills to work on both those moves and the shots that follow the moves. Shoot against an outdoor target or at the net before or after practice.

- ✔ **Inside-slide move, across the top of the zone, or an outside-slide move and shoot:** If you're working with a friend or teammate, ask him to hit you while running or shooting.

- ✔ **Inside- or outside-spin move and shoot:** Practice shooting while running.

- ✔ **Outside body fake and shoot:** Fake outside, cut inside, and shoot.

- ✔ **Inside body fake and shoot:** Fake inside, cut outside, and shoot.

- ✔ **Fake shot, cut to outside, back to inside, and shoot.**

- ✔ **Fake shot, cut to the middle in front of the crease, and shoot.**

- ✔ **Fake shot while sidestepping down the side, and then cut across the top in front of the crease for a shot.**

- ✔ **Fake shot while sidestepping down the side, and then spin outside and in for a shot.**

- ✔ **Bait move while being checked:** Expose your stick over your shoulder, and when the defender goes after it, pull it back in and shoot.

When you take the shot, aim for an area behind the goaltender because he'll probably move. So if you look toward the goalie, the shot will probably wind up hitting him. Shooting with a quick release is also an effective weapon in scoring goals. For starters, it often prevents the defense from getting in position to throw a check. Plus, it prevents the goaltender from getting set up to make a save.

# Chapter 6

# Putting the Ball in the Goal: Shooting Fundamentals

## In This Chapter

▶ Improving your shooting skills

▶ Taking outside shots

▶ Taking shots from close in

▶ Practicing shooting drills

Shooting is one of the most important skills a lacrosse player can have. And great shooters have the knack of not only shooting the ball straight — and hard — but also "thinking" their way around a goalie. Shooting is just like passing a ball against a wall, but a little bit harder. (In fact, later in this chapter, we explain how using an actual wall can help you improve your shooting skills.)

In lacrosse, every player on the field is allowed to shoot and potentially score — even goaltenders (though on extremely rare occasions). And that's a good thing, because scoring is the *fun* part of lacrosse. There's nothing quite like hitting the back of the net behind a goalie.

In this chapter, we offer the fundamentals of shooting to score, as well as the skills you should work on and some drills to help you build those skills.

## Becoming a Great Shooter

Some lacrosse players seem to be able to score at will; others couldn't get the ball in the water if they fell out of a boat, to borrow a saying that shows how bad some players can be at it. If you work on your shooting form, you'll definitely improve your *shooting percentage* (the number of goals you make divided by the number of shots you take), making you a better shooter.

Some players just don't have the touch or feel for shooting. Whether it's their technique, their body size (usually too bulky), their stick, the way they hold their stick, their confidence, their selection of shots, or their timing, one or more of these traits is keeping them from being good shooters.

## Acquiring a shooter's stick

The tool of the trade for the shooter is the stick (also known as the *crosse*). The great shooters can take the head of a stick apart and restring it the way they like it. The pocket is crucial to becoming a great shooter.

Great shooters' sticks have a few things in common:

✔ **A pocket that's located high:** You'll never meet a great shooter who has any of the following: a pocket that is at the *throat* of the stick (where the head joins the handle of the stick). Some shooters like the feel of the ball hitting the end of the plastic frame of the head just slightly so that they know the ball has left the stick. A high pocket, which is near the scoop of the head, is ideal for perimeter shooting in the field game and is the pocket of preference for box players, too.

✔ **A pocket depth that's about equal to a ball's depth:** Great shooters don't have a pocket that's too shallow (because the ball has a hard time staying in a shallow pocket) or too deep (because then the stick can't be used to pass and shoot quickly and accurately). They have to get the pocket depth just right — about a ball's depth — and the ball should come out of the pocket nice and smooth.

   Depending on the type of shooter you are, you may find different types of pockets to be more effective. The deeper the pocket, the more whip and power it has. Outside shooters generally employ deeper pockets to put more power behind their shots. Inside players don't need as much power; they benefit more from a shallower pocket that zips the ball right off the stick.

✔ **A pocket with shooting strings:** *Shooting strings* are adjustable strings that run horizontally below the head of the stick. The ball should rest at the tip of the pocket on the last shooting string.

## Getting the ball past the goalie

To shoot a little white ball behind a goalie into a net takes more than just the ability to hit an open spot. Why? Because goalies tend to move. If goalies just stood there and gave you the shot, lacrosse wouldn't be much of a game. So the first trick to shooting is to learn to read the goalie.

---

# Can great shooting be taught?

Do great shooters have a touch, a natural thing, something they're born with? Some players were born with *soft hands* — they can catch, throw, and shoot effortlessly and accurately. But most players have to put in the practice time to make themselves better shooters.

After you've mastered the proper mechanics of shooting, you have to practice every day to take your shooting skill to the next level. Confidence comes from taking 100 to 200 shots a day until you feel confident about where the ball is going and can hit that spot on the wall almost every time.

---

Some goalies, called *reflex goalies,* show you an open spot and then take it away. Others come out on an angle to take away openings. They're ready to move sideways, anticipating where you're going to shoot by reading your eyes, reading the position of your stick, or just plain guessing where they think the shot is going. (For more about the types of saves that goalies make, see Chapter 8.)

The great shooters believe that they can shoot faster than a goalie can move, so if they see an open spot, they just shoot it. Goalies can be scored on because they have more to contend with than just a stationary shooter. Goalies have to move according to where the ball is, watch for cutters, and be aware of opponents around the net.

## Focusing on form

To become a player with "the touch" — someone who can shoot hard with the ball always going where it should — you have to be aware of your shooting form. Great form means never looking as if you're forcing your shot.

*Soft hands* (see the nearby sidebar, "Can great shooting be taught?") come from having proper form: using your wrists, holding the stick with your fingers loose, extending your wrists back when cocking your stick, and then extending your wrists fully on the follow-through.

## Resolving shooting problems

If you've mastered a shot in practice, why can't you make it in a game? A number of things can contribute to this problem:

✔ **You may have stopped believing in yourself.** By practicing your shooting until you know you can hit whatever you're aiming at, your confidence will soar again.

✔ **You may be *telegraphing* your shot (looking directly at where you're going to shoot).** Limiting your windup — just catching and shooting — keeps the goalie on his toes.

✔ **You may be taking bad shots (for example, from a bad angle or from the wrong side of field), or maybe you're being pressured or checked when you shoot.**

✔ **You may be rushing or hurrying your shot.** Be patient. If you don't have a good shot, don't shoot.

✔ **You may be *bombing* your shot (just winding up and shooting at no particular spot).** Winding up is essential for perimeter shots, but you need to have a target in mind when you take them. Aiming to either side of the goal is helpful.

✔ **You may lack concentration by not focusing on the open spot.** Great shooters can focus on one thing — the open spot left by the goalie — and block out everything else.

If your fundamentals are fine, but you're still having trouble shooting, you may be in a scoring slump. Sometimes players play uptight, so remember to have fun and relax. Or you may be trying too hard, so remember not to force your shot. Finally, just go back to the basics and practice, practice, practice.

# Shooting from a Long Distance

The variety of long shots that you can work on include the overhand shot, the sidearm shot, the underhand shot, and the backhand shot (see Figure 6-1). It doesn't matter what type of shot you use. The options for long shots include the straight long shot for either top corner of the net, the long bounce shot for either top corner or mid-corner, and the long low shot for either bottom corner. You also have in your repertoire the fake long shot, which takes a quick *stick fake* — bringing your stick across your body while stepping to the outside and then back in for the shot.

When you're working on your perimeter shot, keep in mind the following:

✔ **Look at the whole net on your shot and pick the open spot.** Avoid looking directly at the spot you're shooting at because some goalies watch your eyes. Some players try to trick the goalies by looking at one corner and shooting to the other corner.

✔ **Shoot with rhythm rather than flat footed.** Players, whether they know it or not, *hop-step* (hop with the back leg, and step with the front foot) into their shot to synchronize all their body parts with the stick. In addition to the hop-step, at the end of your shot you should take a forward step to create a wide stance for the all-important transfer of body weight from the back foot to the front foot. This motion helps to get more power into your shot.

✔ **Make sure that you *cock* the stick by dropping your stick straight back to wind up for your shot.** Cocking the stick gives you the much-needed power to shoot long.

✔ **Shoot the ball when it's in the stick and still behind your head.** This technique gives you more power than releasing the ball when it's beside your head or in front of your body. The actual release of the ball from the stick is important in getting velocity in your shot.

You want to shoot hard but you don't want to sacrifice accuracy for speed. The most important thing to focus on is getting your shot on goal so that the goaltender has to make a save.

**Figure 6-1:** Clockwise from upper left, the overhand shot, the sidearm shot, the underhand shot, and the backhand shot.

Former Syracuse University standout Paul Carcaterra, now a television analyst with CBS College Sports and the MSG Network, says shooting is all about the follow-through. "Your hands should be away from your body," he says. "That way, the head of the stick will be outside as well. One thing leads to another. *Remember:* No alligator arms, because then, you'll be pushing the ball. Rotate your hips while shooting and then complete your follow-through almost as if you're sweeping the stick toward the ground after releasing the shot."

Great shooters know that they can shoot faster than a goalie can move.

✔ **Shoot in your range.** If you're in your range and you feel able to make your shot, the shot will be more relaxed. If you aren't in your range — if you're too far out from the goal to feel comfortable about the shot — you'll probably force your shot, trying to make up for the distance. For great shooters, the fastest shots are the ones they swing easy with. They don't try to swing or force the shot too much.

If you don't have a good shot or don't see an opening to shoot at, don't shoot. Shooting discipline is critical. Many players end up just shooting at the goalie, regardless of whether they have something to shoot at.

✔ **Before you shoot, make sure your stick is not being interfered with.** That means no stick or body is directly in front of your shot. You may be able to use defenders not directly in front as screens — but there needs to be a gap between you and the defender so he doesn't interfere with your shot. Don't shoot around opponents unless they're playing back from you and can't interfere with your stick. If you've beaten your defender, you should be one step ahead of him and be wide open before you shoot.

✔ **You should be able to hit the open spot you're shooting at.** Have patience when shooting. Just before you shoot, take a split second to look at where you're going to shoot. Some players rush their shots — they take *automatics* (shots without thinking) and end up hitting the goalie in the chest area or *playing catch* with the goalie (shooting a shot that's easy for him to save).

✔ **"Think" your way around the goalie.** Positioning and strategy are critical to developing good shooting accuracy. Sometimes you don't need to just shoot the ball straight and hard. Instead, make it look as if you're going to shoot to the far corner by holding your stick in the sidearm position, and then bringing it over your shoulder in an overhand shot, shooting for the near side.

If you're shooting straight on with the goalie, step into the middle in front of the crease to move the goalie sideways and get him away from his near goalpost. This move gives you two options to shoot at: the far corner or the near corner.

## Knowing the two best areas to shoot long

Striving to get a high shooting percentage gives your team a higher chance of winning. To help your team achieve a high percentage, here are the two best areas on the floor from which to shoot long shots:

- ✔ **Exactly in the middle, where you have many options to pick from on the goalie:** Here, you still have good options from the far corner (high or low) and the near side (high or low).
- ✔ **Off-center on your proper shooting side.**

Shooters commonly aim their shots for opposite the goalie's stick side, because it takes more time for a goalie to move his stick to make the save. But keep in mind that goalies are conditioned to expect shots to be taken there. So a more effective move is to look toward an area before shooting, such as the low-left corner so the goalie expects the shot to go there, and then fire it to the opposite side (in this case, the high right side).

## Nailing the overhand shot

When you're trying to make an overhand shot, your stance is important because, in a real game, you'll typically be turned sideways to protect your stick from your check.

Hold the stick with your fingers loosely, with the top hand just below the half-way point on the shaft. Your stick should be high and behind your head, vertically at a slight 45-degree angle. If you're really winding up to shoot, move your stick backward, level to the field in a cocked position.

The shot originates from behind your head and you release the ball when it's behind your head, but you follow through after the ball is gone. Pull the stick forward by extending your top-hand arm forward and snapping the wrists. On the follow-through, make sure you fully extend your top-hand arm and that the head of your stick points at the target.

The stick motion is directly over your shooting shoulder or to the side of that shoulder for the overhand shot. To get power, synchronization, and rhythm in your shot, step or hop-step into it. Step with your front foot to give yourself a wide stance, which adds power to your shot. Arm extension is crucial: Extend your arm as if you're throwing a football downfield, with your arm fully extended.

# Shooting Closer to the Goal

Crease players need to step out in front of the net to execute close-in shots and not stand on the side of the crease. Timid players tend to stand beside the crease instead of taking the step out in front of the net to get a better shot because they're worried about getting hit from behind.

When you're taking a straight close-in shot, no fake, just look at one corner and shoot at the other corner of the net. If you're taking a close-in shot to the far side of the net, you can take three types of shots:

✔ Start from an overhand shooting position to an overhand shot.

✔ Start from an overhand shooting position to a sidearm shot.

✔ Start from a sidearm shooting position to a sidearm shot.

When you're taking a close-in shot to the near side of the net, you can

✔ Start from an overhand shooting position to an overhand shot.

✔ Start from a sidearm shooting position to an overhand shot.

## Developing a great fake

Most faking in lacrosse happens around the net, but you may sometimes do it when you're far out with the ball or when you're in trouble with the ball. Faking is used in lacrosse more than any other sport in the world.

You need to develop different fakes for different situations:

✔ **Fake with your body.** Jab your foot one way and go the other way.

✔ **Fake a long shot with your stick.** This fake freezes your defender and allows you to go around him.

✔ **Fake a close-in shot against a goalie.** This fake allows you to get the goalie's reaction or to freeze the goalie, and you can then shoot to the open spot.

✔ **Fake a pass.** You freeze your defender to get yourself out of trouble when you're being pressured by a defender and you don't know what to do. A good fake pass against a defender checking you either freezes him or gets him to react by looking to intercept the pass, giving you time to go around him or at least giving you time to make a play.

---

# What to do on a breakaway

Breakaways are common in the box game, because of the limited length. Breakaways can occur two to three times a game and usually originate from the defensive end when a defensive player anticipates an opponent's shot and heads for his offensive zone early, although you sometimes can pass to an open player coming off the bench.

If you get a breakaway in a game, make sure that you run down the floor off-center, not down the middle or straight at the goalie. This gives you the option of cutting across the crease to move the goalie so that you can shoot to the near or far side of the net.

---

## *Becoming a good close-in shooter*

Patience is an extremely important asset around the net. But the longer you hang onto the ball around the net, the greater your chance of getting hit. So if you want to be a good player in close, you can't be afraid to get hit, because you will.

When you're cutting or running across in front of the net, the general rule is to put the ball back where you came from — that is, in the near side of the net.

When you fake a shot at a goalie and he doesn't move, shoot at the corner you just faked at. You can fake right at a big goalie's body, knowing he won't move, but you'll freeze him so that you can then pick and shoot. The other option you have against a big goalie is not to fake at all — just pick and shoot. The bigger goalies tend to rely more on angles.

# *Practicing Shooting Drills*

You can work on shooting drills on your own with some kind of target that matches the dimensions of the net, or with a friend or teammate acting as the goalie. These drills, however, focus on what you can do in practice or with a group of teammates.

# Focusing on long-ball shooting drills

As you're working on your long-ball shots, here are a few fundamentals to keep in mind:

- ✔ On your windup to shoot, your stick should be level to the field.
- ✔ Release the ball when it's behind your head.
- ✔ Cock or twist your wrists before you release the ball to make sure it's in the shooting pocket.
- ✔ Visualize a perfect shot.
- ✔ When you're incorporating cutting into your drills, cut hard to the ball or pass the ball hard to the cutter. Before you cut, fake a cut the opposite way in which you want to cut, and cut with your stick up and ready to shoot.

Mix up the spots on goal. You may want a teammate or a coach to shout out where to aim. Alternate between shots at each corner, mix bounce shots in with shots aimed to the top or bottom of the net. And don't forget to practice your fakes.

Work with several teammates to practice the following perimeter shooting drills. Remember to alternate right- and left-handed shooters in the drills.

### Single-line drill

Every player has a ball and lines up in the center. Players run down and take a straight, perimeter shot from near the top of the box. Change shot locations each time down the field.

### Semicircle long-ball shooting drill

Form three lines in a semicircle near the top of the box. Each line shoots continuously, first around the horn and then alternating from side to side. After a player shoots, he should fade off to the side.

### Two-line shooting drills

With each player cradling a ball, start the two lines from the top of the box and then from the top middle. The lines can alternate sides shooting, first all right shots and then all left shots.

- ✔ Lines start from the top side of the field and cut across the top, alternating among planting their feet and shooting an overhand shot; shooting on the run; and faking a shot, pulling the stick across their body, and shooting.
- ✔ Lines start from the top side of the field, facing an imaginary defender, and just wind up and shoot.
- ✔ Lines start from one side of the field and cut across the top, alternating among planting their feet and shooting an overhand shot; shooting on

the run; and planting, faking a windup, pulling the stick across the body, and shooting.

✓ Lines start from the top corner area of the zone and then cut across the top, shooting on the run.

## *Working on close-in shooting drills*

When practicing your close-in shots, don't forget these tips:

✓ **Follow your rebound.**

✓ **Make sure that you step around in front of the net before you shoot.**

✓ **Place your top hand higher on your stick when you're faking.** You can fake with your wrists only (no arm action), or you can fake with your wrists and arms together.

✓ **On faking, turn your wrists in and fake hard.** Think to yourself, "I'm going to shoot," so you make your fake look real. But remember to check back so that you don't end up shooting instead.

✓ **Against bigger goalies, don't fake — just pick and shoot.**

Mix up the spots on goal. You may want a teammate or a coach to shout out where to aim. Alternate types of fakes before shooting to alternating corners — for example, fake high and then shoot low or fake low and then shoot high.

---

## Shooting games

Here are a couple games that you can work into your shooting practice routine:

✓ **Shooting game "21":** Make up two teams, usually left shots against right shots. Players can take any type of shot. You get one point for a close-in shot, two points for a long shot, and three points for a long bounce shot. For variation, try close-in shooting only. A game goes to 21 points.

✓ **Breakaway shooting game "15":** In this game, the stick handler runs the full length of the field, and the coach calls out which shot to take: a straight close-in fake and shot, a long shot on the run, or a long shot

from a stationary position just inside the box. The game is played to 15 points.

And here's a game that you can do on your own to practice shooting:

1. **Bring a bucket with about 60 balls with you to the field along with nine cones.**

2. **Place the cones at nine different spots inside the box, along with six balls.**

3. **Starting from the spot farthest from the goal, go from each spot to the next, shooting six balls on goal from each of the nine positions.**

Work with several teammates to practice the following close-in shooting drills. Remember to alternate right-shot and left-shot shooters in the drills.

### Single-line drill

Every player has a ball, and all the players line up at midfield. Players run down the field, one right after the other, and take straight, close-in shots in rapid succession. Run the line of players again, this time giving players the option to fake or just shoot.

### 2-on-0 shooting drill

Players form two lines — right shots and left shots — one on each side of the crease. Each player cradles a ball. On the run, the players alternate from side to side and shoot around a cone, which is placed in the middle of the crease.

So that you don't have players running into each other, keep the left shots inside and the right shots outside.

### 2-on-0 passing drill

One line, the passing line, is in the side position, passing diagonally to players in the other line. The passer passes to a stationary player in the crease area, who takes a quick shot. The passer should work on looking at the net while passing.

## Don't forget the goalie

If you're a coach and you're working on shooting drills with your team, remember to tell your goalie what's expected of him during the drill. You want your goalie to improve along with your shooters.

Here are some important guidelines:

✔ The goalie needs to be properly warmed up before a game or practice. This means taking shots from a designated "warm-up" shooter, who is often a coach or assistant coach.

✔ The goalie should stand in a standard possession in the middle of the net so that he's ready to react to whatever types of varying shots he'll face.

✔ The goalie should keep his body in a balanced position, so he can easily adjust his position depending on the shot.

✔ The goalie should remain patient and not get jittery or jumpy while waiting for the opposing team to get a shot off.

✔ The goalie should make his own arc, or imaginary semicircle. This is an area in the middle about 2 feet from the goal line that covers shots that arrive at both the left and right of the goalie at varying angles and heights.

Rotating his body positioning will help both the shooter and the goalie. The goalie will become comfortable defending the net from different positioning perspectives, and the shooter will be able to practice against a goalie in a variety of different positions.

# Chapter 7

# Keeping the Ball out of the Goal: Developing Defensive Skills

*In This Chapter*

▶ Defending the stick handler

▶ Defending other offensive players

▶ Drilling defensively

The fast pace of a lacrosse game is generally dictated by the offense. But that speedy offensive pace requires quickness and stamina from lacrosse players on the defensive side of the field, too.

This chapter gives you the strategies and tactics you need to make yourself a better individual defender. For information about building team defensive skills, see Chapter 10.

## Stopping the Ball: Taking On the Stick Handler

Keeping up with the stick handler requires the solid combination of a number of skills, both physical and mental. This section reviews some of the skills that you need in order to play good individual defense.

### Communicating with your teammates

For some reason, most lacrosse players have a hard time communicating on the field. Being vocal is a must because of all the action and movement that happens in a game — and this is especially true when you're on defense.

Good defensive communication in a game should cover the following:

- **Picks and screens:** Warn your teammates when they're about to be picked off or become the victim of a set screen. (Picks and screens help free up an offensive player so that he can get a more open look at the net or cut to an open spot for a pass.)

- **Cuts:** Let your teammates know when an offensive player is cutting toward another spot to receive a pass, usually a position that allows an easier shot on goal.

- **Who's guarding whom:** When defending an offensive player, let your teammates know who you're playing against, especially when a pick or screen causes you and another defender to switch checks. By not communicating, you may create a situation where two defenders are inadvertently guarding the same offensive player, leaving someone somewhere wide open for an easy shot.

- **Helping:** Some game situations dictate when it's okay to have two defenders guarding the same offensive player (called *double-teaming*). If you leave your matchup to double-team the stick handler or another offensive player, let the teammate you're helping know so that he can apply more defensive pressure and play more aggressively than usual.

## Playing with your feet

One of the keys to defending well is to keep your body in balance. Your feet play the biggest role in keeping your body in balance. You play defense with your feet to maintain good position. As the offensive player moves, you move your feet while staying in your position of readiness with your knees bent, back straight, looking directly at your opponent's chest, not at his stick or the ball.

A few strategies can help you defend in certain situations:

- **Drop step.** You drop step when the stick handler makes a move to the net to maintain a cushion. The drop step allows you to be ready to throw a check by having weight on your front foot so that you can push off from this front foot to stay with the stick handler. This way, if the stick handler decides to attack the net quickly, you're in the position to move back quickly. The defender should remain centered and ready to adjust if the offensive player moves forward, rolls back, or changes direction.

- **Defend the body, not the stick.** Don't play an offensive player's stick on a windup for a shot — you don't want to challenge what you think may be an upcoming shot. The stick handler could fake his shot and go around you, looking for an easier shot or for a teammate cutting to the net. Play your opponent's body, not his stick.

✔ **Shuffle step.** As you move with the stick handler, often down the side-lines as he tries to beat you, take short shuffle steps, or lateral side-steps, shuffling sideways to stay with him (as shown in Figure 7-1).

Keep a wide stance as you shuffle. Don't bring your feet close together or you may lose your balance. Also, don't cross your feet when shuffling. You're more likely to trip over them than gain any advantage against the stick handler.

A good way to improve your footwork is to jump rope, including weighted ropes. To start, jump rope 50 times. Then increase that amount each day in increments of 25.

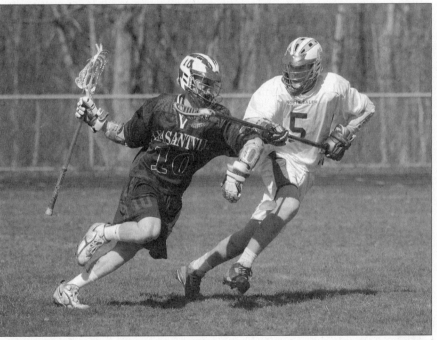

**Figure 7-1:**
Proper defensive footwork is crucial in lacrosse.

Photo by Jim Stout/MaxPreps.com

## Playing with your head

We're not suggesting you make a header as you would in soccer — although lacrosse balls have been known to ricochet off helmets. Instead, we're talking about on-the-spot thinking.

On defense, you have to play with your head differently from the way you do when you're on offense. On offense, you can do all kinds of things without thinking. But on defense, you're *always* thinking and trying to anticipate what's going to happen before it does.

Knowing your opponent's strengths, favorite moves, and tendencies helps you in this anticipation. Which is his dominant hand? Is he quick? Does he like to shoot from the outside? Does he like to work inside?

Offensive players are creatures of habit, always trying to make the same move. As a defender, you have to know what your opponent is trying to do so that you can take away his primary move.

## Establishing effective defensive positioning

Defensive positioning simply means being in the right place at the right time. In fact, many coaches feel that establishing good defensive positioning is half the battle of playing solid defense.

Play with your knees bent to make sure that you stay low, and with your feet placed shoulder-width apart for balance. Taking this low body position allows you to make quicker and stronger moves against the offensive player.

Also, make sure that you keep your head up by keeping your eyes directed to the top of the offensive player's chest area or the top of the numbers on his jersey. Avoid looking directly at the ball, because you'll probably end up trying to go after the ball, stick-checking, and being beaten off the ball. Also, if you drop your eyes to look at the waist area, you'll end up dropping your head — again giving the offensive player the chance to beat you.

Checking is important, but taking the correct position against the stick handler helps you prevent more scoring opportunities. Never give up body position to throw a stick check. Plus, when the offensive player is a threat to feed, the defender should constantly keep the stick out in front to apply pressure to the bottom hand.

The key area to defend on the field is often referred to as the *hole.* It's the 7-yard radius around the goal. According to Adam Lodewick, defensive coordinator at Yorktown High School in New York's Hudson Valley, "If offensive players are moving in there freely, then your defense isn't doing its job." To help protect the hole, players should *slough in,* or stay tight toward the crease. This concept of protecting the crease area forces the offense into settling for lower-percentage shots from the perimeter.

## Slashing or checking?

Especially in the National Lacrosse League (NLL), you'll see wraparound checks. These checks occur when the defender works around the stick handler to get at the ball, poke-checking to dislodge the ball and pressuring the stick handler. The poke-check is a move to dislodge the ball. The defender tries to poke his stick between the offensive player's stick and body to pry the ball loose.

Slashing also has a place in lacrosse. When coaching slashing, be sure to encourage players to give a two-handed slash on the stick handler, just to let him know what kind of game he's going to be in. But even while using the stick to slash, the players have to stay down. Of course, in field lacrosse this kind of slashing is illegal. Checking players with a stick is just that: a check.

In most game situations in box, the most effective defensive positioning against the stick handler is to force him to the sideboards. To do so, overplay the stick handler *half a man* — in other words, turn your shoulders to the sideboards either a quarter-turn or parallel to the boards.

## Playing hard and with heart

You have to play hard and with heart. Maintain an attitude that suggests you'll never give up. More often than not, getting to ground balls and playing solid defense are the result of who wants it the most.

Lacrosse is an aggressive game. To defend well, you need to be aggressive — not only in your play but also in your attitude. Defenders who have a reputation for being cocky and mouthy are thought of as pests. They bother people defensively, irritate their opponents, and generally tick people off. They're also usually thought of as good defenders.

## Defending the field of play

The distance from one end line to another on a lacrosse field is pretty long. So too are the sticks of the defensemen. Field lacrosse teams generally use three long-stick defensemen at once, though a fourth can be deployed as a midfielder. So space is important — a defensive player needs to use his stick to hold off and keep the midfielder or attackman at a distance.

# Cross-checking

A significant way in which box lacrosse differs from field lacrosse is that cross-checking is legal in the box game. In a cross-check, a defensive player applies pressure to the stick handler with his stick.

The defender holds the stick with two hands and applies it to the stick handler's upper-body area. This defensive strategy works to slow down the stick handler's drive toward the goal, perhaps forcing him to try an off-balance shot or pass off to a teammate.

When holding the stick to cross-check, your hands should be about body-width apart and your arms should be cocked. The open face of your stick should point backward to allow for easier pickups of loose balls by just turning your handle. Cross-checking should only be used to stop a stick handler, so you should keep both hands on the stick.

Good defense requires the defensive player to make two or three good cross-checks on a play, rather than one big hit. He has to move his feet constantly to keep up with the stick handler so that he can make multiple cross-checks.

Patience is the key in not getting beaten by the stick handler. One of the most important things to do to play good defense is to wait for the stick handler to come to you instead of reaching for or lunging at him. While waiting, make sure that you keep your feet active and ready to move. So get low, relax the muscles, and wait.

On contact, try to remain stationary so that you have a solid base with your feet. On the cross-check, try to keep the stick handler in the middle of the stick, between both hands. Follow these steps to deliver an effective cross-check:

1. **When you hit, extend your arms upward and outward.**

   Never overextend on your check, because you'll become vulnerable and off-balance.

2. **As you hit up and under, make contact on your opponent's arm between his elbow and shoulder and stay down.**

   If you stand up on the hit, you'll lose your power and quickness.

3. **During the hit, make sure that your feet are under your body for balance.**

4. **Cross-check and get off the stick handler.**

   Make your hits short and hard, and then recoil, filling the gap you created with the hit by shuffling out with small steps. Just keep continually cross-checking. If you lean on the stick handler's body with your stick when cross-checking, he'll roll and slide past you.

You want to force the stick handler toward the boards by overplaying him half-a-man. In other words, don't stand directly in front of him — stand slightly off to the side of him toward the center of the floor. This defensive stance essentially gives you a one-player defensive advantage, except that the extra "player" is really the sideboards. Make sure that your hips are parallel to the sideboards and your head is aligned with the head of your opponent's stick.

You may have to move out on the stick handler to maintain pressure, but you still have to wait for him to come to you.

Now this may sound like a contradiction. But really when you go after the stick handler, you should shuffle the last two steps so that you maintain control, keeping a safe distance away so that he can't make his way around you, but effectively moving toward him to prevent a quick shot.

Against a good long-ball shooter, you can't afford the luxury of thinking that a player can't score from a certain scoring distance and then letting him shoot. Defenders can't stay back and let shooters shoot because they *will* score.

If you get too close, the offensive player can make a quick move and zoom away. Defensemen need time to recover and that requires a space buffer with the offensive player.

Another important element of defense in field lacrosse is keeping your head on a swivel — figuratively, of course. Always keep your eyes moving between your man and the man with the ball.

Defensemen play with both hands on their stick, but they can't use the space between their hands to check an opposing player.

One hand on the stick may be extended toward the offensive player to keep him at bay so that the head of the stick is used for this poke check.

Both hands can be involved in the same check if they're used together, generally at the bottom of the shaft, to push off the opponent. Contact between each stick head is common, as the defensive player tries to check the ball out of the opponent's possession. Defensemen can also use their bodies to hold off offensive players.

# Stopping the Player: Defending Offensive Players without the Ball

Defensive positioning is the primary weapon a defender has against offensive players who don't have the ball. Your goal as a defender is to maintain a position that limits the possibility of the player you're covering receiving a pass or cutting to get closer to the net. How you achieve that goal depends on which side of the field the ball is on.

## Off-ball-side defending

When defending an offensive player on the off-ball side of the defense, you should form a flat triangle. In this triangle, you're at the apex of the triangle, and the stick handler and the offensive player you're covering form the base of the triangle. It's called a flat triangle because you should play off the player you're covering slightly and toward the stick handler in case you need to be in a position to help, so you're flattening the triangle a bit.

If your defense takes the shape of a deeper triangle, you're more likely to be protecting the net than keeping yourself available to help against the stick handler. In this situation, the opponent could cut very easily for a pass and shot.

On the off-ball side, always keep your opponent in front of you. If you play your check even — that is, parallel to the goal — he could fake up and cut behind you for a quick pass and shot. If your opponent goes behind you (called a *backdoor cut*), always assume that a pass is coming and turn and play his stick hard.

Off-ball defenders should play an open stance, facing down the field using their peripheral vision to see both their man and the ball. A helpful rule for defenders is "Two looks to your man, one look to the ball."

In the National Lacrosse League (NLL), which has highly skilled offensive players, off-ball defenders play closer to their opponents, using more of a closed stance, belly to belly.

## Ball-side defending

The defenders defending non–stick handlers on the ball side of the field should look over their shoulders at the stick handler in case their teammate needs help.

If the stick handler passes the ball, drop to the level of the ball immediately and then adjust your position according to your check. You're now in a position to collapse, help, and rotate, especially from the top of the defense.

## Moving before the ball

The final rule for positioning when defending against offensive players without the ball is that the defense moves before the offense moves on any movement of the ball.

Here are a few more tips for this type of individual defense:

- ✔ **Never let a player lean on your stick without the ball.** He can equalize pressure, giving himself the chance to catch the ball and score before you can adjust using your stick.

- ✔ **Never let a player lean against you while cutting through the middle.** He can neutralize your ability to use your body to stop a pass.

- ✔ **Play your man to deny him the ball.** Stay between him and the ball, not between him and the net.

# Drills to Build Your Defensive Skills

The drills in this section can help you improve the skills you need to be a strong defensive player. You'll be able to practice defending the stick handler and other offensive players, as well as develop the agility you need to successfully defend the ball. From footwork to stick work to defensive stance, you can work on these drills alone or with teammates.

## Developing defensive agility

These drills are designed to help you improve your footwork. The majority of defensive drills deal with lateral action, footwork, communication, and quickness, all actions that are part of every successful defensive player's repertoire. Remember to keep your drills short, quick, and hard.

- ✔ **Footwork:** More often than not, running on defense involves moving backward or sideways, rather than forward. An effective way to work on improving your footwork is running backward (say, the length of the field and back). While facing the sidelines, run sideways the length of the field, taking lateral steps and keeping your body low.

- ✔ **Defensive steps:** To develop some of the defensive steps you need for defensive situations, this drill focuses on repeating each step in order. Start with an advance step, move into the retreat step, and swing sideways with the shuffle. When working on this drill, make sure to keep your body low, as you would in a game situation.

- ✔ **Reaction:** This wave drill prepares you for game situations in which you need to react to a quickly passed ball or a cutting player. Working with a teammate or with your whole team, you react to the direction your partner or coach waves to, simulating the movement of the ball, for example. You can alternate the steps you take with the reaction, using a shuffle step during one set or a slide step during another. Again, make sure that your knees are bent and you're in the proper stance.

- ✔ **Covering the defender:** In this shadow drill, work with a teammate to practice following the movements of an offensive player. To do this, you just need to mirror the other player's movements for 10 seconds, alternating so that your partner can also work on his defensive skills. Work on this drill both with contact and without contact.

- ✔ **Slide steps:** This defensive slide drill asks you to do the slide step back and forth ten times within a 10-foot area, timing yourself so that you have a way to gauge your progress. Alternatively, you can practice this slide drill in 30-second time periods, counting how many times you can slide back and forth in the area before the 30-second period ends.

✔ **Lateral movement:** This defensive square drill works on lateral motion, agility, and quickness. Place four cones (or other objects) to mark a square. The distance between the cones should match the distance you would normally move in a game. Move laterally around the cones both clockwise and counterclockwise. Try going around the square four times, or time it for 20 seconds.

✔ **Stopping and starting:** Using the same square setup, this drill lets you practice for those game situations when you have to stop or start suddenly. Start in the middle of the square, run to a corner, backpedal to the middle, and go to another corner. Do this with all four corners. You can also sprint to the corner and sprint back to the middle or slide to the corner and slide back to the middle.

Ric Beardsley, a four-time all-American defenseman at Syracuse University who also played in Major League Lacrosse, offers some methods you can use to develop defensive agility:

✔ **Stretch.** The more flexible you are, the faster you'll be and the stronger you can get. As a defenseman, your hips and lower back need to be flexible for power.

✔ **Work on drills.** Drills are boring but essential. A good defenseman needs to know the basics — you'll use the basics more than any other player on the field. So doing those boring drills and taking them seriously will actually make you better.

✔ **Work on postion-specific training.** Training for your position in the workouts that you do outside of practice is the key to success. Run and practice using a 20-pound weight vest, do explosive squats, and jump rope for quick feet. Another trick is to play with a weighted stick — a stick filled with sand.

## Drills for defending the stick handler

The drills in this section help you work on some of the skills discussed earlier in this chapter for defending the stick handler.

### 1-on-1 defensive progression

This drill is best with the whole team broken into partners — one offensive and one defensive. The offensive players play token offense so that the defensive players can work on defending different situations.

Here's how it works:

1. **The defender leans on the stick handler and experiences what happens when the offensive player steps backs or rolls.**

2. **While stationary, the stick handler leans into the defender and rolls to try to beat the defender.**

3. **The stick handler just stands and lets the defender check him, feeling what it's like to hit and fill the gap created by the hit.**

4. **The stick handler fakes one way, with the defender reacting to catch up to the fake, and then the stick handler fakes the other way.**

   This becomes a reaction drill for the defender.

5. **The stick handler fakes a cut inside and then cuts outside and down.**

   The defender hits and slides down to prevent the stick handler from beating him on the outside.

6. **The stick handler fakes an outside cut and cuts inside.**

   The defender hits and moves to prevent the stick handler from getting an inside position to go to the net.

7. **The stick handler runs down the outside, and then stops and rolls back into middle for a shot.**

   The defender works on his footwork to stop the stick handler from coming back.

8. **The stick handler fakes a shot, and cuts outside and back in.**

   The defender stays low, keeping his stick up to interfere with the shot, but he doesn't stick-check.

### 1-on-1 closing-out drill

Run this drill with a teammate or with the whole team. Partners are spaced 5 yards apart. One partner passes to other and *closes out* hard on him — that is, he follows the pass to his partner and takes his defensive stance, shuffling the last two steps. Then he moves back to his original position, and the partner with the ball passes and closes out on him.

### 1-on-1 steal-the-ball drill

Two players go one-on-one against each other. The stick handler is trying to score, and the defender can only poke and wrap around to get the ball from the stick handler.

### 2-on-1 fight-through-pick drill

This drill uses three players: a defender, a stick handler, and another offensive player. The defender plays the stick handler, while the second offensive player tries to set a pick on the defender. The drill is designed so that the defender can either step back or step up to work around the pick and get back to defending the stick handler.

For variation, use three offensive players with two trying to set picks for the stick handler, from either side or with double picks. The defender then has to fight through both picks.

# Drills for defending other offensive players

The drills in this section help you work on some of the skills discussed earlier in this chapter for defending other offensive players.

### 2-on-1 denying man on ball side or off-ball side

This drill uses three players: two offensive players and one defender. The defender covers one offensive player, while the other offensive player tries to pass to his offensive teammate. The defender takes a closed stance, belly to belly, to deny the pass away. Deny the pass from the same side of the field or floor or from the opposite side of the field or floor.

### 1-on-1 multiple defensive teaching drill

This progression drill for the box game works best with two coaches controlling the ball, and it stresses stance, positioning, and communication. When communicating, players should call out "cutter," "help right," or "pick right." The defender starts on the side, defending an offensive player without the ball; the coaches set up on opposite sides of the floor, one with the ball.

Here's how it works:

1. **Positioned on the ball side, the defender denies the entry pass using a closed stance, close to the offensive player as he goes in and out to get in the clear for a pass from a coach or another teammate.**

   One coach throws a cross-floor pass to the other coach.

2. **Switching to the off-ball side, the defender denies the cross-floor pass using an open stance, following the offensive player as he moves up and down the sidelines trying to get into the clear for a pass.**

3. **The offensive player tries to cut in front of the defender to the ball while the defender yells "cutter" and takes away the cut.**

4. **The offensive player circles the net and then fakes a cut in front of the defender before cutting backdoor (behind the defender). The defender yells "cutter," turns his back to the ball, and plays the cutter's stick hard with a slash.**

5. After the cut, the offensive player circles the net and comes back to the cornerman's spot, while the defender is playing between him and the ball.

6. On the off-ball side, the defender calls "help right" and helps on penetration by the coach or other teammate with the ball and makes a quick recovery back to his check.

7. On the recovery following the help, the defender closes out on the pass back to his check by the coach.

8. Bring another offensive player into the drill, starting him in the crease before moving to set an *up pick*, where the offensive player picks the defender from behind, between the net and the defender.

9. The defender steps back and plays the picker as he rolls or slides down to the net for a pass.

10. The stick handler cuts outside down the sidelines while the picker runs back to the top for a return pass from the stick handler, who is now in the crease area.

11. The defender defends the cross pick-and-roll on the ball by stepping back and playing the picker rolling to the net while the stick handler makes a cut across the top to pass down to the picker.

12. After his cut to the net, the picker goes to the crease position to receive a down pass and the defender defends a down pick-and-roll by stepping back on the pick and switching to the picker.

13. Another defensive player calls out "pick right" and the stick handler comes out of the pick and then runs the ball back down into the corner area while the defender follows his check to the top.

    The defender is now in the top area and his check is going to set a screen for the stick handler in the corner area.

14. The defender fights off the screen to get position between his check and the ball. When the stick handler comes off the screen, the defender comes out from the side or goes around the screen and comes out on the net side to switch and check him.

    The defender is now on the stick handler who backpedals to the top to finally go one-on-one.

# Chapter 8

# Goaltending

*In This Chapter*

▶ Assessing who has the right stuff

▶ Picking up the goaltending basics

▶ Making saves

▶ Starting the offense

▶ Communicating with your defense

*T*he most important task of a goaltender is to stop the ball from getting into the net. How to do that is what this chapter is all about.

Unfortunately, some coaches leave goaltenders on their own to learn how to play the position through trial and error. Practice sessions in which the goaltender is simply someone to shoot at rather than a vital team member who needs coaching also don't help.

The fact is, the goaltender position may be the most complex one on the field. It requires a wide variety of attributes, such as quick reflexes, an even-keeled temperament, poise, athleticism, communication skills, and leadership qualities.

In this chapter, we take a look at the skills necessary to be a standout goaltender and tell you how you can become a better goalie. We also examine some of the attributes found among the game's best goalies.

# Recognizing What It Takes to Play in Goal

No doubt about it, goaltender is a glamorous position in both hockey and soccer. One of the primary reasons why goalies get so much attention in those sports is that they have many opportunities to put up some impressive numbers, such as saves and shutouts. You wouldn't see hockey or soccer goaltenders gain that type of notoriety if they allowed 14 goals a game.

But allowing double-figure goals is a regular occurrence for a lacrosse goalie. So, to be a successful goalie in lacrosse, you need to recognize that you're going to get scored upon.

The most successful goalies are the ones who have the ability to bounce back and make a big save after letting in a goal. But there are other attributes essential to playing the position effectively. We explore them in this section.

## Focus

A good lacrosse goalie should have the ability to stay focused during a game. Face it, your mind has a tendency to wander no matter what you may be doing. Keeping yourself mentally in the game at all times is important.

Being a goalie doesn't reward a wandering mind. You have to keep your eye on the ball no matter how many offensive players run in front of you, how many picks and screens take place off to your side, or how many fans are constantly chanting from the stands.

## Desire

Being a goaltender requires a special type of personality. You must not only want to take on the role of being the last line of defense, but thrive on it. This means that you'll be under the microscope. When a goal is scored, you'll be the one people see holding your stick at your side in front of the net. But when you make a big save, that can change the momentum of a game and you'll be the one people see as sparking the team.

Being a goaltender involves all kinds of mental and emotional peaks and valleys. There are also plenty of physical challenges. After all, you'll be getting routinely hit with a hard rubber ball coming at you at eye-popping speeds.

## Stick-to-itiveness

Many players are comfortable and confident when things are going well. In order to be an effective goaltender, you must display those traits when things *aren't* going your way. After all, if you get down or rattled after allowing a goal or two, there's a good chance the other team will capitalize by scoring even more goals. You need to shake off goals when you allow them, and look forward, not back.

When the game is over, you can analyze what occurred that allowed the goal to be scored. But during the game, concentrate on preventing the next goal from being scored.

## Communication

As goaltender, you're the captain of the defense. Only you can see the entire defensive zone — including who is playing where and how the offense is maneuvering. Your defensemen are too busy guarding their opposing players to be able to get this vantage point. So, make the most of this advantage. Shout out help to them early and often. Also, be supportive of your teammates when they may be responsible for a player getting in position to score. Giving them that support could very well give them the confidence they need to prevent another similar play from occurring.

BOX LACROSSE

## How playing goalie differs in box lacrosse

Goaltending in box lacrosse is a whole different animal in many ways. With so much less space to cover in goal (4 feet wide and 4 feet high), the body is the most important tool for box lacrosse goalies when it comes to making saves.

But that isn't the only difference between field and box goalies: Unlike field goalies, box goalies stand with the stick of the head on the floor, as opposed to keeping the head of the stick upright.

One-on-one breakaways, which are rare in field lacrosse, are common in box lacrosse. But box lacrosse goalies don't have to worry about players setting up plays behind the net as they do in field lacrosse, where there is 15 yards between the goal and end line.

Despite the smaller size of the goals, box lacrosse generally has more scoring than field lacrosse, where scores average around 20 goals combined per game, while impressive save percentages for NCAA goalies average in the mid-60s. Shutouts are almost unheard of in box lacrosse. This is because scoring overall is higher in box lacrosse.

# The Basics of Goaltending

Goaltending can be broken down into six basic tasks:

- ✔ Staying in your ready stance for the shot and forming an arc
- ✔ Staying centered
- ✔ Following the ball, using your eyes and your body
- ✔ Challenging the shooter
- ✔ Communicating with the defense
- ✔ Anticipating what's going to happen as the play evolves

We cover each of these points in greater detail in the following sections.

## Where it all starts: The ready stance

As a goalie, you have to take a stance, the *ready stance*. You have to be balanced and relaxed so that you're ready to react quickly forward, backward, and sideways.

Take a crouching position with your knees bent, back straight, and shoulders and chest square to the ball — that is, with your body on the goal line facing the ball.

Your feet should be shoulder-width apart, and your body weight should be on the balls of your feet. Hold the stick upright, with very little space between the net of the stick and your helmet.

The goalie should make his own imaginary semicircle, or arc. This is an area in the middle that stretches roughly 2 feet from the goal line and uses the goalposts as a reference point. Forming this arc helps the goalie be in position to make saves on shots that arrive at both the left and right of the goalie at varying angles and heights. All movement should be started from this centering position.

Another key for a goalie is hand positioning. The goalie's top hand should be on the throat of the stick, with the bottom hand toward the middle. The distance between the hands should be about the length of your waistline.

## Staying centered

Position yourself a step above the goal line in the center of the net — that is, between the goal posts. This center position gives you the best flexibility to move your body with the ball.

Just as you need to stay centered physically, you need to stay centered mentally. "Lacrosse is a head game," says former Yorktown (New York) High School all-American goaltender and Cornell University standout long-stick midfielder Ethan Vedder. "You'll either win it or lose it. You can do a lot as a goalie before even facing a shot in terms of organizing your defense, putting your body in the right position, and knowing where the offense is going to shoot from and how you're going to react to it."

## Following the ball

Because your primary task as goalie is to allow as few goals to be scored as possible, you need to make every effort to know where the ball is at all times, even when it's behind you.

Knowing where the ball is involves more than just keeping your *eye* on the ball. You need to follow the ball with your *body* as well. Following the ball with your body involves moving your body when the ball moves, keeping it square to the ball in the shooter's stick. When the ball swings to your right side, swing your body to the right, keeping it parallel between the ball and the net.

## Working on your stick saves

If you arrive at any high school lacrosse venue a half-hour or so before game time, you're sure to see a coach or player warming up the goalie while the rest of the team does pre-game warm-ups and drills. This activity may look leisurely, but it's not. The goalie must treat every shot as if it's in an actual game situation and make his best effort to stop each shot.

Whoever warms up the goalie should start with an array of either low or high shots and then switch off. Then he should shoot some bounce shots as well, or mix in the bounce shots in between the assortment of high and low shots.

The following drills are designed to help you work on your stick saves:

✔ **For long, low shots:** A semicircle of shooters shoots long, low shots. Focus on moving the stick to the ball with your body backing up the stick.

✔ **For mid-waist shots:** A semicircle of players shoots mid-waist shots. Use only your stick to stop shots.

✔ **For bounce shots:** A semicircle of players shoot bounce shots to any target in the net. Use only your stick to stop shots.

Following the ball is especially important because, often, the play will be behind you — in the 15-yard area behind each goal — not in front of you. Much of a team's offense flows through this 15-yard space, and you have to actually turn around completely so that you face the goal to watch the ball. Then, when the ball swings to the front, you should take a couple extra steps out to slice a shooter's angle.

You also have to negotiate a large area when clearing the ball. After possession is gained, according to the college rules a team has 20 seconds to advance past the restraining line (35 yards from the end line) and out of its defensive end.

Attackmen don't sprint away after possession is lost. They stick around to help scramble your effort to clear the ball out of the defensive end. This means that you need to be athletic enough to run around and coordinated enough to handle the ball in the open field.

Keep your eye on the ball, following it around the playing area. And you not only want to follow the ball on a shot on goal but also as it's passed around from player to player.

## Challenging the shooter

As the goalie, you need to move out one or two steps from the goal line to challenge the shooter. You're not likely to be a successful goalie if you're looking at the position as one of comfort, waiting around for the occasional shot. By moving out from the goal line, you also cut down the available angles and space for your opponent to place the ball.

Playing in goal requires you to challenge the shooter so that he's more likely to rush a shot and send it off-line or decide not to shoot at all.

How far out you move depends on how far away the shooter is, who's shooting, and how big you are. You have to test your positioning to find the perfect spot that reduces your opponent's shooting area. Generally, though, three steps out, or at the top of the crease, is a bit much, unless the shooter is way out and definitely shooting. If you're that far out in the crease and the shooter fakes a shot, he can easily attack and put the ball over your shoulder.

The biggest problem for goaltenders is getting caught moving out when the shot is taken. When you move out, you can't move laterally. If the shooter picks his shot, he'll score.

When you do step out, remember that recovery is just as important as coming out. As the ball moves from side to side, shuffle your feet by taking small sidesteps and keep your stick on the ground.

If the ball is passed down low in the zone, retreat by stepping back and to the post. If the ball is passed up high, step out to challenge.

Coaches can run these drills for three distinct save styles:

- **Soft toss.** From a distance of about 6 feet away, the coach tosses the ball to the goalie, who does not use a stick. As a result, the goalie will catch the ball with his top hand. The coach tosses the ball to all areas around the goal area in order to simulate the variety of saves that a goalie will have to make in the course of a game.
- **The goalie steps to the ball.** Players take controlled shots so that the goalie can work on his technique and positioning.
- **The goalie stays back in his net for reflexive saves.** Players take rapid-fire shots so that the goalie can work on his reflexes and quickness.
- **The goalie takes a step out for angle saves.** The coach calls out, at random, the types of shots for players to take:
  - Long, top-corner shots
  - Long, bottom-corner shots
  - Long shots directed at the mid-waist
  - Long bounce shots for top corner
  - Long bounce shots for mid-waist
  - Close-in shots, without a fake
  - Close-in shots with one strong fake

## Don't bite on the fake

As a goaltender, you're sure to see your share of stick fakes. In fact, you're likely to see stick fakes of stick fakes, before yet another stick fake that leads to a shot.

The idea, of course, is that the shooter wants you to move in one direction to block a shot that he fakes so that he can score on a shot the other way. Not only does a successful stick fake lead to a goal for the other team, but it can also make even the best goalies look a little silly.

You can do a couple of things to protect against the fake:

- ✔ **Practice patience.** If you can wait out a shooter's stick fakes, you're more likely to be able to react effectively against the shooter's actual shot.

- ✔ **Follow the shooter's stick, not his or her body movements.** Don't look at head fakes, look for the ball. And if the player hides or drops his or her stick, react to it as soon as it's visible again.

Actual practice may not help against stick fakes as much as knowing your opponents' tendencies. Knowing which shooters are more likely to try a stick fake, and which shooters are more likely to just shoot away, will help you be the most effective against stick fakes.

Bob Watson of the Toronto Rock, two-time National Lacrosse League goaltender of the year, says about playing the stick fake: "When you see a stick fake, you must stay square to the shooter's stick and rely on your angles. Have patience and don't overreact. Let the shooter make the first move."

Do a progression as the goalie warms up. For example, many goalies prefer to start stick-side high for shot/hard pass placement then work to non-stick-side high. Next would be stick-side waist high, follow by non-stick side waist high, and work your way down to low and eventually bounce shots. A total of about two minutes should be spent on each area.

The step out can be a good strategy for goalies in defending against the breakaway — that is, when an offensive player breaks away from the rest of the players on the floor and anticipates a one-on-one opportunity against the goalie.

## Communicating with the defense

A shy goaltender is not an effective goaltender. You need to speak out throughout the game, calling out assignments and helping your defensemen know where to be. You also need to be consistent in the specific words you use so that your defensemen understand and quickly identify whatever lingo your team is familiar with.

## Talking it up

According to Ethan Vedder, as a goaltender, the six teammates in front of you in your zone are your six best friends. That means you're hard on them at times, but always supportive. And, like any good friendship, communication is vital.

"You're sitting in the middle of it all and you have the luxury of seeing what's happening as it unfolds," Vedder said. "They have other tasks, so you need to help them get in the right position as much as possible."

That means communicating, often in a forceful way. You shouldn't order around your defensive players — you just want to instruct them quickly and forcefully as far as positioning goes. After all, a split second may be the difference between a goal and a save. Often, the difference between a good goalie and a great goalie is communication and vocal leadership.

## Anticipating what's going to happen next

A vital part of what you need to do as a goaltender is to look ahead. You need to be aware of the tendencies of the other team's shooters. For example, if an opposing attackman is weak with his right hand and is controlling the ball with his right hand under heavy pressure, he probably won't shoot, so look for him to pass it off. Conversely, if a strong right-handed shooter makes a clean catch with his right hand in a position to shoot, be ready to try to stop his best shot.

## Making the Reflex Save

The reflexive part of goaltending relies on your athletic ability to get your body in front of shots. No matter how much you're able to cut down on the angle that a shooter may have on goal, you still have to move laterally or step sideways to make saves, whether it's with your stick or your body.

 Beginning goalies have a tendency to turn their body on a shot so that the ball hits their sides or their backs. Coaches can help them build confidence by using tennis balls in shooting drills so that goalies know that they can't get hurt and are well protected.

## The Goalie on Offense

The goaltender plays a key role in a team's offense, primarily by starting the offense following a stopped shot. A crisp, accurate clearing pass can set the offense off on a fast break.

# Making the angle save

Because of the confined space in box lacrosse, it's important that goaltenders play the angles as best they can to prevent opposing shooters from having a large amount of the net area to target.

The angle part of goaltending involves getting good body positioning, being in the right place at the right time, stepping out and cutting down with the body some of the open areas of the net to shoot at. As a goalie, you want to be out and set in a ready stance before the shot is taken. You have to know how to play angles to stop shots.

Here are a few drills to help you develop your angle-save skills:

✔ Form a triangle with a rope attached to you and to both posts. Learn to stay in the center of the posts — that is, in the middle of the net.

✔ Find an ideal spot against shooter. The shooter takes a position within good scoring range and shoots at you. If he scores, he tells you to move slightly over because you're giving him too much to shoot at.

✔ Five players spread out on the floor just to pass ball the around quickly. They shoot at you quickly and randomly.

When you're inside the crease, defenders may not make contact with you. But you're fair game when you're out of the crease. This means you can get hit by opposing defenders. It also means that, not only can you set up the fast break, but you can start it. At times, opposing players are so surprised to see the goalie ranging beyond midfield on a clear that they fail to defend him. On more than one occasion, this has led to the goaltender accomplishing the ultimate of rarities — scoring a goal.

# Chapter 9

# The Possession Game

## In This Chapter

▶ Everything you need to know about faceoffs

▶ Understanding why ground balls are so important

▶ Focusing on rides and clears

*Y*ou can't score if you don't have the ball. That's why there are few — if any — things more important in lacrosse than getting and maintaining possession. This chapter takes a look at ways to do it.

The first way — the *faceoff* — is probably the most important. The faceoff determines who gets the ball at the beginning of the game, at the start of each subsequent quarter, and following each goal. If a team can dominate in the *faceoff X* (the area at midfield in which faceoffs are held), it can make up for deficiencies in many other areas. Faceoffs can also help a team trailing by several goals late in a game get right back in the game — and possibly even pull out the win.

Another way to get possession occurs when neither team has gained control of a ground ball. The team that successfully winds up scooping it up could wind up giving itself a big shift in momentum as well.

In this chapter, we also take a look at two areas that are often overlooked in the possession game:

✔ **Rides:** A *ride* occurs when the defensive team tries to prevent the team with possession from advancing the ball from its defensive end to the offensive zone.

✔ **Clears:** A *clear* occurs when the ball moves from the defensive half of the field into the offensive zone.

# The Art of the Faceoff

Throughout this book, we mention that lacrosse is similar to hockey, basketball, and football. But there's another sport lacrosse is similar to: wrestling. Wrestling? Yes, wrestling. At least one aspect of lacrosse is very similar to wrestling — and it also happens to be one of the most important aspects of the sport: the faceoff.

Faceoffs, which often resemble a wrestling match for control of the ball, are held at the start of each game, the start of each subsequent quarter, and after a goal is scored. Because of this rule, lacrosse is one of the few sports where you can score and then get the ball right back — possession doesn't automatically shift to the opposing team the way it does with, say, basketball and football.

Faceoffs are such a vital part of the game that many teams have players who specialize in faceoffs. After possession is decided, those players sprint right off the field. In the sport, they're known as FOGOs (which stands for *face off, get off*). Even though FOGOs may not be on the field when goals are scored, they're often the most responsible for goals because they win the faceoffs that lead to the possessions during which goals are scored.

Michael Bartomioli, a midfielder on the University of Michigan's 2009 Men's Collegiate Club Lacrosse Association national championship team, says that the trend toward specialization in sports has been especially prevalent for lacrosse in the faceoff X. "Facing off becomes almost like a chess game — faceoff guys have become so skilled," said Bartomioli. "When players can concentrate solely on facing off, they can master a number of different moves."

## X marks the spot

All the action occurs in the *faceoff X,* or the area right at midfield in which the faceoffs are conducted. After the official rests the ball in the middle of the centerline, two opposing players position themselves parallel to the line and as close to the line as possible without crossing it. They squat into their stances, with their elbows inside their knees and their backsides slanted toward the ball and facing the side of the field their goal is on (as shown in Figure 9-1).

# Drawing instead of facing off

The women's lacrosse equivalent of the faceoff is called a *draw*. Like faceoffs, draws occur at the beginning of the game, at the beginning of each subsequent half, and after each score. Draws begin between two players who stand facing one another with their sticks held horizontally and their feet about shoulder-width apart, with one foot toeing the center line. Any player may take the draw, and a maximum of five players may be positioned on the field either on the center circle or between the two restraining lines during a draw. All other field players must be below the restraining line.

The heads, or crosses, of their sticks' faces are held back-to-back, hip-level in the air over the centerline. Each player's stick is between the ball and the goal she's defending. The backs of the crosses are lined up against each other with the bottoms of each crosse parallel, and the ball is placed by the official between the two crosses. A player taking the draw must not have either hand near the crosse of the stick or the ball when preparing to take the draw. On the word *ready,* the official signals the two players taking the draw to remain motionless. Then, after a whistle is blown, both players draw their crosses up and away from the other, in an attempt to get the ball to a teammate or to themselves. The ball is required to go above the head level of both players taking the draw.

Photos by Raymond J. Nelson/MaxPreps.com

**Figure 9-1:**
Players get
set for a
faceoff.

*Photo by Jim Stout/MaxPreps.com*

Most players prefer to use short sticks rather than long sticks for faceoffs, because short sticks offer better control.

After the official blows his whistle to start play, the battle begins. That's when timing and technique — two of the most critical aspects to success — come in.

Also of vital importance are the faceoff man's two teammates perched in the wing areas. Oftentimes, a faceoff isn't won cleanly by either player; instead, the ball is jarred loose and one of the charging wing players scoops it up.

The wings may go after the ball as soon as the whistle sounds. Other players have to wait until the ball goes over the defensive-area line or either team gains possession.

## Techniques of the trade

Faceoff specialists use a variety of techniques. We cover the most common ones in the following sections.

- ✔ **Clamp:** The clamp is probably the most popular grip. Here, the player places the back of the head of the stick over the ball before trying to pull the ball back toward him.

- ✔ **Jump:** In a jump, the player traps the ball with the face of the stick head, rather than the back of the stick head. A jump is basically a reverse clamp.

- ✔ **Rake:** In the rake, the player sweeps his stick like a rake to get the ball to one of his wing players.

- ✔ **Plunger:** Similar to the clamp, in the plunger, the player places the back of the stick head over the ball. Then he lifts his back hand while applying pressure with his front hand, pinching the ball with the stick head to allow him to control the ball and pull it around his opponent. If he pulls the ball around his opponent, this often leads to a fast break.

- ✔ **Double over:** In the double over, both hands face downward (allowing for more power) and are positioned high on the stick. The double over is also known as a motorcycle grip. This grip is the one used by former University of Delaware star Alex Smith. (For more on Alex, see the nearby sidebar, "Faceoff star, final four.")

- ✔ **Push:** In the push, the player pushes the head of the stick forward as the top sidewall is facing toward him so that the ball moves forward, behind the opposing faceoff player, where it can be scooped up by either the faceoff player himself or a wingman, often leading to a fast break.

## Faceoff fundamentals

The concepts and strategies for faceoffs are similar in both field and box lacrosse. The goal is for the player facing off to either *pull* the ball and collect it himself or *push* it toward a teammate. Players in the wing area should be the team's fastest players and the players most adept at picking up the ball off the ground.

### Faceoff star, final four

Winning a flurry of faceoffs often allows teams to overcome late-game deficits that may have seemed insurmountable. It can also lift programs to new heights. Case in point: the University of Delaware, whose unlikely run to its first Division I semifinal appearance in 2007 would not have been possible without Alex Smith, who rewrote NCAA faceoff records. (Smith won nearly 70 percent of his faceoffs in his college career.) Prior to the 2007 season, Delaware had won just one postseason game in its history.

# Getting the edge on the faceoff

During a faceoff in box lacrosse, you need to out-loose-ball the other team, each player outfighting the player beside him for possession. This may sound easy, but it takes team effort, not just one good faceoff player. Here are some tips to help your team improve its faceoff success:

✔ **Get the jump on the opposition.** Try to anticipate when the referee will blow the whistle. You don't want to leave early, just before the whistle, even though refs don't always call this violation. But try to pick up on some of the referee's quirks — what he does just before he blows the whistle. Some players count from the time the referee leaves the small circle until he blows his whistle, hoping to pick up a pattern.

✔ **Attack all loose balls.** On most faceoffs, the ball comes loose, so players have to be ready to battle for the loose ball. You need tough players on the faceoff unit — quick, big, not afraid to get hit — and good stick handlers who can pick up the ball in a crowd. If the opposition gets to the ball first, players shouldn't back off. Play your opponent's stick hard to stop him from picking it up or bang him into the boards. Coaches should send two players after every loose ball.

✔ **Line up on the opponent's stick side.** If you line up in this way, you can interfere with your opponent's stick.

✔ **Protect the ball.** You want your team to use their bodies to protect the ball and keep both hands on the stick. Don't pick up the ball with just one hand on an exposed stick.

✔ **Back each other up on loose balls.** On a loose ball, the defender on the ball side moves in for the loose ball, while the other defender balances the floor by going back on defense. The offensive forward (creaseman) also cheats on the line and can be extra-aggressive, because he doesn't have to worry about being scored on while the off-ball forward (creaseman) goes back to the middle or even farther back, depending on the situation, to balance the floor defensively.

In the National Lacrosse League (NLL), all centermen, who are assigned to take faceoffs, are right-hand shots because they have to stay on their own side of the centerline. A centerman can grip only the shaft of the stick; he isn't allowed to touch the plastic head of his stick.

Here are some specific faceoff tips:

✔ Line up as close to the ball as you can.

✔ Be consistent in the way you grip the stick for each faceoff, so you can refine and improve your technique.

✔ Keep weight off your hands when lining up for the faceoff, so you can quickly move to an upright position while maintaining balance.

Each faceoff midfielder has his own technique that works especially well for him. Matt Witko, one of the leading players at Tufts University, distinguished himself as one of the premier faceoff specialists in the lacrosse hotbed of New York's Hudson Valley during his playing days at Horace Greeley High School in Chappaqua. Here are some tips from Matt on how to improve your faceoff technique:

✔ **Stand with your feet about shoulder-width apart, with both feet facing the ball.** You want to be comfortable in your stance, while at the same time being able to explode in either direction in order to get to the ball, and this stance allows you to do exactly that. Being in the right position to start is the most crucial part of facing off.

✔ **Be quick.** Timing is everything in facing off. The best faceoff players have the quickest hands. When you go out on the field for the opening draw, you should know what move you're going to do and do it confidently.

Make sure you're always on the "front side" of the whistle. If you're too early, it's a violation. But if you're too late, you almost certainly will lose the faceoff.

✔ **Know your opponent.** After the opening faceoff, you should have a good idea of what you're up against and what your opponent's go-to move is. Use this information to your advantage. Knowing what he can do allows you to counter his move.

You have an array of moves at your disposal, from the plunger to the rake to the jump, all of which work well. The best faceoff men can do all of them, but being really good at one is often better than being average at a few.

✔ **Pay attention to footwork.** Footwork, such as stepping toward the ball or stepping upfield (toward the opponent's goal), is a big part of your move. Use your feet and your eyes to be a great faceoff player. Once possession is gained, footwork is key in creating a scoring opportunity.

✔ **Work with your teammates to get possession.** The part of the faceoff after the draw is won separates the best faceoff players from the rest. Being able to control the ball and read the situation is one of the hardest skills to pick up and only comes with a lot of practice. Winning the draw is half the battle — getting possession is the hardest part. A great faceoff specialist works with his wings to get possession of the ball.

✔ **Be confident.** Many faceoff players don't have confidence with the ball — they do well in the faceoff, but when they have possession of the ball, they struggle with getting it into the offensive zone. As a result, teams often scheme to put a long-stick midfieldman on the faceoff player after he picks up the ball. Have confidence in your own stick skills. Be an athlete and run the ball into the box. Always be a threat to score — if a team doesn't slide to you, don't be afraid to shoot.

# Ground-Ball Wars

Faceoffs are critical when it comes to the possession game, but there is no area in lacrosse in which possessions are decided as frequently as ground balls. A *ground ball,* as the name suggests, occurs when a player scoops a ball up off the ground (as shown in Figure 9-2). It may sound simple, but as you'll see, it's anything but.

The importance of ground balls is unquestionable. Because they determine possession and because of their frequency, ground balls are arguably as important as any other aspect of the game — maybe more so. In fact, it's not too much of a stretch to say that ground balls are the key to victory. If your team outplays your opponent in collecting ground balls, there's a good chance it will win the game.

Ground balls may be even more important at youth levels than at the more advanced levels, because younger players' stick skills are not as advanced, so ground balls occur much more frequently.

**Figure 9-2:**
A player
gets set to
scoop up a
ground ball.

Photo by Jim Stout/MaxPreps.com

In box lacrosse, ground balls are known as *loose balls* — and they're every bit as important.

## When ground balls happen

Here are a few of the game situations during which ground balls become available:

- ✔ When recovering a rebound off a missed shot
- ✔ When stealing the ball from the stick handler
- ✔ When forcing the opposition to take a bad shot
- ✔ When forcing the opposition to make a bad pass
- ✔ On any faceoff

Trying for the ground ball in these situations and actually gaining possession of it are two very different matters.

## How to make a ground ball yours

Determination, anticipation, and hustle are the three most important attributes when it comes to getting ground balls. But some important technique is involved, too. In order to be effective at getting ground balls, you need to practice them diligently and frequently — like any other lacrosse skill.

It all starts with anticipation. You have to believe that every possession is going to end up with a ground ball. That means anticipating how you're going to get to the ball area as quickly and effectively as possible if the player you're guarding is not the one with the ball.

Next, you want to think about your approach to the ball. Bend your knees, stay low, keep a wide stance, and bend over to protect the ball. You should always have two hands on the stick, with your top hand near the throat and your bottom hand at the butt or end of the stick. And remember to keep this butt end low to the field or floor to make it easier to scoop through the ball.

When it comes to actually picking up the ground ball, you have a few moves to choose from:

- ✔ **Scoop pickup:** The scoop pickup is probably the most common pickup in lacrosse because it's so fast and simple. Aim for the area just *behind* where the ball is so that you can scoop the ball through in a motion somewhat similar to the one you use when shoveling snow. When you get the ball into your stick, make sure that you protect the stick by pulling it in close to your body and then start to cradle immediately, to make sure that you have the ball.

✔ **Trap and scoop:** Cover the ball with your pocket and then scoop up the ball.

✔ **Indian pickup:** The politically incorrect name *Indian pickup* refers to placing the backside of the head of your stick over the ball and knocking the ball with the side of the frame while turning the head of your stick over.

You probably won't have time to try the fancier, less-effective moves of trap and scoop and Indian pickup, so focus your attention on the scoop pickup.

When you go after a ground ball with an opponent beside you, get your body between the ball and your opponent. With this positioning, you can use your body to shield the ball from your opponent while you pick it up.

After you get in front of your opponent, you may want to slow down a bit, maybe even backing up slightly so that you can prevent him from slashing at your stick as you try to pick up the ground ball.

The way you approach going after a ground ball could be the difference of two goals — a possible goal for your team and a possible goal for the opposition — so don't take it casually. You want to attack ground balls aggressively instead of waiting for them to come to you. Attacking versus watching makes all the difference.

Don't be the only player to go after a ground ball. Your team stands a better chance of picking up a ground ball if you're consistently meeting one or more of your teammates at the ball. By outnumbering your opponent, you can more easily gain possession of the ground ball. Plus, with two or three teammates around a ground ball, you may be able to use one or two players to fend off opposing players so that the best stick handler can pick up the ground ball and do something with it.

Coaches need to have their players practice a wide variety of ground-ball situations. Some of these situations — including ground balls toward the sideline and ground balls toward the end line, for example — require different techniques. A basic ground-ball drill is to have two players line up hip to hip, and then roll the ball out.

*Wall ball* (when a player practices individually by throwing and catching a ball against a wall) is not only good for honing your shooting technique. You can also use it to work on your ground-ball skills, too. Just throw the ball against the wall hard and low, and scoop it up.

All ground-ball drills should include a pass so that players can work on getting the ball out of danger and igniting their offense.

## Ground-ball tips from an all-American

Brian Dalton, a former all-American midfielder at Springfield College in Massachusetts, who is now an assistant coach at St. John's University in New York City, offers some tips on getting ground balls:

✔ **Box out your opponent.** When you see that the ball is on the ground, get in front of the opposing player or players who are also in pursuit, and position your body between the ball and them. Then quickly get as low and wide to the ground as you can to prevent them from picking up the ground ball before you do.

✔ **Get as low as possible.** Position both your body and the butt end of your stick low to the ground.

✔ **Use two hands.** Unless you're in an awkward position and have no choice but to take a stab at the ball with one hand, use

two hands. Then scoop the ball through and bring it up toward your face mask.

✔ **Find an opening.** Spring to explode to an open spot on the field as soon as you have possession. Within 2 seconds of getting the ground ball, get the ball moving.

✔ **Create transition.** You got the ground ball — now capitalize on it. Look to create a transition opportunity for your team. That will likely mean passing the ball to a teammate (preferably a short stick) who is open and in position to advance the ball. Try to outlet the ball within 5 to 10 seconds of coming away with the ground ball.

✔ **Umbrella the ball.** The most effective way to create a fast-break opportunity is for the wing players to get to either side of their teammate who just picked up the ground ball — with one on the left side and one on the right side of the player with possession.

## What to do after you gain possession

After you get possession of the ground ball, you have a few options as far as what to do next:

✔ You can tuck the ball into your body to protect the ball.

✔ You can pass the ball back to your goalie, if you're in your own defensive zone.

✔ You can pass the ball to the closest available teammate.

If you can't pick up the ball, knock it back to your goalie or to a teammate.

# Riding High

A *ride* is a play that aims to prevent the team with possession of the ball from advancing the ball from the team's defensive end to the offensive zone.

Because the ride starts in the defensive end, the defending team's attackmen, who are stationed in the offensive zone, are the key players to effectively execute rides.

One of the unique aspects of lacrosse is that the most talented offensive players on the field quickly transition to key defensive players in a matter of seconds. In fact, one of the most effective riding attackmen in recent years at the collegiate level was also one of the game's premier offensive stars: former Syracuse star Casey Powell.

The most effective riders are players with quickness, athleticism, and agility (traits often more common in midfielders than in attackmen). Because the attackmen are the most crucial riders, some may be lacking in one or more of those areas, but they can make up for it with stick-to-itiveness.

## Why rides matter

Rides allow a team the opportunity to get the ball back as soon as it loses possession — whether on a shot on goal or on a turnover. If effective, rides can lead not only to changes in possession, but also to huge momentum shifts.

Teams that invest a lot of time, effort, and energy into riding are almost always rewarded for it. Strong riding often allows teams with inferior talent to stay in games. Think of rides as a key *x* factor that could very well determine the outcome of a game.

## The most effective ride techniques

In order for rides to be effective, the attacking team has to transition to a defensive team that works together to prevent the offense from clearing the ball in just a few seconds.

After the offensive team becomes a riding team, it needs to be mindful of the following:

- ✔ **Cover the deep guys.** The clearing team will look to outlet the ball. If the deep players are well guarded, their first option will be eliminated.

- ✔ **Make up for your shortcomings.** Because of the presence of the goalie, the clearing team will always have a one-player advantage. Make up for it with aggressive play right away.

- ✔ **Know who to cover.** Applying pressure on the player with the ball right away is the main priority.

✓ **Take a chance.** Because of the inherent man disadvantage, you can never play a straight man-to-man in a ride. So you'll have to take chances. To free up a player for the ride, leave the player farthest from the ball open — while still covering the other deep offensive players.

A ride is effective if it causes a turnover — or if it forces the team with possession to throw the ball toward either sideline. To that aim, attackmen must *not* go for big checks that could result in a penalty or could allow opposing players — usually defensemen on the clear — to break free. One of the riding attackmen should be a chaser, who is free to roam to whoever has the ball.

An effective alignment for a ten-man ride is to have your goaltender, a defenseman, and two midfielders play deep and two defenders and a midfielder form a triangle upfield, with the three attackmen pressuring the opposing goaltender and defenders.

# Clearing Things Up

A clear occurs when the ball moves from the defensive half of the field into the offensive zone. Clears are an often underappreciated aspect of the game because they often lead to scoring opportunities. Often, clears are only noticed when they aren't completed successfully. There's a reason for that: At the highest levels of lacrosse, teams will be able to successfully clear the ball the overwhelming majority of the time. But when they don't, it can be the difference in a game.

## Understanding why clears are crucial

Clears are important to a winning team's success. Performing them successfully not only keeps the ball away from the opponent's hands, but allows you to advance the ball offensively in a situation where you very nearly allowed a goal to be scored.

Here are two good, basic clears for your team to master:

✓ **Off of a save:** Two defenders cut to their respective sideline — the goal line extended — with the third defender remaining close to the crease in case the clear fails. The three midfielders break up the field: the outside midfielders cut toward the sidelines and the third inside midfielder finds space in the middle of the field. If the goalie throws the ball to the corner defenseman, the midfielders move back toward the ball, finding space.

✔ **Off of a sideline clear:** Have a midfielder pick the ball up, with two defensemen and the goalie parallel to him so that there are four players equally spaced from sideline to sideline. The other two midfielders and remaining defensemen are equally spaced across the midfield line. This will provide enough room for the player with the ball to find an open man.

## Starting with the goalie

When it comes to clearing, the goaltender is in the center of the action (see Figure 9-3). If he's not the one actually triggering the clear, then he, in effect, becomes an air-traffic controller.

If the goalie is the player triggering the clear, he has the advantage of being able to retreat into the crease, so that the riding team may not immediately check him.

Goalies also have the advantage because they can see the entire field and see which players are open before firing an outlet pass.

**Figure 9-3:**
A goaltender makes a clearing pass.

Photo by Jim Stout/MaxPreps.com

# Chapter 10

# Practicing Team Offense and Defense

## In This Chapter

▶ Fitting the players into the team offense or defense

▶ Working within a team offensive structure

▶ Defending as a team

A game that involves nine players plus a goaltender on each side of the ball requires team cooperation. Successful lacrosse teams work together, with each individual player displaying his greatest skills within the structure of the team's offense or defense.

All offensive and defensive systems are team systems. We discuss the specifics of these systems — that is, the way teams play the game, either offensively or defensively — in Chapters 14 and 15. This chapter sets the foundation for understanding how a team works together so that it can successfully run its offensive and defensive systems.

# How the Players Fit In: Roles and Positions in Team Offenses and Defenses

There are six players on offense — three attackmen and three midfielders. These players all use short sticks except in some instances, usually in transition, when a long-stick player will bring the ball into the offensive zone.

Attackmen are the players who account for the majority of the scoring. They're the players with the strongest stick skills and hardest, most accurate shots. Attackmen are also the most stationary players on the field. Some attackmen plant themselves in front of the crease and simply dunk home feeds; others operate behind the goal — or the X position — and direct the offense almost like a quarterback. Stick skills, speed, and size are an attackman's greatest attribute, with some coaches rating speed and quickness over size and others putting more emphasis on stick skills or size.

Conversely, speed may be the *most* important attribute for a midfielder. Midfielders must run up and down the field and are the most mobile players on the field. They also regularly play both offense and defense.

## The attackman's role

Some attackmen spend most of their time setting up teammates for scoring plays with passes. They're known as *feeding attackmen.* Many feeding attackmen use the large amount of real estate behind the net to engineer the offense. This strategy allows them to see the entire offensive zone, including cuts that are made as well as the position of the goaltender and defense.

*Crease attackmen* are those who finish plays by scoring goals. They often operate right on the crease.

Not only do attackmen need to have the best stick skills of all the players on the team, but they need to have the quickest releases and most accurate shots as well. Attackmen also need to be able to get their shots off quickly, before slides come. They need to be adept at fakes — both stick fakes and head fakes. And they must have excellent hand-eye coordination, which is vital for catching as well as scoring from the crease area.

Attackmen have an important role on defense when it comes to rides: They must quickly transition from offense to defense as the defensive team is attempting to clear the ball.

## The midfielder's role

Midfielders need to be versatile and flexible in their roles when it comes to running an offense. Sometimes, they have scoring opportunities from close range (though not nearly as often as attackmen do), so they have to be able to catch and shoot quickly. They also have to be able to find the open man, especially on fast-break opportunities, which they often trigger because fast breaks start with either a faceoff win or ground ball at midfield.

Because midfielders are usually stationed at the top of the box in a set offense, they have to be adept long-range shooters as well. Long-range shooting is a difficult skill to acquire and one that requires persistent and diligent daily practice.

# The box lacrosse offense

In box lacrosse, the offense is made up of two creasemen, two cornermen, and a pointman. The two creasemen start play low in the corner area of the floor. One creaseman is a right shot who plays on the left side of the floor. The other creaseman is a left shot who plays on the right side of the floor.

✔ **The creaseman:** The creaseman is like a forward or a winger in hockey or soccer. He tries to get out in front of the fast break and get down the floor as quickly as he can. He positions himself at the crease until any possibility of a fast break or odd-man situation has been eliminated. When the break is over, he has the option of staying low on the offense or coming up and setting a pick against the cornerman's defender. He's usually one of the fastest players on the team.

On any missed shot, the creaseman's job is to go after the loose ball if he has a chance to get it. If he can't get it, he can delay the opposition's break by pressing the stick handler or trying to steal the ball from him. Or he can go to the bench if he's in a system that replaces offensive and defensive players on the fly (that is, an *offense-defense system*).

The creaseman must be able to get down the floor very quickly, either from the bench or out of the defense. Therefore, he must have a great ability to catch the ball while running at top speed. He must also have great ability to score on the run, either straight on at the goalie or cutting across close to the crease. Finally, he must be able to run plays such as the pick-and-roll and then have the ability to catch the ball in traffic and score in tight.

✔ **The cornerman:** The cornerman is usually the quarterback-type player who starts the offense and handles the ball while on

offense — he's the player you want to play through. He starts at the top of the offense and is always a threat to shoot long or go one-on-one. He's a strong long-ball shooter yet can cut inside and score. His options, if he doesn't shoot or go one-on-one, are to wait for a pick by a creaseman, to pass off and cut for a return pass, to hang back at the top of the offense for a return pass, or to set a pick for a teammate. He also is designated as the defensive safety on any shot at the net, either going all the way back to protect his own net or running to the bench to get a defensive player on the floor.

The two cornermen — a right shot and a left shot — play above and behind the creasemen. They may start from this position, but they could end up anywhere on the floor, depending on the flow of the offense and where their teammates are on the floor. Their best bet is to stay on their own side of the floor so that they can always be an instant threat to shoot when receiving the ball.

✔ **The pointman:** This position can be either behind the cornerman on his proper side of the floor or in the middle of the floor. He can start in the middle, but after the passing and cutting begins, he can cut, pick, or stay where he is for a return pass.

The pointman's role is similar to a cornerman's role except that whichever side he's on becomes the strong side of the offense (that is, the side with three offensive players). A good pointman is always a threat to score and he knows which of his teammates has the best chance of scoring if he passes the ball. He can also pass off and clear out to the opposite side of his pass or he can pass to a cornerman and run a pick-and-roll with him. Finally, he should have great anticipation as to when to get back on defense.

## Offense in the women's game

Attackers are the focal point of the offense in the women's game. Three home positions dominate the attack. The primary jobs of the first home, who is stationed closest to the goal, are to shoot and finish offensive plays.

If the first home is the finisher of the offense, then the second home is the feeder. In addition to setting up plays, she must also be a capable shooter from every possible scoring position.

The third home is also a playmaker. But she usually triggers the start of a scoring play, often leading the shift to offense from defense.

However, the position the offensive unit is attacking from usually determines who the true playmaker will be. For example, it will vary based on whether the ball is on top of the 8-meter arc or behind the goal area.

Attack wings perform duties similar to those of the third home. They must also be able to run well and pass effectively.

Former Syracuse University standout Paul Carcaterra, now a TV analyst with CBS College Sports and the MSG Network, offers some pointers for effective shooting for both attackmen and midfielders:

- ✔ Top scorers must have a feel for the cage and where to place their shots and when to release them.

- ✔ You can never work on your shooting and shooting situations too much. Practice your shot by yourself as often as you can, practice with a defenseman and goaltender, and practice the shots you get in a game.

- ✔ Be patient. Shooting is the skill in lacrosse that takes the most time to develop. It won't come overnight, so give it time — and lots of hard work.

# Practicing a Team Offensive Philosophy

The primary objective of an offensive team is, of course, to score. Scoring may come from defensive pressure, steals, checking, ground balls, fast breaks, or a set offense. It really doesn't matter where the goal originates, as long as the team scores.

A secondary objective for an offensive team is to keep itself in position to defend against the abrupt change of possession. We discuss both of these objectives in this section.

## Keep it simple

In general, a team should try to run a very simple offensive system, especially at the youth levels. Try to avoid fancy and complex plays. Instead use simple concepts that don't take much time to set up.

Keep things fundamentally sound. The key is not what you do but how you do it. Make good crisp passes. Make sure the offensive players are not stagnant so that you keep your opponents moving. Know your teammates' tendencies. Keep moving — with and without the ball.

Good execution and timing on your plays comes from skill with sound fundamentals. The two best things a player can offer on offense are a perfect pass and help to set up an open teammate with a pick or a screen.

## Balance freedom and structure

Freedom to move with the ball is an effective tool in lacrosse. It often can lead to a one-on-one scoring opportunity. However, it can also lead to selfish play and grandstanding, keeping other offensive players out of the flow of a game.

One-on-one play serves as more of a starting point for offenses. And that translates into more of an emphasis on team offense and defense. More often than not, it turns into a six-on-six game in the offensive attack area, making it similar to basketball. The player with the ball tries to dodge by his man, draw a slide from another defender (when a defender leaves his cover for another player), and then find an open teammate.

Try to maintain a balance by allowing appropriate freedom within a structured or disciplined system. You may want to set goals so that your team aims for 50 percent one-on-one plays and 50 percent team play.

Giving players too much individual freedom usually means that lacrosse is being played out of control. You want to be aggressive on offense, but with patience and control. You want to keep moving and cutting rather than constantly forcing plays and shots. Constant movement not only leads to more open scoring opportunities but also wears down the defenders.

## Offensive mistakes that drive coaches crazy

Help your coach avoid premature graying by staying away from some of the following offensive no-no's:

✔ **Poor stick-handling:** Remember that opponents are always stick-checking, trying to steal the ball. A stick handler's highest priority is to protect the ball at all times.

✔ **Unforced turnovers:** Losing the ball when not under pressure, badly thrown passes, or dropped passes are equally maddening. Take care with your passing and catching.

✔ **Too much passing:** Some players spend too much time looking to make the perfect pretty pass rather than looking to go one-on-one to beat their defenders or looking to shoot. As long as their shooting percentage is good, the greatest players are those who are known for their ability to beat defenders and score, not so much their ability to pass and get assists. Now don't get us wrong here — seeing the floor and the ability to make a perfect pass into a teammate's stick for a score is naturally important, but it's secondary to scoring in a team's offensive weaponry.

✔ **The inability to set a pick:** You have to know how to set a pick on a pick-and-roll as well as how to come off a pick. This play is so effective in a team's offensive scheme that it has to be an automatic play between two teammates. The most common mistake is to come off the pick looking to pass rather than looking to shoot. The play is designed to free up an offensive player for a clear shot on goal.

✔ **Not knowing your cuts:** Successful offensive systems require precise timing. Some players don't have the proper timing on their cuts — either cutting too early, when the stick handler isn't ready to pass, or being checked out of a cutting opportunity. Keep working to make cuts happen, to collapse the defense, and to just wear out the defenders.

✔ **Not getting back on turnovers:** Another major area that drives coaches crazy is when their team is scored upon in transition. On any shot, players need to be ready to react back down the field to take away the breakaway, instead of admiring the shot.

## *Attack! Attack!*

Attack the opposition and keep them off balance before they get a chance to attack you. Any offensive action will get a defensive reaction. By attacking on offense, you're more likely to be facing a defense that is a split second behind you. Always tell defenders to be proactive, not reactive. Defenders can do a lot to dictate what the offense can or can't do, so they shouldn't wait to attack. Forcing the offense to weak areas and positions is extremely effective.

An aggressive offense is usually going to be met with an aggressive defense. You'll be taking shots both from the perimeter and from the crease area. You'll have defensive players coming at you from all angles. You can't be afraid to get hit — and you *will* be hit, especially when you cut toward the crease, the prime scoring area.

## *Focus on good shot selection*

It stands to reason that if the primary objective of an offense is to score, then the number-one way to achieve that objective is to maintain a high shooting percentage. Players must know what a good shot is. Getting high percentage shots requires having discipline when taking shots, which reflects a team attitude.

Here are some pointers that will help you become the best shooter you can be:

- ✔ Don't show off or be selfish with the ball when shooting.
- ✔ Pass up a so-so shot and pass to a teammate who has a better shot.
- ✔ Shoot smartly. If the goalie is not giving you anything to shoot at, shoot at the top corners or bounce a shot at him to try to mix him up.
- ✔ Keep moving. An offense with motion and cutting is much more difficult to defend against than one that is stationary.
- ✔ Take only good shots. Don't bail out the goaltender and defense with poor shots.

Your shooting rule should be that you can't shoot when an opponent's stick or body is in front of your shot. The exception is when the defender backs off from the shooter, so that you can use him for a screen shot.

Offensive possessions are generally shorter in box lacrosse than they are in field lacrosse. They're also less calculated in box lacrosse. There is less structure and coordination. It's more common in box lacrosse for a player to take a shot without beating his defender.

## A sampling of offensive sets

The most popular offensive formations in lacrosse are the 1-3-2 (with one player behind the net) and the 2-2-2 (putting two players in front of the crease).

Another set, the invert, is becoming more popular, especially against teams with dominant defensemen. *Inverting* means teams switch and move their middies behind the goal and push the attackmen out in front. This strategy forces the

long sticks, who most often defend the attackmen, out in front of the goal and away from the area where most of the offense is created.

Since long sticks are so much tougher to play against (because of the length of the stick and the fact that all they play is defense), a large part of offense involves trying to move around so that the player with the ball is going against a player with a short stick.

# Building the Team Offense through Drills

In this section, we suggest drills that your team can practice to help establish a team attitude when on offense.

## Zero passing

This drill is ideal to do before practice in place of the standard line drills. It's beneficial because it's much more realistic than normal line drills and concentrates on clearing.

There are three lines — one on the 25-yard line, one on the 50-yard line, and one on the opposite 25-yard line. The drill starts when the goalie outlets the ball to the first line. Each person continues to pass the ball up the field until the ball reaches the other goalie on the opposite side of the field. That goalie then outlets the ball to the other line opposite from where the ball drill started. So, in total, there are six lines parallel with each other.

## Quarterback drill

In this drill, there are three lines 5 yards from the goal line. There is one line in front of the goalie, one line to the right of the goalie, and one line on the left of the goalie. You need three players for this drill in order to outlet the ball, and ideally, three goalies as well. The middle goalie is responsible for saying "Break!" The three lines then break up the field. The lines on the right and left both run 15 yards and break hard toward the sideline. The middle line breaks just slightly to the right. After the three players catch the pass from the goalies, they need to get the ball out of their stick as quickly as possible, and pass it up to the waiting attackmen. The attackmen can pass it back to the middies for them to shoot, or the attackmen can shoot it themselves.

This drill is great for clearing and can really help a team looking to excel in transition opportunities.

## Ball perimeter work

In this drill, there are a total of four lines:

- ✔ One at the X position (behind the net)
- ✔ One on the wing
- ✔ One up top
- ✔ One on the opposite wing

There are three balls in the drill at all times and each player is responsible for giving an accurate pass every time. Each player cuts hard toward the goal for eight to ten steps and then quickly pops back out to receive the pass.

The cut is important because it creates separation from the player and the opponent.

## X shooting drill

In this drill, there are two lines 5 yards from the goal and another two lines on the goal line. The two bottom lines are responsible for giving an accurate pass to the player who's cutting down opposite from where the lines are (hence, an X formation). The player cutting down must catch and shoot the ball very quickly into the lower corners.

This drill helps to improve hand-eye coordination, as well as passing and shooting accuracy.

BOX LACROSSE

## Offensive drills for box lacrosse teams

Your box lacrosse team can run a variety of drills geared specifically toward box offensive positions.

In the **2-on-2 screen on the ball drill**, the cornerman passes down and sets a down screen for the creaseman on his side of the floor. He fights to get an inside position on the defender to stop him from switching. The man who sets the screen pops back after the cutter passes him for defensive safety.

There are a variety of 3-on-3 pointman drills, which are set plays for the pointman at the top of the offense. He usually starts the drill and initiates the offense at the top of the offense.

✔ **3-on-3 pointman cross pick-and-roll on the off-ball side drill:** The pointman passes to either cornerman, runs to the opposite side, and sets a cross pick-and-roll for the other cornerman.

✔ **3-on-3 pointman down pick-and-roll drill:** The pointman passes to the cornerman and runs a down pick for the cornerman on the opposite side of the floor. The creaseman on that side of the floor just stays on the crease.

✔ **3-on-3 pointman give-and-go drill:** The pointman passes to either cornerman and cuts for a return pass down the middle.

✔ **5-on-5 pointman double drill:** The pointman passes to the cornerman, who passes to the creaseman, and both the pointman and the cornerman set a double screen for the creaseman. On the double screen, the top screener reads the play and comes back on defense.

In the **3-on-3 defensive safety drill (full floor)**, you have three lines. Two of the lines play three-on-three live at one end; on the shot, two defenders stay on floor while one defender runs to the bench for a substitution. The three former offensive players react back accordingly. The new offensive team gets one shot. After a shot by the new offensive team, the play is over. Now the new offensive team brings the ball up against a new defensive team.

# *Practicing a Team Defensive Philosophy*

A good defense stresses a team concept — that is, six defensive players playing as one. A team-oriented defensive system helps players perform as one. Players are able to anticipate the movements of their teammates. In this kind of team-focused and disciplined system, players are more likely to be where they're supposed to be and doing what they're supposed to do, instead of freelancing wherever the action is.

Within this defensive system, your team is trying to take away the strength of your opponent. Rules on defense can improve your chances of success, but against certain teams, your system needs to be flexible enough to make adjustments during the game.

A solid team defensive philosophy centers on placing your most talented defensive players in key positions. For example, in most cases, a coach whose team employs a man-to-man defense will assign his best defender to guard the opposing team's most dangerous offensive player. In some cases, the coach may even decide to *shut off* that offensive player: The defensive player will shadow that offensive player extremely closely all over the field to deny him possession of the ball — let alone a shot on goal (if the strategy works to perfection, that is).

Defensive rules alone don't get the job done. Knowing how to play defense alone doesn't get the job done. The force of the personalities of players and coaches is what determines the quality and intensity of defense — that, and the guidelines discussed in this section.

## Communicating on the field

This rule is probably the most important for defense: Players must talk to each other on the field. Communicating helps to get rid of any defensive indecision about who is guarding whom and, at the same time, builds team cohesion.

Here are some of the things that you need to communicate while playing defense:

- ✔ Let your teammates know when you're defending a certain player. Call out, "I've got number four," when picking up a check.

- ✔ Yell out "Who's hot?" (meaning, "Who has the first slide?"). This call should elicit a quick response, "I'm hot," from the player who has the first slide. Call out who the second and third slides are as well.

- ✔ If you spot a ground ball, call out something like "Ball!" This call warns the rest of the defenders to look for it, and the direction of the call gives them a general idea of where the ball is before they see it.

- ✔ When you gain possession of the ball, let your teammates know that it's time to switch from defensive to offensive mode. Call out something like "Break!" to encourage the rest of the defenders to break for a breakaway or to run to the bench to let offensive players on the field.

- ✔ When you move over to help out a teammate, let him know that you're there. Call out something like "I'm left" to let your teammate know — usually the one who's defending the stick handler — that he has help.

- ✔ Likewise, if you need help, such as on a pick or a defensive switch, seek it. Call out something like "Pick left" and then, if necessary, "Switch" or "Stay" depending on whether you're going to switch assignments because of the pick.

## Defensive mistakes that drive coaches crazy

Improve your team's defense by following these steps so that you can avoid making defensive blunders:

✔ **Pressure the stick handler.** Some defenders are content to stand in front of the stick handler and either just watch him or wave their sticks in front of his stick to delay a pass or look to intercept a pass. Instead, you have to pressure him with checking and slashing, giving yourself the best chance to avoid getting beaten by the stick handler faking a pass or a shot, and then cutting around you.

✔ **Defend the pick-and-roll.** All you have to do to defend the pick-and-roll is warn your teammate that a pick is coming. Speak up. If you don't, both you and your teammate will end up trailing the cutter who is wide open for the pass.

✔ **Close to the net, defend in front of your opponent.** A basic offensive play is when an offensive player stands in front of the crease, waiting for a pass. Many defenders play behind him and try to check him out of the way. However, the offensive player can just lean on his defender, equalizing the defensive pressure and putting himself in a "relaxed" position to catch the ball and turn to shoot. The best way to defend this situation is to play on the ball side of the opponent. This way, you're in a position to help your teammate on the stick handler if he gets beaten; plus, you can deny the pass to this offensive player very easily by just playing his stick with yours.

The flow of the game will dictate many more opportunities for you to communicate on defense.

In an effective defensive system, communication is just as important as playing ability. Constantly remind yourself to talk to your teammates during a game — in fact, make sure that you remind yourself out loud, not just inside your head. And remember to talk during practice sessions as well, which will only serve to help you remember to keep on talking.

Adam Lodewick, the defensive coordinator of Yorktown High School in New York's Hudson Valley, which has won 28 sectional titles since 1980, confirms the importance of communication: "You can throw any six guys out there who have never played together before, but if they communicate with one another, you can have a successful defense."

## Pressuring the stick handler

It doesn't matter what style or type of defense you play — if you can't stop the stick handler, you're going to have a long season. Stopping the stick handler is the foundation behind all defenses. So having the right technique is extremely important.

The basic defensive stance is taking what is called a *position of readiness,* which means staying down on your opponent by keeping your knees bent, staying balanced by spreading your feet wide apart, keeping your back straight, and looking at the stick handler at his chest rather than at the ball or his stick.

If the player doesn't have the ball, hold your stick at chest level with your arms bent, ready to explode out. If he does have the ball, you always want your stick in front of the player's gloves.

Naturally, you want to be between the ball and the net to stop penetration, but your position should also overplay him (that is, keep your body slightly off-center from your opponent, trying to force him to the sideline). In this position, you can best pressure the stick handler.

Be a pest. Check the stick handler's body, and check him on his stick and glove; don't just wave your stick in the air to try to intercept a pass — force the action. Create defensive pressure. Stop his movement toward the net. Be the aggressor.

When you check the stick handler, you're really pushing him away from you, creating a gap between you and him. If you don't quickly fill this gap by moving out on him, he'll use you as a screen and shoot around you.

In the National Lacrosse League (NLL), players are always trying to get the ball off the stick handler by using a wraparound check, slashing, or poking, increasing their chances of being beaten or getting a penalty. Referees are unpredictable regarding the slash. At one point in a game, they'll call it; other times, they'll let it go. So consider your chances and the consequences as you make your defensive moves.

A key to playing defense is using space as a buffer with the offensive player. Overly aggressive defensemen are easily burned. You need to try to force the player with the ball away from his strong hand. For example, if a player is right-handed, force him so that he is going left, even if that's toward the goal. *Sliding* (that is, picking up the open man) is the most important part of team defense. Slide packages can be complex, frequently involving more than two players.

With long sticks looming at the other end, it's uncommon for a goalie to simply launch a clearing pass downfield. Clears are more deliberate, involving multiple steps as defensemen move the ball out of the defensive area past pressuring attackmen. Goalies need to communicate with their defensemen where the attackmen are and how to move the ball up the field.

---

## Defense is an attitude

Another key to defense is having the right attitude — being aggressive, mean, physically tough, intimidating, and irritating, as well as ticking people off. It may help you to think of defense as a stormy day with lightning and thunder. Play this type of aggressive defense to get the ball, to run, and to score.

To play good defense, a defensive player needs about 75 percent attitude and 25 percent skill. Attitude can make up for lack of skill. If you do get beaten because of weak technique, an aggressive attitude can still help you recover by pursuing the stick handler or cutter and preventing him from scoring.

---

## Forcing the ball

Your team defensive strategy should be to force the action. Always be aggressive against the opponent so that you try to dictate where the ball is going instead of allowing the offense to dictate it.

When you force the action, you force the ball. By playing an offensive player a certain way, you may be able to get him to pass to a less-skilled shooter or to shoot from an angle that's not his best shot. This section suggests some ways to force the ball from various points on the playing surface.

### When the ball is at the top side

When the ball is at the top side of the offensive zone, play the stick handler to the inside part of the field to force that player to the sideline. Your goal in forcing the ball in this situation is to take away the first option; the stick handler's strongest move is the pass to the cutter across the top for a shot.

A defensive strategy that forces the stick handler to the sideline gives him only the second option, the weaker of the two. When the stick handler is in an outside lane, try to keep him in the *alley* (the lane between the defender and the side of the offensive zone).

### When the ball is in the corner

When the ball is low in the corner area, you want to force the stick handler back into the middle; again, this is where your help is. If you're beaten to the outside when in the corner area, your defensive teammate will have to come over from the off-ball side to help with the stick handler, who now just passes across to his teammate for an easy goal.

Ric Beardsley, a four-time all-American defenseman at Syracuse University who also starred in both Major League Lacrosse (MLL) and the NLL, offers some tips for defensemen:

- **Find your man.** Call out who you have on each dead ball.

- **Be flexible.** When playing defense, you need to keep your head on a swivel and hips open to the stick handler and your man off ball. This allows you to keep an eye on the ball and an eye on your man.

- **Position yourself properly.** Always stay between your offensive player and the goal.

- **Communicate**. Communicating with your defensive teammates is essential to good team defense and slide packages.

## Defending picks: To switch or not to switch

*Switching* on defense means exchanging defensive assignments with a teammate during the play of the game. Switching occurs when two offensive players come close to each other, where one tries to interfere with the other's defender in order to force the defenders to switch defensive assignments. One reason why picks are used so much is that, if they work, they create a moment of indecision for the defense or they create a gap for the stick handler to shoot or go one-on-one.

The first thing you do is stop your opponent from setting the pick as he goes to set it. You can do this by checking the picker and pushing him out of the way so that you don't get tied up with the picker. By getting tied up, you create a screen for the stick handler, which gives him a number of options, including moving toward the net for a more open shot or passing to an open teammate.

How can you defend a pick? First, you have to anticipate being picked before it occurs. The job of the defender on the picker is to verbally warn you that you're about to be picked by calling out "Pick left" or "Pick right." Then you can jump out hard at the stick handler, instead of waiting for him to come to you. Or if you do get picked, you can go to him hard to fill the gap created by the pick.

When you hear your teammate calling out an upcoming pick, you can neutralize the pick by stepping back and switching checking assignments with your teammate. On this switch, make sure that you, as the defender on the stick handler, get on the inside position of your new check — that is, between your new check and the net — and play his body to prevent him from receiving the pass as he rolls to the net.

If it's a poor pick, you don't need to switch with your teammate; instead, you can stay with your own check by fighting or sliding through the pick and staying even with your opponent. In fact, when you get past the picker, you can show yourself to the stick handler at an angle to force him back to the sidelines. Be aware, though, that the stick handler may fake to go one way and then go the opposite way off the pick as an element of surprise.

If you don't switch, the defender on the picker should call "Stay" to let you know that you're not going to switch. He can even show himself to the stick handler while still staying with the picker just to slow down the stick handler and help you out.

## Defending screens on the ball side: To switch or not to switch, part 2

To defend against the screen, the defender on the screener must stay between his check and the ball. He plays on the ball side, or top side, of the screener, putting his stick over the screener's stick. He definitely does not stand behind the screener.

Now if the stick handler beats you, as the defender, and goes to the net, your teammate is in a position to leave his screener and stop him. But if the stick handler comes out of the corner to use the screen, your teammate (the one defending the screener) can move around behind the screener, to the other side, or even stay in the front, to get into a position to switch and jump out at the stick handler aggressively as he comes off the screen. When this happens, you can switch defensive assignments, going to the screener who may try to roll to the net.

What's the difference between a screen and a pick? A screen is interference that happens away from the ball. A pick is interference that happens on the ball.

Ric Beardsley, the former Syracuse University and MLL star defenseman, has these words of wisdoms for defending players with the ball:

- ✔ **Keep a half-step in front of your man.** This is called *being even with your man*.

- ✔ **Your stick should always be under or on the free hand.** If you can take one of the stick handler's hands away, he's forced to play with one hand. If he can shoot and pass with one hand, well, then he deserves to score.

If the stick handler coming out of the corner can't get close enough to the screen to rub his check out of the play, the defenders just stay with their checks.

BOX LACROSSE

## Maintaining floor position

When defending on the off-ball side of the defense in box lacrosse, your defense should form a flat triangle. You're at the apex of the triangle (toward the center lane), and the stick handler (up top) and your check (in the outside lane) form the base of the triangle. It's called a flat triangle because you play off your check slightly and toward the stick handler to be in a position to help.

If you play a deep triangle, where you're closer to the net, with your check and the stick handler at about equal distances from you, you're protecting the net more than playing your check and watching the stick handler. In this situation, your check could cut very easily for a pass and shot. And in the flat triangle, you should always keep your opponent in front of you, never play-

ing him even, or parallel to the net, because he could fake up and cut behind you for a quick pass and shot. If your opponent goes behind you on a backdoor cut, always assume that a pass is coming his way and turn and play his stick hard.

Solid team defense related to the position of the ball suggests that if your stick handler passes the ball, you should move to the level of the ball immediately and then adjust your position according to your check. You're now in a position ready to collapse, help, and rotate, especially from the top of the defense.

The final rule for positioning is that the defense moves before the offense moves on any movement of the ball.

# Building the Team Defense through Drills

This section suggests a few drills that your team can practice to help establish a team attitude when on defense.

## 2-on-1 defending the pick-and-roll on the ball

In this drill, you can put the defender on the stick-handler first to learn to step back when being picked, or to fight through the pick (if it's a poor pick), before reestablishing pressure on the ball. Then you can put the defender on the picker, who must call out "Pick" to the imaginary defender and jump out on the stick handler.

The next progression is to let the offensive player go one-on-one against the defender when he jumps out.

## 4-on-4 shell drill to practice defensive positioning

This drill is a great one to do during every defensive practice. First, get the offense to stay stationary and move the ball around. After the defenders have taken the proper position regarding their checks and the ball, the offensive players without the ball can move to get in the clear; the stick handler can't move.

Practice several scenarios with each drill, including moving with and without the ball, using and not using picks or screens, penetration or no penetration, and shot or no shot.

## 3-on-2 help-side defense

Break the 4-on-4 drill down into a 3-on-2 situation. The stick handler tries to make a pass to the 2-on-2 on the off-ball side, with offensive players remaining stationary. Then the offensive players can interchange, move up and down the side, try to cut to the ball for a pass, and work a pick. The defenders work to defend against each offensive scenario.

## Box-specific defensive drills

Here are a couple of drills specific to box lacrosse defensive positions:

✔ **4-on-4 defending screens on the ball or off-ball drill:** Defending the off-ball screen, the top offensive player passes outside to a teammate and then sets a screen for the bottom offensive player by tying up or getting inside position on his defender on the way down. The defender on the screener must be ready to switch onto the cutter coming off the screen. He does this by not getting tied up and fighting to get inside position on the screener so that he's in a position to fire out on the cutter.

You can also work this drill on the ball side of the floor with the stick handler passing down to the creaseman and then trying to

set a screen on his defender as he looks for a phony return pass. The stick handler comes out of the corner area looking to use the screen. The defenders play the screen accordingly.

✔ **3-on-2 half-floor defensive drill:** A group of five players rotate in and out of the defense and offense. Two defenders try to stop three offensive players from scoring for 10 seconds, or until they drop the ball. Give one group of two defenders five opportunities to stop the offense. This drill stresses aggressive and intense defensive play, communication on the floor, concentration, anticipation, helping out a teammate, totally recovering or rotating, and defensive coordination.

# Chapter 11

# Calling on the Special Forces: Specialty Teams

## In This Chapter

▶ Revving up the offense with the man-up and power-play units

▶ Overcoming a player deficit with the man-down and man-short units

▶ Running drills for the specialty units

The most underappreciated part of lacrosse is its specialty teams: the man-up offense and the man-down defense in field lacrosse, and the power-play offense and the man-short defense in box lacrosse.

If you have a strong man-up offense that you can run when your opponent is down a player because of a penalty, your odds of scoring a goal are significantly higher. In the case of non-releasable penalties (such as an illegal stick penalty), teams are often able to score two goals — sometimes even three goals or more — using their specialty teams.

Most field lacrosse penalties last 30 seconds or a minute, limiting your man-up offense's ability to be patient. With the added space in field lacrosse, man-up units rely on set plays. Though penalty opportunities are few during games, most college teams spend as much time practicing their man-up plays as they do their six-on-six offenses. This is because in these often-elaborate offensive man-up sets, everyone has a role and execution is crucial to succeed in these extremely important scoring opportunities.

In box lacrosse, penalties are usually two minutes or five minutes in length. If you have a strong man-down defense that can keep an opponent's man-up unit at bay, limiting the number of goals per shot attempts, you'll also be very competitive. In many cases the closest, toughest games are won by the specialty teams.

Good teams, more often than not, are ones that are not penalized frequently and also take advantage of penalties called against the opposition by cashing in with goals that often are crucial for swinging the momentum in a game.

In this chapter, we tell you the ingredients for effective specialty teams, including how to make the most of your man-up opportunities, and what to do when you're short-handed.

# Operating When You Have a Player Advantage

Man-up opportunities occur when an opposing player commits a penalty and is sent off to sit out of action for the designated amount of time. That player is not replaced, so the non-penalized team has a player advantage for the duration of the penalty period (or until it scores a goal, in the case of the releasable penalties). (See Chapter 4 for more information about the rules involved in man-up and power-play situations.)

## Practicing patience on the man-up/power play

A key element for players on the man-up or power play is patience. Many players think they have to get the shot off right away or feel as though they'd better shoot because they may not get the ball back from their teammates.

The man-down team *wants* you to take quick shots, because quick shots usually aren't as successful. Quick shots are okay occasionally, but they shouldn't be the norm. Usually, they're successful when you use them as an element of surprise.

Take your time by reversing the ball around the zone or among the three top players of your man-up or power play. Unless you have a no-brainer wide-open shot, you never want to make one pass and then shoot, because the man-down players are usually in their best defensive position at the beginning of a penalty-killing situation, and they're alert and active. Also, the goalie is in his best position to see the pass and shot.

Quick ball movement is crucial. Because a man-down defense has to rotate, the offensive team should strive to move the ball faster than they can rotate, creating an opportunity for an open shot.

On the flip side, you don't want to just pass the ball and pass the ball and pass the ball and then shoot only when you realize you're running out of time. A great man-up or power play not only moves the ball but also moves the defensive players out of their alignment by penetrating or attacking the gaps.

## *Aligning your players on the man-up/power play*

In field lacrosse, when you're up a man, the opposing team's man-down alignment is usually similar to what the team uses when it's defending a six-on-five transition — namely, a five-man zone.

In box lacrosse, the man-short defense is likely to be a simple box alignment with two players up top and two players down low. Your pointman should play at the top of the zone between the top two defenders. The standard practice is to line up other players behind the defenders, not beside them. Players tend to gravitate to their opponents, which makes it easier for the defensive team to check your players.

In box lacrosse, the shooters stand outside and behind the two top defenders. By playing your shooters behind the two top defenders — in fact, by playing them almost equidistant from the top and bottom defenders — you may be able to create uncertainty for the man-down players. On a pass to a shooter, which defender will move to play him — the top one or the bottom one? With this slight uncertainty, your shooter may get that split second he needs to get an open shot or pass. The creasemen can choose to move in and out of the middle — in front of or behind the defenders — to create an additional passing lane on power-play opportunities.

## *Singling out good man-up/ power-play players*

To be successful on man-up and power-play chances, your players must practice discipline — they shouldn't take any retaliatory penalties, mouth off to the referee, or do anything else irresponsible that would negate the advantage you have. They also need to commit to being at practice all the time because the man-up and power play require precise execution, which must be practiced all the time.

If a player can't or won't give you this kind of discipline, that doesn't mean you can't use him. But you probably don't want to waste your time with him on the man-up or power-play unit. He can still play a regular shift for the team, though.

Here are some important fundamental principles to remember on the man-up or power play:

✔ **Make your passes count.** Practice throwing *shooting passes* (passes that the receiver can catch and shoot all in one motion). Have your players work together to get to know their teammates' best shooting positions. For example, if one shooter has a great sidearm shot, a shooting pass to him would be off to the side of his shooting arm.

Also, try to avoid making predetermined passes, unless you're running a set play. Instead, move the ball randomly, counting on your players to spot defensive weaknesses and get the ball to that area of the zone.

✔ **Be ready to shoot before you get the ball.** Encourage your top offensive players to be ready to shoot before receiving the pass. Their sticks should be back, level to the field or floor, and their feet should be planted for a quick step into their shots. This ready position helps a player get a quick and accurate shot off as soon after he catches the ball as possible.

✔ **Keep your players moving.** By moving the ball and moving your players, your man-up or power play can make the defense move or shift, potentially creating openings for penetration or shots. Don't resort to only passing the ball around the outside.

✔ **Keep your players properly aligned.** This will allow them to pass and move into the play freely instead of catching and then retreating because of pressure.

When selecting your man-up units, choose your team's top offensive players, regardless of position. An athletic midfielder may be able to get up and down the field and run on the first line, but a fourth attackman with more pure offensive skills to feed, shoot, and dodge will be more valuable to a man-up unit.

## Running set plays in the man-up/ power-play offense

You may have your best chance of scoring on the man advantage without running a set play. The freedom that your players have to read what the defense gives them is usually your best offensive weapon. However, having a set play does give a lift to a team whose ball and player movement have become stagnant.

Starting your man advantage with a set play in place gives the unit a clear plan of attack that can be adjusted based upon what the defense is allowing.

The best man-up plays for an offense are often similar to the ones it employs in settled situations. In the following sections, we give you a look at some effective man-up plays from LaxLessons.com.

## Don't miss the point on the power play

In box lacrosse, the pointman is definitely the most important player on the power play. If you don't have a great pointman, you probably won't have a great power play. Here are the signature qualities of a great pointman:

✔ A great long-ball shot, usually overhand or sidearm

✔ Great passing skills with the ability to pass quickly and accurately

✔ The ability to see the whole floor and read the defensive setup

✔ Decisiveness with the ball

The pointman has several options during a power-play set, including scoring with a long shot from the top, following passes to either shooter by taking a step toward the pass, and being ready to reverse the ball.

The two shooters (cornermen, in a regular set), left shot and right shot, play on each side during the power play and are your primary shooters from the side. They should be excellent shooters with the ability to hit the far top corner or far side of the net as their primary shot and the near side of the net as their secondary shot. They also have to be good passers who can dump a pass to the near creaseman or fire a level pass to the opposite side of the floor to the far creaseman or the other shooter.

The shooters should not pass to a creaseman unless a bottom defender comes up after the shooter. You should limit your passes to the crease unless you have a clear chance to score. They can also decoy the first pass by trying to fool the man-short players into thinking that you're going to attack from one side, and then reverse the ball and look to attack from the other side.

Stress to your players that even with the decoy, as they swing the ball quickly to the other side, they should always look for an open shot. They should also swing the ball around quickly to get the goalie and the man-short players moving out of their positions. Too many teams slow down the ball while looking for a shot, giving the man-short players time to recover and interfere with a shot.

Give your plays unique names so you can call them out without revealing to your opponent what play you're running. For example, if you're running the 3-3 set with a screen, and you yell out, "3-3!", your opponent will know immediately what you're planning to do. But if you've told your team ahead of time that the "3-3" is called "Emma," you can shout out, "Emma!", and the opposition will be none the wiser.

### Crease pass and shoot

After one clockwise rotation, Player 4 carries the ball before throwing it to Player 3, who then passes it off to Player 2, who rotates up from behind the net before passing it off to Player 3. As Player 3 holds the ball, Player 1, as a decoy, cuts in his direction. Player 2 then gets the ball back at the goal line extended. After the defense rotates, Player 5 sets a screen that frees Player 6 on the backside for a pass across the crease from Player 2.

The crease pass and shoot (shown in Figure 11-1) is effective against a four-man rotating set.

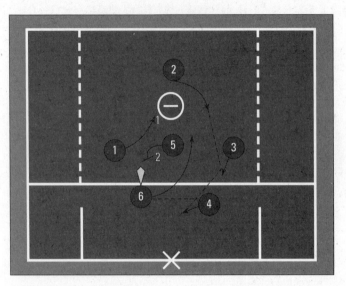

### 3-3 set with a screen

The ball is passed around once clockwise. The last player to catch it, Player 4, brings it up top. Player 4 then throws it to Player 2, who just moved from a wing position behind the cage to a position off the crease. As the pass is made, Player 5 cuts hard, using Player 2 as a decoy. Player 2 then throws the ball across the crease to Player 1. At the same time, Player 6 sets a pick on the top defenseman on the wing and Player 3 comes across to the right side of the screen by Player 5. If the defenseman getting screened comes out to cover Player 4, then Player 5 cuts to the goal for a pick and roll.

The 3-3 set with a screen is shown in Figure 11-2.

### 1-4-1

Following one rotation of the ball, Player 4 passes it off to Player 3, who rotated off the crease in a 1-4-1 set. Player 3 then passes to Player 2, who also came off the crease. Player 6, who is stationed behind the net, cuts to free himself for a pass from Player 2. Player 1, meanwhile, cuts from the wing to the backside and gets a pass from Player 6. He then looks for Player 5 up top or Player 6 on the crease.

The 1-4-1 is shown in Figure 11-3.

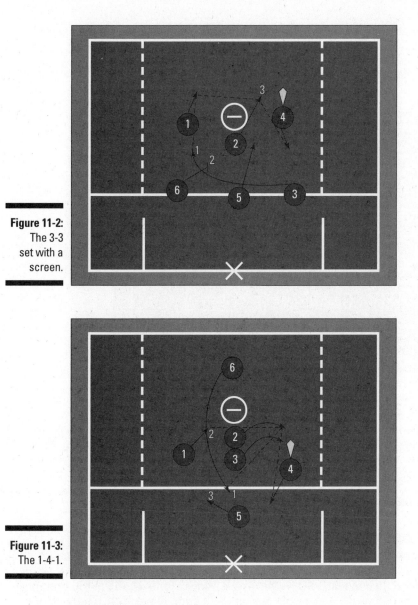

**Figure 11-2:**
The 3-3
set with a
screen.

**Figure 11-3:**
The 1-4-1.

### Roll with the rotation

After the ball is rotated counterclockwise, Player 6 reverses it to Player 4. Player 4 then passes to Player 5, who throws it off to Player 1, who is rotating from behind the crease. As Player 5 controls, Player 6 serves as a decoy by cutting toward him. Player 1 gets the ball near the crease, forcing the defense to rotate. Player 3 sets a screen on the last defender that rotates. Player 2 should be open on the back side from a feed from Player 1.

The roll with the rotation play is shown in Figure 11-4.

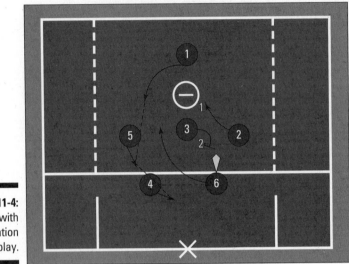

**Figure 11-4:**
The roll with the rotation play.

## Wide 2-2-2 set

Following a counterclockwise rotation, Player 2 throws a reverse pass to Player 4, who then gets the ball to Player 5. Then Player 5 passes to Player 1 after the ball moves clockwise as Player 2 moves to get a pass. If nothing develops, Player 1 moves the ball to Player 6, who looks for Player 4.

The wide 2-2-2 set is shown in Figure 11-5.

## 3-3 camouflage

This play is set up so that the play that is run out of the 3-3 is disguised. After Player 3 moves the ball upfield, Player 4 rotates to the middle of the 3-3 set. Player 6 then moves toward the crease, Player 5 moves to the top-right position, and Player 1 goes to the bottom-right spot. Player 2 then moves from the crease to the lower-left spot.

The 3-3 camouflage is shown in Figure 11-6.

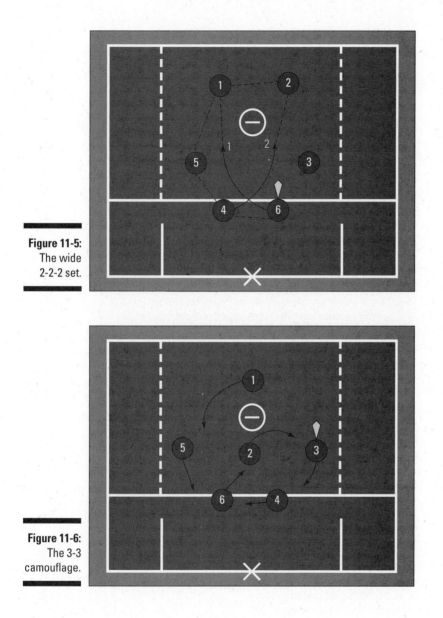

**Figure 11-5:**
The wide
2-2-2 set.

**Figure 11-6:**
The 3-3
camouflage.

# Ready, set for some man-short plays

Here are a few set plays to try against a box alignment in the man-short defense in box lacrosse:

✔ **Cutter play:** Sending cutters through the man-short can create confusion and chaos. The first pass of this play goes from the pointman to the shooter. The second pass goes back to the pointman, who makes the third pass by reversing the ball to the other shooter.

✔ **Swing play:** The pointman passes to the shooter on the side of the floor from which the play runs. The shooter passes back to the pointman who continues the reversal to the other shooter. When this shooter catches the ball, the off-ball creaseman cuts into the middle while the off-ball shooter slides down into the creaseman's spot for a pass and shot.

✔ **Diagonal play:** When you call this play, the creaseman on the side on which the play occurs moves behind the defender or out at an angle so that he creates a passing lane. Following a reversal sequence, the pointman passes to the shooter who then makes a diagonal pass to the opposite creaseman.

✔ **Middle play:** This play calls for the pointman to cut down the middle of the man-short. You should run this play only periodically; it's a great surprise play to catch the man-short off guard. If the pointman is a left shot, he passes to the right-shot shooter, who passes to the right-shot creaseman, who passes to the pointman cutting down the middle of the zone. If the pointman is a right-hand shot, reverse the sequence.

The diamond alignment of the man-short plays three defenders (a point defender and two wing defenders) against the three top players in the power-play alignment. The fourth defender (the back defender) plays between the two crease-men in the middle of the zone, creating the fourth point on the diamond.

To beat a diamond man short, look for diagonal passes, send cutters through the middle of the zone, pick defenders in the zone, and get the ball to the crease. Here are a few set plays to run against the diamond-man short:

✔ **Up pick play:** The off-ball creaseman sets an up pick (that is, picking him up toward the top of the zone) on the off-ball wing defender while the off-ball shooter drops to the crease for a pass and shot from the opposite shooter or creaseman.

✔ **Top pick play:** To start this play, the left-shot pointman passes to the right-shot shooter. The left-shot shooter sets a top pick (toward the top of the zone) on the point defender while the left-shot pointman cuts to the left-shot shooter's position for a pass and shot.

✔ **Diagonal pass to crease:** The pointman passes to the shooter who returns the ball back to the pointman who reverses the ball to the other shooter. This shooter looks to make the diagonal pass to the opposite creaseman.

## Attacking the six-on-five situation

In certain game situations, you have a chance to pull your goalie off the floor and send a sixth offensive player onto the floor. These situations usually occur on a delayed penalty, during the last 10 seconds of a period, or at the end of the game when you're behind.

Try these plays to take advantage of this type of power play:

✔ **Bench play:** Just get the ball on the opposite side of the bench and run a player off the bench right through the zone defense. This can be an element-of-surprise to run even when the defense is not expecting you to pull your goalie.

✔ **Regular play:** If the opposition plays a 2-1-2 zone, put a player in the middle of the zone and attack the zone as if in a power play.

✔ **High play:** Against a 1-2-2 zone defense, place a man in the top middle of the zone. He can set a pick on the top defender for the pointman to get a shot.

✔ **Low play:** Place a good scoring creaseman in the bottom middle of the zone. He looks to receive a pass in the middle, usually from a creaseman, for a shot.

# Playing defense on the man-up/power play

When the man-down/power-play unit is playing defense, it can double-team the stick handler to try to create a turnover, or it can play a zone defense with some extra pressure on the stick handler (often a 2-1-2).

The best way for the man-down unit to get the ball back quickly is to pressure the man-up players to force them to turn the ball over.

After a shot, the man-up/power-play unit does need to be prepared to play defense should the shot miss and the man-down team get the rebound. On the shot, each player goes to a previously assigned defensive player.

Most man-down defenses are set up with players near the goal trying to prevent higher-percentage shots from being unleashed from just outside the crease. This often forces the man-up offense to settle for lower-percentage perimeter shots.

# Defending at a Disadvantage: The Man-Down/Man-Short Defense

Maintaining discipline is even more critical for the man-down and man-short defense than for the man-up and power-play offense. If one of your man-down players ends up taking a retaliatory penalty or protests to a referee, you're going to soon find your team on the short end of a two-man advantage.

Man-down defenses most often rely on a basic box-and-one scheme in field lacrosse. Defense may form a box around the offensive player who is responsible for the ball-side crease area. This requires a four-man rotation. The alternative to this set is a five-man rotation in which the responsibility for the crease goes to the defender who is furthest from the ball.

As with man-up units, the best pure defensive players should play man-down. Lateral movement, the ability to knock down passes, and take-away ability are more important than the speed to start a fast break.

After the defense gets the ball into the opposing offensive box, the penalty is released (unless it's a harsher non-releasable call). Teams can then push the ball toward goal, but it's usually advisable to pull the offense back and substitute your offensive players back in.

To execute man-down defenses, you need aggressive, quick, and smart players. Your decision to play a box-and-one or a diamond man-short formation should be based on where the man-up or power-play offense set up its best shooters — and how many of its best shooters are on the field or floor.

Play in a box if the man-up/power-play unit keeps working the ball to the sides; rotate into a diamond when the ball stays at the top of the zone.

## Building your man-down/ man-short defense

The two bottom defenders should be big and physical — all the better if they also have a long reach to deter passes and make that little check on the offensive player's hands and arms. They should be good at getting ground balls and quick enough to get back into the play on any rotation by his defensive teammates.

---

# Thinking inside the box

The box alignment is the common man-short defensive formation in indoor lacrosse. Quite simply, the four defensive players play in a box formation — two players at the top of the zone, and two players at the bottom. The two top defenders play the three top offensive players, while the bottom defenders play the creasemen.

From this formation, either of your two top defenders can easily break down the floor on a shot. In this formation, if the shooter on the power play cuts through the middle of the zone, the opposite-side bottom defender must leave his creaseman and cross-check the shooter with the ball.

The diamond alignment of the man-short defense is just a box alignment turned on its corner. Three defenders (a point defender and two wing defenders) play against the three top players in the power-play alignment. The fourth defender (the back defender) plays between the two creasemen in the middle of the zone, creating the fourth point on the diamond.

---

The two top defenders are usually a little quicker than the bottom defenders; they need to be able to anticipate the results of a shot and use their quickness to break for a transition pass.

Though quicker, they still have to play aggressively and be physical on the man down or man short. They should be smart enough to read who has the hot hand on the man-up or power play and overplay him a bit more. And if the two top defenders can score, the man-up or power-play unit may play more cautiously to avoid turning the ball over to the good scorers.

All your man-down/man-short defenders must stay active, both with their body movement and with their sticks. Because a man-up/power-play offense can involve a great deal of passing back and forth, you have to guard against your defenders getting bored and losing defensive focus.

Here are a couple of keys to running a man-down defense:

- ✔ **Pack it inside.** Stationing the majority of the defense toward the crease helps cut down on shots from just outside the crease and forces perimeter shots. It also forces the team on offense to work the ball around, which helps to chew time off the clock and kill the penalty.

- ✔ **Run the 2-1-2 set.** Station your quickest and most athletic player in the middle so he can cover the crease ball-side. The perimeter defensemen pinch in as needed.

## Playing offense on the man-down/man-short

Although the man-down or man-short is definitely a defensive specialty team, occasionally you have to think offense with your defense. Your man-down or man-short defense will be a little stronger if you have players at the top who are a threat to score. The man-up or power-play offense won't play as recklessly if they know that they may have to get back because of this scoring threat.

If the goalie stops a shot, he first looks to throw the long breakaway pass to one of the top players breaking or to a breaking player coming into the game. A breakaway situation can also occur following a ground ball or loose ball. In the chaos that accompanies recovering it, you may be able to beat the man-up or power-play unit down the field or floor. Look to pass the ball up the field or floor rather than run the ball up, because passing is the quickest way to move the ball.

If your man-down or man-short defense can't create a quick scoring opportunity in transition, your best offensive option is to slow down the game to run out the penalty.

## Running man-down/man-short drills

In addition to running the following drills, your best man-down/man-short practice work will come out of game-like situations and scrimmages during practices.

### Rotation drill

Place cones where the man-up/power-play unit would stand. The defensive players rotate together for cohesion.

### Delay drill

In this drill, practice holding the ball by constantly running down picks on the off-ball side and throwing passes to the player coming off the pick and also by running a straight motion, spread offense.

# Chapter 12

# Becoming a Better Lacrosse Player — Physically and Mentally

### In This Chapter

▶ Exploring the physical and mental challenges of lacrosse

▶ Getting in shape — and why

▶ Starting your workouts with stretching

▶ Conditioning for lacrosse

▶ Gaining quickness and flexibility

▶ Increasing strength with weight training

▶ Getting mentally ready to play

*L*acrosse players are among the fittest athletes in the world. They must have speed and quickness, as well as upper-body strength to take all the pounding that happens during the course of a game — whether it's a check or a good, clean hit. You should do your best to be in game-ready shape when your team gathers to start workouts for an upcoming season. After all, pre-season training camps don't always focus on getting into shape; instead, they usually concentrate on skills and team play.

Here are a few more things to keep in mind as you get in playing shape for lacrosse:

- **No rest for the weary, so train to minimize weariness.** A lacrosse game consists of endurance running, short bursts of speed, stop-and-start running with high intensity, and a lot of body and stick contact thrown in, with only brief rests before returning to action.

- **Practice sprint marathoning.** Lacrosse players have to run short bursts of speed over a long period of time, so players have to train for both types of running.

- **Even a flat surface has its ups and downs.** In a lacrosse game, if you're in shape, you feel like you're running downhill. If you're not in very good shape, you feel like you're running uphill — and the game can be drudgery.

## Staying in the zone

Being in game shape is a mental challenge for lacrosse players. You should be able to stay in the *zone,* which encourages great performance. This chapter discusses getting ready to play mentally. Here are a few tips to get you started:

✔ **Be positive.** Lacrosse is, after all, a game, and your mental attitude toward it should be a positive one. Remember, too, that staying positive is easy when you're winning; the tough part is staying positive after you lose or make mistakes.

✔ **Accept the challenge.** Look forward to each upcoming game, to the challenge of the opponent (both your team's opponent and any particular individual opponent you have in mind) and to the fundamentals of the challenge that awaits.

✔ **Plan for success.** The players who anticipate that each game will be a good game are usually the successful ones.

✔ **Use your nervousness.** Try to focus and quiet your mind before the game. But remember that feeling a little bit nervous is okay, too. Use your nerves to help you get physically energized and ready to play. Let your mind keep things loose.

✔ **Have fun.** Lacrosse is a game. Enjoy yourself!

The result of these good feelings is that you get into the zone. Being in the zone means that you play alert and can anticipate things before they happen — all the activity around you seems to happen in slow motion. Your mental focus is totally absorbed in playing the game and blocking out all distractions. You play with self-confidence and you're emotionally controlled. Being in the zone helps you play the game effortlessly and you react more by instinct than by rote.

In this chapter, we give you the information you need to be at the top of your game, both mentally and physically.

# Understanding the Benefits of Being in Condition

Being in great shape allows you to perform at the highest level your body (and mind) can. Here are a few reasons why you should strive for top physical conditioning:

✔ **You prevent injuries.** Injuries are part of lacrosse. Whether it's a cut, a skinned knee, a pulled muscle, a broken arm or leg, or a sprained ankle, if you play lacrosse, you *will* get injured. How often you get injured and how fast you recover depends a great deal on the condition you're in.

Eating right, stretching, and getting plenty of sleep can help limit injuries — with a little help from plain old good luck.

✔ **You improve your lacrosse performance.** If you're in top physical condition, you can improve your speed, increase your ability to take a hit, become more agile, react quicker, run faster, and play longer at maximum efficiency.

✔ **You get mentally tough.** When you start to tire in your conditioning drills, that's when you should start to push yourself more.

Your team has to play together as one, so mental toughness as part of top physical conditioning is a team goal as well as a personal one. When working on conditioning, coaches need to make sure that all players reach the goals set for the team on any particular day. If one player falls behind, everyone goes again.

# Stretching to Be Your Best

As with any physical conditioning, your best workout is only as effective as your best pre-workout stretch.

Stretching helps to reduce strains, sprains, spasms, and muscle tears and prevent muscles from being tight and inflexible. Stretching also helps to prevent injuries common to running, such as pulled muscles, shin splints, ankle sprains, hamstring pulls, pulled groins, and *Achilles tendonitis* (also known as an *Achilles heel,* an inflamed heel cord).

Stretching before and after practices and games will keep you flexible — it reduces muscle tension by increasing your range of motion, which makes you a better lacrosse player.

## How to stretch

Before you stretch, it's a good idea to warm up a little with a light jog, running backward, or even enough carioca to work up a sweat. (*Carioca* is a sideways running exercise in which you cross-step laterally up and down the playing surface.)

Conduct your stretching sessions in just about the same way every time you work out. Work your larger muscles first, and then move on to your smaller muscles. In other words, start with your back, hips, hamstrings, groin, and quads (calves, ankles, and feet), and then follow up by stretching your shoulders, arms, wrists, and neck.

When you stretch, hold the stretch in a fixed position for a sustained period of time — aim for 20 to 30 seconds. Avoid bouncing up and down when stretching; save any movement for the practice or the game.

When stretching, you should feel a mild tension or a moderate burning sensation in your muscles, but no pain. If you feel pain, your body is telling you to stop.

## Stretching exercises for lacrosse

Any kind of stretching is a good habit to get into before working out with your team or before a game, and some stretching methods are especially helpful for getting ready for lacrosse activity. This section introduces these drills.

### Back stretches

Whether you're playing on a grass or turf field or the hard indoor surface of a box lacrosse arena, your constant running — not to mention the convoluted body positions you may end up in as a result of a check or an awkward shot on goal — will put some strain on your back.

Here are some good stretches to get your back limbered up for practice or a game:

- **Rollover:** Lie on your back, with your arms flat on the field at your sides. Bring both your legs together over your head and back. While keeping your legs straight, and your arms on the field, try to touch the field with your feet.

- **Pretzel stretch:** This stretch works on your lower back. Sitting upright, place your right hand on the field behind you and rotate your head and shoulders toward your right hand. Then cross your left leg over your right leg. Pull your left knee across your body with your left arm until you feel the stretch in the hip and torso of your left side. Repeat the stretch on the other side.

- **Lying gluteal stretch:** Lie on your back. Bend your right knee and pull it toward your chest until you feel a good stretch in the lower-back area. Repeat the stretch on the other side.

## Leg stretches

Because lacrosse requires constant motion on your part, stretching your legs in preparation for playing is critical. These stationary exercises are a good start:

✓ **Side-to-side leg swings:** Swing one leg at a time from one side of your body to the other. Work on this exercise doing ten repetitions per leg. You may want to hang onto a teammate for balance.

✓ **Front-to-back kicks:** Swing one leg at a time, forward and backward, not using so much thrust that you risk kicking off your shoe. *Remember:* You're just warming up here. Again, you may want to hang onto a teammate for balance. Work on ten repetitions per leg.

✓ **Sitting leg stretch:** Sit on the field with both legs straight and together. Bring your chest to your knees and hold for 20 seconds. This exercise stretches the backs of your legs as well as your hamstrings.

✓ **Straddle leg stretch:** Sit with your legs spread out flat on the field, forming a V, and slowly bend forward from the hips toward one foot. Keep your head forward and your back straight, bring your chest to one knee, until you feel tension in your hamstrings, and hold for 20 seconds. Then move to the other leg.

## Hamstring and quad stretches

These leg-stretching exercises are designed to loosen up and improve the flexibility of your calf and thigh muscles:

✓ **Sitting hamstring stretch:** Sit on the field and bend your right leg, bringing the sole of your right foot to rest on the inside and upper part of your left leg. Lean slightly forward, bringing your chest to the left leg and stretch the hamstring of the left leg. Hold the stretch for 20 seconds. Repeat on the other side.

✓ **Standing hamstring stretch:** In a standing position, put your right leg up on a bench in a straight position and bring your chest to your right knee. Hold the stretch for 20 seconds. Repeat on the other side.

✓ **Standing hamstring and calf stretch (iliotibial band stretch):** In a standing position, cross your right leg over your left leg and then slowly bend, moving your hands down toward your left ankle. Hold the stretch for 20 seconds. Repeat on the other side.

✓ **Stork stand:** For this quad stretch, stand on your right leg, balancing yourself by holding onto a teammate. Grab your left foot near the toes, and pull your toes toward your buttocks. Stretch for 20 seconds. Repeat on the other side.

✔ **Quad sit:** Kneel on the field and then sit down on both legs. Lean back to stretch your quads. Hold for 20 seconds.

✔ **Hurdler's stretch:** Start in a sitting position. Straighten your right leg in front of you, and bend your left knee, bringing your left leg behind you. Slowly lean back to stretch your left leg's front thigh (the quad). Hold for 20 seconds. Then slowly lean forward while grasping the right foot, to stretch your right leg's back thigh (the hamstring). Hold the stretch for 20 seconds. Repeat on the other side.

✔ **Achilles stretch:** This exercise works on your calf muscles. Stand a little away from a wall and lean on it with your hands, bending your right leg and placing your left leg straight behind you. Slowly move your hips forward until you feel a stretch in your left calf. Keep your left heel on the ground. Hold the stretch for 20 seconds. Repeat on the other side.

### Abdomen and groin stretches

These stretching exercises will improve your flexibility, which can come in handy when you reach for loose balls or create an awkward shot opportunity:

✔ **Crunches:** This exercise stretches your abdominal muscles. Lying on your back with your knees bent and your feet on the field, pull yourself up into a sit-up position, holding briefly in a 45-degree angle to the field before lying back down. Start with one set of 25 crunches, and work up to a set of 100. Add more sets as your routine becomes more advanced.

✔ **Sitting straddle stretch:** Sit with your legs spread out flat on the field, forming a V, and slowly lean forward at the hips bringing your chest toward the ground until you feel a slight pull in your groin and hamstring area. Keep your back straight and hold this stretch for 20 seconds.

✔ **Groin sit:** Sit with your knees bent and your heels together. Use your elbows to press your knees toward the field. Stretch until you feel tension in the inner thigh or groin area, and hold for 20 seconds.

✔ **Forward lunge:** Also for the groin and hamstring, this exercise starts from a standing position. Lunge forward with your right foot, and then push the hip of your left leg forward. Hold for 20 seconds. Switch legs and repeat.

# Stretching for speed during and before the season

Some stretching exercises not only can be targeted to certain activities but also provide your body with an opportunity to loosen up and prepare for a workout. Here are a few exercises to help you increase your running speed for a game:

✔ **High-knee marching:** In this drill, you try to improve your *high-knee drive* (your ability to lift your knee as high as possible on each stride), which you need when you accelerate during a game. Drive your knee upward, thigh parallel to the ground, and repeat on the other side. Keep your feet moving quickly. Try this drill for 20 yards with a marching or skipping motion.

✔ **High knee with straight leg reach:** With your legs straight, run while trying to extend your stride length. Keep your legs straight and your knees locked, pushing back off the ground. Focus on driving forward off the ground. Try this drill for 20 yards.

✔ **Heel kicks:** Run 20 yards aggressively, focusing on how rapidly your feet move to touch your buttocks with your heels. Keep your toes pointed, try to keep your upper leg from moving, and run with a slight forward lean and proper arm action.

✔ **Shuffle:** Across a 10-foot-wide section of the field, shuffle, focusing on lateral movement and low hip strength. If you work on keeping your center of gravity low, you can change direction more quickly.

### Stretching your neck and shoulders

Designed to loosen up your neck and shoulders, these exercises work well for reducing tension — both physical and mental:

✔ **Shoulder stretch #1:** Wrap your right arm around in front of your neck as your left arm presses the right elbow back. Hold for 20 seconds. Repeat on the other side.

✔ **Shoulder stretch #2:** Reach over your head and down the back with your right arm as your left arm presses down at the elbow. Hold for 20 seconds. Repeat on the other side.

✔ **Shoulder stretch #3:** Reach straight backward with both arms and press both arms upward toward your back. Hold for 20 seconds.

✔ **Neck stretch:** Tilt your head to the left, stretching the right side of your neck. Hold that position for 5 seconds. Then tilt your head to the right, holding that position for 5 seconds. Repeat six times (for a total of three times per side).

# Running for Top Physical Conditioning

You have to run both long and short distances in lacrosse because of the nature of the game. All that running requires you to stay in running shape with long-distance conditioning, sprint conditioning to increase speed, and endurance training. This section offers advice for this kind of training.

Although you can run for game-shape conditioning at any time during the year, long-distance and endurance training are best reserved for the off-season or during pre-season training, and conditioning for speed is ideal for in-season workouts.

## Off-season and pre-season conditioning

A typical off-season lacrosse program may include a two-hour workout for total conditioning: 30 minutes of stretching, 30 minutes of weight training (strength training), 30 minutes of distance running (aerobic activity), and 30 minutes of sports activity (basketball, field hockey, lacrosse).

### Long-distance and endurance conditioning

Long-distance running is what you do first to build up a base for the cardiovascular part of the game. By building up your cardiovascular system, you can recover quickly so that you can run, rest, and then quickly give it a go again. Usually, a good long-distance run lasts from 12 to 15 minutes.

Because running is a high-impact exercise, try to run on a soft surface (such as grass or field turf) to reduce any potential knee and back problems. Avoid running on pavement.

Endurance, or interval, training is good for the off-season and pre-season because you can stop and start in the middle of an extended workout. Here's an example of an endurance-training set:

- ✔ **Inside single-line run:** This is a 10- to 12-minute run around the perimeter of a field. If you're working out with a group of teammates, you can add a sprint element by making sure that the player at the back of the line sprints to the front of the line after each lap.

- ✔ **Outside 1-mile run:** Record your time for this shorter long-distance run so that you can gauge your improvement. Less than six minutes is a fast time. Around seven minutes offers a high-fitness workout. A good average time is around eight minutes.

- ✔ **Outside 1½-mile run:** Do another long-distance run and aim for between nine and ten minutes. Anything less than 12 minutes is good.

✔ **Outside 2-mile run:** Keep this run to less than 14 minutes for a good workout. Remember to record your time.

✔ **20-yard shuffle run:** Wind down with some 20-yard back-and-forth shuffle runs. This is a good run to close an endurance workout with.

Endurance training gets you in the best shape possible for training camp. Training camp isn't the place to work yourself into shape. To make a team today, you have to be in shape going *into* training camp to impress the coaches.

### Sprint conditioning

Speed is in the genes. You either have it or you don't. But you can increase your speed to a certain degree. Here are a few different ways to increase running speed during the off-season:

✔ **Weight training:** To develop leg strength for longer strides, work out with squats, leg curls, leg extensions, leg presses, dead lifts, and step-ups.

✔ **Resistance training:** Also for leg strength (and longer strides), workouts may include running uphill, running up steps, running in water, and running with weights.

✔ **Over-speed training:** To develop your *stride frequency* (the number of strides in your sprint), try running in sand, running on a treadmill, or sprinting on a gradual downhill slope.

✔ **Plyometrics:** Plyometrics are exercises in which muscles are stretched with the goal of creating explosive strength through quick movements that increase performance. Examples include jumps, hops, and bounding exercises, all of which work to contract your muscles more quickly, increasing your power.

# In-season conditioning

Beyond lacrosse games and practices, your in-season training regimen should focus on increasing efficiency — efficiency in endurance, efficiency in speed, and efficiency in transitioning between the two.

The primary way to achieve maximum efficiency in your workouts is with the correct form:

✔ Relax your torso, shoulders, hands, and jaw.

✔ Lean your upper body slightly forward, but don't bend at the waist.

✔ Swing your arms without crossing the midpoint of the body. The faster your arms move, the faster your feet move.

✔ Keep your head upright and relaxed, focusing straight ahead.

✔ Move your feet in a straight line, not inward or outward.

✔ Drive your lead leg out and up, not just lifting it upward. Snap your down leg back beneath your hips with full extension. You want a pushing action off the balls of your feet.

✔ Don't run on your toes. Your body is better at pushing than pulling, so make a pushing action with your feet against the ground.

To increase speed efficiency in a lacrosse game, stress short strides to begin with, and then, in the open field, generate more speed by opening up your stride. You run faster by increasing your stride length and moving your legs faster.

You can tailor your interval training during the season to your lacrosse practices. Focus the workouts on simulating lacrosse game conditions — that is, going for short intensive spurts of activity before a period of rest.

The shorter your work period, the higher its intensity should be. With shorter work periods, increase your rest or recovery period.

Here are some examples of efficient interval training sessions for endurance, power, and speed:

✔ **Interval endurance training:** Run 400 yards in consecutive 40-yard increments. This workout is relatively light (about 60 percent maximum effort) and should be done in 60 to 70 seconds. Your rest period should be about 180 seconds, about a 1:3 work-to-rest ratio. Complete three repetitions.

✔ **Interval power training:** This drill increases endurance for repeated high-speed sprints and is performed with 100 percent maximum effort. Run a 40-yard sprint within 6 seconds. Your rest period is 30 seconds, a 1:5 work-to-rest ratio. Complete eight to ten repetitions.

✔ **Interval sprint training:** Sprint up and down the playing surface for 40 to 45 seconds at 75 percent maximum effort. (This workout simulates the time and game speed of an average lacrosse game shift.) Rest for 120 seconds, about a 1:3 work-to-rest ratio. Complete five repetitions.

The beauty of interval training is that these variables can be changed to your age and level of conditioning. Keep the distance a constant, but you can vary the time of the run and rest.

All in-season drills should focus on keeping in game-shape throughout the season. This outcome is best achieved with continuous movement during practice, rather than extra conditioning after practice. During the season, coaches should avoid conditioning after practice because players may hold back during practice if they know they'll be expected to run later. Try motivating your players: If they run an all-out effort during practice, there will be no conditioning after practice.

If you do run conditioning drills during in-season practices, here are a few tips to keep in mind:

- ✔ **Go all-out.** All running drills are at full speed and use the full length of the field.

- ✔ **Set goals.** Let your team know how much you're expecting them to run, as well as the number of quality workout repetitions that you expect. Or set a time limit for completing certain drills.

- ✔ **Toss a ball in the mix.** Players run the hardest when a ball is involved in the drill. That's why the best way to prepare for playing lacrosse is to scrimmage.

- ✔ **Mix things up.** Try to change the style, intensity, and order of drills conducted during practices, or your players will get bored.

- ✔ **Create a challenge.** Make your drills challenging and competitive. Your players are on the team for a reason — they want to succeed in a competitive environment. Try to make your practices almost as rewarding in that way as an actual game.

If you play three lines, players will go on the field every third shift, so try to relate your training to these variables. Make the training demands slightly greater than in game situations. Hard practice days should be followed by easy practice days or days off during the season. A hard practice should not be done on the day before an important game.

Recovery from a hard day or a game can take 24 to 48 hours.

### Conditioning drills without a ball

Not every drill needs to have a ball to be successful. Here are a few drills to run during in-season practices that may be a blast for your team.

### Sprints down and back

Run five sprints from one end of the field to the other, adding one sprint if any player comes in over a predetermined set time. Use three groups of players — fast, medium, and slow — with target times for each group.

### Suicide runs down and back

Suicide runs have three stages: Groups of players start at one end of the field and run to the first line and back, then to the far line and back, and finally to midfield and back. Use three groups of players — fast, medium, and slow — with target times for each group. Let your players know ahead of time how many repetitions they'll run, adding one repetition for each time a player comes in over a predetermined time.

### Variety run

This drill incorporates four separate styles of running. In the end, each player will run the length of the field and back twice. Set target times for each player.

1. **Run half the length of the field.**

2. **Run backward back to the other end.**

3. **Zigzag through the cones to the other end.**

4. **Run the length of field chasing loose balls rolled to them.**

## Conditioning drills with a ball

In this section, we offer some drills to run *with* a ball.

As an alternative to running or other conditioning drills at the end of an intense practice, stage brief (three- or four-minute) games without line changes.

### 2-on-0 run and pass

Pair up players to run the length of the field while passing the ball back and forth. Each player should call out the receiver's name when passing, and each pass should be thrown after no more than two steps with the ball.

The goal is to keep the ball moving forward (that is, passing in front of the other player and not behind or short of the receiver).

### 5-on-0 run, pass, and shoot

Line up five players across one goal line. The players run down half the length of the field and back together, passing the ball from one player to the next. When the line reaches just inside the offensive zone, the player who controls the ball shoots. The drill continues until every player shoots at least once.

*Shoot and break out on a loose ball*

Roll a ball into a corner of the field and send a player after it. The player runs the ball down to the other end of the field and shoots on the goalie. Alternate left-hand and right-hand shots, switching sides when every player has run the drill at least once.

# Improving Your Quickness and Agility

Quickness comes into play when you take a speedy first step with which you're able to beat your defender and explosively go by her. This first quick step is important because it can get you past your defender or create space between you and your defender to be able to take a shot or make a pass.

If you have average speed, however, you may be able to beat your defender because of your agility, your flexibility, and your ability to change direction quickly. You can set up an opponent by making her think you're going one way by your body language and instead you fake and go the other way. This kind of flexibility can cause your defender to lean one way while you make your offensive move the other way, again creating an opening for a shot or a pass.

Quickness and agility are critical to defensive play as well. A quick defender is able to react to offensive movement, possibly catching up to an opponent who has beaten him. Agility and flexibility on defense can combine with smarts to anticipate when an offensive player may try to beat you to the punch.

This section offers some quickness and agility drills to improve your offensive and defensive games.

## Offensive drills

These drills work on your footwork and foot speed, skills required for quick and agile movement on the lacrosse playing surface:

- ✔ **Faking:** While jogging around the field, take short, quick steps in an opposite direction. Push right, step left, and then push left, step right.

- ✔ **Pivoting (for a left-shot player):** Fake right with your right foot, step inside with your left foot, pivot (or spin) on your left foot while pulling your right foot over your left foot, and then go left.

- ✔ **Pivoting (for a right-shot player):** Fake left with your left foot, step inside with your right foot, pivot (or spin) on your right foot while pulling your left foot over your right foot, and then go right.

- ✔ **Agility obstacle run:** Run up and down the field through and around cones. You can add faking drills to this run as well.

- ✔ **Sprints:** Set up a cone about 12 feet from the sideline. Run back and forth from the cone to the sideline, touching the sideline marker with your stick. Run in 30-second repetitions.

- ✔ **Agility square:** Start in a corner and run down the field for a pass, making a one-on-one move across the top of the zone. Then after a pass, make a V-cut to the crease area to set a cross pick before rolling back to the original corner for another pass.

# Defensive drills

To improve footwork, most defensive drills deal with lateral action, footwork, communication, and quickness. Make your drills short, quick, and hard.

## Footwork drills

Some examples of footwork drills are running backward (up and down the length of the field) and carioca (crossover runs facing the sideline and down the length of the field).

## The wave drill

The team reacts to the direction in which the coach points. Your reaction motions should be step and slide down and back or drop-step and slide across. Work on keeping your knees bent and maintaining a proper defensive stance.

## The shadow drill

With a partner, one player mirrors the other for 10 seconds. This drill can be a non-contact drill (the stick handler moves side to side and can't beat the defender) or a contact drill (the stick handler works the defender but can't beat him).

## Defensive square drills

To work on lateral motion, agility, and quickness, place four cones to mark a square that equals the distance a player would move during a game. You can run this drill clockwise or counterclockwise. Do four repetitions or target a set time.

Here are a few types of square drills you can run:

✔ Facing the same direction at all times, backpedal, shuffle, sprint forward, and shuffle from cone to cone to complete a square.

✔ Shuffle down to the first cone in a defensive stance (facing the boards). Open your stance and shuffle across to the next cone (facing the goal). Turn and run up the sideline to the third cone, changing to a shuffle for the last two steps. Close out the drill by shuffling back across to the original cone.

✔ Starting in the middle of the square, run to a corner and backpedal back to the middle. Repeat with all four corners. You can run the same drill with sprints or slides back and forth from middle to corner.

# Getting into Shape with Weights

Strength is one of the keys to success in today's lacrosse, and strength can best be developed through a properly organized weight-training program. You're hit when you're going after ground balls. You're checked hard across your upper body and arms to stop you from going to the net. You're stopped from cutting toward the goal. And you're required to sprint to the other end of the field to score. In all these situations, weight training will help you improve your performance by increasing your endurance, flexibility, agility, running speed, and overall physical strength. Besides improving all these qualities, weight training helps to prevent injuries.

Weight training works on the overload principle. You demand a muscle to do something it doesn't want to do by increasing the amount of weight or increasing the number of repetitions that you can do.

What you do during the off-season determines what you do during the season, and a solid off-season training program should include weight training. (Many players don't regularly lift during the season because of the physical demands of games and practices — to say nothing of being stretched for time.) As with any training that you take on, keep a record or chart to gauge your progress, as well as to motivate you to greater heights.

For more information about training with weights, check out *Weight Training For Dummies,* 2nd Edition, by Liz Neporent and Suzanne Schlosberg (Wiley).

Here are some tips to keep in mind when weight training:

✔ **Repeat consistent repetitions.** Start with enough weight to do about eight reps each set, working your way up to ten reps. Repeat each exercise eight to ten times, working with 75 percent of your *maximum weight* (the most weight you're capable of lifting for a single repetition of a given exercise). After you can complete ten repetitions without straining too much, increase the weight. It's important to work with the weight that's best for you — not too heavy yet challenging enough to make you work.

✔ **Train in sets.** You may want to start with one set, and then progress, working up to three sets. Some people recommend one set to total fatigue. A set is doing one type of exercise for eight to ten reps.

✔ **Maintain consistency in your order of exercises.** Start with the largest muscle groups first (shoulders, back, abdomen, chest, quadriceps, and calves), and then work with the smallest muscle groups (shoulders, arms, and ankles).

✔ **Lift with proper form.** The technique must be correct, slow, controlled, and smooth. Concentrate on your form and don't cheat, such as arching your back when bench-pressing in order to get more leverage or bouncing or swinging the weight when doing arm curls. Lift weights up in 2 seconds and lower weights down in 4 seconds.

✔ **Breathe consistently.** Some people recommend no scheme to breathing when lifting weights, but say you just shouldn't hold your breath. Others recommend that you breathe in while raising the weights or working the muscles and breathe out while you lower the weights. Whatever you choose to do, do it the same way every time.

✔ **Raise and lower the weight through a full range of motion.** This maintains or increases flexibility, which is important for preventing injuries.

✔ **Take time between exercises.** In a weight-training program, if you're working on endurance, cut down your recovery time to 15 to 45 seconds between exercises, or even no rest. If you're working on strength, rest for one to two minutes between exercises.

✔ **Maintain a consistent training schedule.** During the off-season, you can train three times a week on alternate days. Your muscles need time to recover and grow. An alternative that some players practice is to train six days a week by working the upper body one day and the lower body the next day.

During the season, you can train two times a week to maintain if you have the time, but be careful, because rest is important during the playing season.

✔ **Manage your training time.** Spend no longer than 45 minutes (for endurance training) to one hour (for strength training) in the weight room. It's a good idea to work in teams so that one of you can be a spotter, and you can push each other.

Here are some standard weight-training exercises that you can start with for both the upper and lower body:

- **Crunch (for abdominal muscles):** Lie on your back on a mat, knees bent, and feet flat on the ground with your fingers lightly touching your ears. Slowly curl your torso until your shoulder blades leave the mat. Hold this position a few seconds, and then lower slowly back down to the mat.

- **Bench press (for chest muscles):** Lie on an exercise bench with your knees bent so your feet are flat on the ground. Grasp the barbell from the rack with your hands slightly wider than shoulder width apart. Slowly lower the barbell to your chest, and then press the barbell up until your arms are fully extended.

- **Military press (for shoulder muscles):** Sitting at the end of the bench, grasp the barbell, and plant your feet firmly on the ground. Lift the weight over your head and rest it on the back of your shoulders; push the bar up to arm's length, and then lower it to the starting position and repeat.

- **Bicep curl (for bicep muscles):** In a standing position, hold the barbell with an underhand grip, allowing it to rest against your thigh. Slowly bring the bar up to your chest, bending your elbows but keeping your upper arms motionless against your sides. Hold the bar against your chest and then slowly lower it to the starting position.

- **Lat pull-down (for back muscles):** Grasp the bar at the lat pull-down station of a weight machine with your hands 3 feet apart, and then sit down, allowing your arms to extend overhead. Pull the bar down slowly until it touches the back of your neck right above your shoulders, and then return to the starting position.

- **Squat (for quads and buttocks):** In a standing position, grip a barbell and place it across your shoulders, behind your head. Holding the bar and placing your hands shoulder-width apart, slowly squat down until your upper thighs are parallel to the ground, and then return to the original position. Make sure you keep your head up and your back straight.

- **Leg curl (for hamstrings):** Sit in the curl machine placing your heels on top of the footpad. To get support, hold onto the front or side of the machine. Curl your legs (that is, bring your heels toward your buttocks), and then slowly let the weights come back up to the original position.

- **Leg extension (for quads):** Sit in the leg-extension machine with your feet under the footpad, raise the weight stack until your legs are parallel to the ground, and return it to the starting position.

## Eating and sleeping your way to game shape

What you eat and how you sleep affect the way you play. Good nutrition alone is not enough to produce a winner, but poor nutrition may be enough to *keep* you from being a winner. Athletes have to eat a balanced diet every day. Recovery is also critical to help you restore your energy — and the best recovery starts with a good night's sleep.

Here are a few eating and sleeping tips to keep in mind to help you achieve your best on the lacrosse field:

- **Stay hydrated.** Water has more impact on performance than any of the foods you eat. The biggest mistake that players make is to wait until they're thirsty to drink. You should drink throughout the day, regardless of whether you're thirsty. Drink a considerable amount of juices, water, or sports drinks before, during, and after a lacrosse game or practice. Aim for at *least* eight glasses of water each day.

- **Eat a simple, balanced diet that leans to the low side in fat content and to the high side in carbohydrates.** (Carbohydrates help you increase endurance.) And stay away from junk foods.

- **Eat and drink every two hours whenever possible.** Aim for four to six meals per day, but eat lightly — for example, three moderately sized meals plus two to three snacks each day. Eat more frequently, but in smaller portions.

- **Try for eight or more hours of sleep every night, especially during the season.** Don't underestimate the value of a nice catnap. During the season, short naps (10 to 15 minutes) will leave you feeling energized and refreshed.

# *Mentally Preparing for Lacrosse*

Because lacrosse is such a physically demanding sport — whether it's the endurance and stamina required for a field lacrosse contest or the quick turns and body banging of a box lacrosse game. Up to this point, the focus of this chapter has been on *physical* readiness, but being ready to play lacrosse takes more than just physical strength. As in any sport, mental toughness is more than just a hackneyed cliché — it's a requirement.

How you mentally approach lacrosse — whether it's your approach before a game or before a practice — is an important factor in how well you'll play. For some players, preparing mentally may mean little more than going over a checklist of emotions and expectations before a game:

- Do I have the proper attitude or outlook?
- Am I calm and composed?

✔ Do I feel optimistic?

✔ Am I self-confident?

✔ Am I alert and totally focused?

✔ Am I ready to have fun?

Other players, however, may need some additional help to prepare mentally for a game. This section discusses a few approaches.

## Setting goals

By setting long-term personal goals, or *outcome goals,* you can become more self-motivated. For example, you may want to be recognized as the best player or the best defender on your team or in your league. If you're motivated to do your best to achieve this goal, you can get mentally ready to play more easily. Outcome goals can also help you get over the rough spots that every player faces during a long season; short-term disappointments are overcome by long-term outcome goals.

These long-term outcome goals, of course, are nothing more than a whole bunch of short-term goals strung together. Your short-term goals may be performance or behavior goals. Either way, you're setting a bar for yourself for the outcome of a game or practice. For example, a short-term performance goal may be to score two or three goals in a game. As well as competing against your opponent, you're competing against yourself and the achievement of your short-term goals.

Coaches may want to have their players create personal plans so that they're aware of goal-setting strategies to help them prepare to play.

## Practicing relaxation

Athletes often fail to achieve their best performance because they're too tight, anxious, or stressed out. Of all the human emotions, nervousness is the greatest enemy of achievement. You can't eliminate pressure situations — they'll always be there because they're a natural part of a lacrosse game. If you're prepared to play, however, the game won't be a stressful situation and you'll have "good pressure" as a result.

Good pressure heightens your senses, makes you more focused and motivated, and helps you play to your maximum potential. Understanding your response to that kind of pressure is one of the best ways to relax in preparation of a game.

Relaxation can help during a game as well. "Give it all you got" is one of the real myths in sports; in reality, giving it all you've got usually leads to tension, stress, and anxiety, slowing down your decision-making skills and hindering your performance. As you perform in a game, relax. A relaxed body and mind are characteristic of all great players.

In the following sections, we cover the various ways you can relax.

### Relaxing with a proper attitude

You create your own pressure by the way you look at a situation and by what you say to yourself about it. Play down the importance of the outcome of a game. Approach each game as a welcome opportunity for success and challenge rather than as dreaded threats. You get "good pressure" if you look at the game as an opportunity to feel the joy of playing a great game against a worthy opponent.

Your anxiety level rises if you put a life-or-death price tag on the outcome of a game. In reality, no loss or setback from a game will ruin your life.

### Relaxing by tightening and relaxing your muscles

Proper deep breathing and muscle-relaxing exercises help you feel loose and calm, relax your muscles, and energize yourself. This strategy involves just tensing and relaxing your muscles, which helps your muscles loosen up. Some players like to shake their arms to feel relaxed. You could also tighten and loosen your grip on your stick until you feel the level that's just right.

### Relaxing with deep breathing

A small amount of pre-game excitement and anticipation is healthy and necessary to get you ready to play a game. But how do you know if you're too excited? Breathing is the first step to recognize your level of arousal. So before the game, check out your breathing.

Because stress influences breathing, be on the lookout for short, shallow breathing. Focus instead on inhaling slowly and deeply through your nose, filling your lungs and diaphragm as completely as possible. Then focus on your exhalation as you relax any muscle tension in your body, letting the air out slowly through your mouth.

The exhale is what relaxes you and reduces stress, which in turn increases performance.

## Visualizing your way to success

Visualization should be a part of mental preparation for every lacrosse player. There is a direct correlation between the mind and the physical body. You visualize in your mind how you want to play in the upcoming game, and when you have that in mind, the physical body just seems to take over.

Before a game, visualize yourself playing a perfect game. You want to visualize success, such as beating your defender, scoring a goal, or stopping your opponent's goal scorer. The more real the experience in your mind, the more effective your performance will be.

Visualization works because it acts like a practice or dress rehearsal before the game. So when the time comes for the real game, you have a sense that you've already done this before.

Most players who visualize imagine all the good things that can happen in the game. But the top players also visualize all the bad things that can happen and how they'll handle them.

## Paying attention to self-talk

What do you say to yourself before a game? Is it positive or negative, or do you not talk to yourself at all? To get into the correct playing mental zone you have to be positive, you have to think you can do it.

The good lacrosse players know that if they don't learn to control their thoughts, their thoughts will control them. Self-talk is basically the skill of replacing a negative inner voice that hurts your performance with a positive inner voice that will help you perform better.

If your thoughts are positive and focused, you'll increase your performance state. Positive self-talk helps you get into the zone by making you feel good, feel optimistic, focus on your performance, feel confident, feel energized and alert, and feel calm and physically relaxed.

If you want to be a good player, you have to learn to play hurt, play when fatigued, and play when you don't feel like it. Great players talk themselves into playing their best when they feel their worst.

You can also use self-talk to relax yourself. If you feel you're trying too hard or tensing up, just tell yourself something like "relax," "just let it happen," "let it flow." You can even talk out loud or give yourself a pep talk. For some players, talking out loud seems to help more than just talking in their heads.

The speed and tone of your voice is as important as what you say. Talking rapidly with a harsh tone will tighten your muscles. Talking slowly and in a low tone can relax you.

Some players also find that talking to the opposition helps them to stay relaxed.

## Controlling your emotions

One player gets upset over a bad call and comes out on his next shift playing brilliantly. Another player might get upset over something and retaliate. Both players get upset, yet one handled it well, and the other didn't. Know your *hot buttons* (what gets you upset and makes you lose your temper). Hot buttons can hurt your performance because powerful negative emotions weaken your decision-making ability.

You may not make the hot button go away, but you can learn to cope with the situation. Instead of allowing the situation to control you, you can control the response you choose. The best way to deal with getting upset is to be prepared for it. A self-control strategy is to make a list of adversities and visualize how you'll react to them.

Have you ever seen a perfect game? There will always be setbacks, adversities, and mistakes in any game and in any season. By planning ahead and anticipating problems, you'll feel confident that you can handle any unexpected situations. Think about all the things that could go wrong and imagine how you would handle them. Problems could happen before the game, in a hotel room or at home, on the bus, in the arena, just before the game, while warming up in the arena, as you step on the field for warm-up, during the game, or at the very end of the game. So the trick is to expect the unexpected and try to prepare for it.

## Focusing on the game

Some players walk around before a game in a trancelike state. What they're doing is focusing on their performance and thinking about the game. When you focus, you force everything out of your mind except your preparation and your performance to minimize as many distractions as possible before the game. You have to focus to avoid the invasion of self-defeating thoughts, such as worry, doubt, and fear, and to enter the game with your own positive thoughts.

### Focusing on what you're doing

Focus your attention on your performance rather than on any desired outcome. Focus your attention on what you *can* control, which is your performance, rather than on things you can't control, such as winning. Just think about doing your best and losing yourself in your performance.

Concentration is the ability to focus all your attention on what you're doing in the present moment, not what happened two plays ago, and not what's going to happen in the next two minutes.

### Trying not to force concentration

Mental preparedness includes being in tune with what's happening on the field and fitting into the flow of the action. When in this zone, you just let your focus happen. If you try too hard to focus, your performance deteriorates, especially when things are going badly: You think too much, you start to force things to happen, you play uptight, and end up getting yourself into more trouble.

When a player is playing well, she isn't really thinking about anything; she's just doing what comes naturally.

### Focusing on the positive

You'll perform better by thinking or focusing on what you have to do instead of on what you don't want to do. If you think negatively, such as "I'm not going to throw the ball away," that thought of not committing an error focuses your mind on committing the error, thereby directing the body to do just that. If you focus positively, such as "I'm going to hit my teammate's stick high and outside," that thought helps your mind to concentrate on a relaxed, positive focus — your teammate's stick.

### Blocking out distractions

To stay mentally alert during an entire lacrosse game takes full concentration. You have to work at it to shut everything out and dismiss all stray thoughts from your mind except what you have to do. You can't have any momentary lapses, so you must play as if every ground ball, every one-on-one confrontation is important. You must concentrate on not letting your mind wander.

Be sure to focus on the here and now when playing in a game and not get caught up in the next game or even a big upcoming game next week or next month.

## Establish a pre-game routine

Jitters and butterflies will always be there before a game. Nervousness keeps you alert, but it could result in nervous exhaustion if you don't learn how to control it. You need a pre-game routine to help you relax before a game, to get rid of nervousness and butterflies, and to help you energize if you aren't in a ready state to play.

Keep the same pre-game routine for every game. This approach prevents panic if things start going wrong. You should have a ritual — a warm-up routine to take control of your mental state and get rid of any negative distractions and thoughts. For example, what can happen before a big game? Players panic and change their approach to the game. A major cause of failure in the big game is altering your routine. You have to establish a pre-game routine that feels comfortable for *you* and then stick to it, no matter what happens.

So what is your routine? Do you take a nap? Do you eat a certain pre-game meal? Do you get dressed in a certain order? Do you never wash your socks and underwear until the end of the season? Do you have a special pre-game warm-up?

Are these idiosyncrasies, habits, good luck charms, superstitions, rituals, or just eccentricities? Call them what you will, they work. Some players like to be quiet; others like to be loud, joke around, and be chatty. Some players like to seclude themselves and listen to quiet music; others like to listen to loud music. Some have a plan to keep busy right up to game time to keep themselves from getting nervous. Some have developed a ritual of putting on their equipment in a certain order. Others just get dressed quickly and put on their equipment in any order. Some like to energize by doing physical exercises such as push-ups, jumping, skipping, or riding a stationary bike. Some like to relax by doing deep breathing and muscle relaxation.

Then there are others who want to watch the video of the opposition to look for habits and weaknesses. Some players go through the mental preparation strategies of relaxation and visualization, imagining their best games in their mind. Others get themselves ready to play by telling themselves how they want to feel and play.

## *Energizing yourself going into a game*

If you're feeling sluggish or fatigued before a game, you likely have some nervous pent-up energy. Physical activities can get the circulation going and pump yourself up; try jumping up and down, skipping, or stationary biking. You may find that these physical activities will wake you up and make you more alert.

You get energy by using energy.

Try listening to upbeat music while you visualize or breathe or practice some other mental preparation. Whatever the activity, your goal is to get your heart pumping and excited for the upcoming challenge.

# Part III
# Coaching Lacrosse

The 5th Wave          By Rich Tennant

©RICHTENNANT

"This guy wants to know if he can play. He says he's fast and agile, and he has his own stick."

# In this part . . .

1f you're a lacrosse coach, especially a new one, you need to know where to look for advice on building your team, developing a game plan, and motivating your players. This part offers all that and more, including specific tips for coaching kids. We also help you decide on a style of play for your offense and defense and give you effective strategies to use on offense against specific defenses, and vice versa.

# Chapter 13

# Fundamentals of Coaching Lacrosse

## In This Chapter

▶ Finding a game plan to match your players

▶ Finding the players to achieve your game plan

▶ Understanding what it takes to coach kids

▶ Building team unity

Successful coaches have all kinds of different techniques. There are motivators, disciplinarians, sympathizers (so-called "players' coaches"), those known for their X's and O's (great strategists), delegators, or micromanagers. But unsuccessful coaches in any sport have also had some or all of these traits, too. What sets the successful coaches apart from their peers is the ability to match the players on their team to a style of play that gives their team the best opportunity to win.

This chapter introduces the fundamentals of coaching as simply that: selecting the best players available and creating a system that will take the fullest advantage of their skills. We also offer a few tips about coaching kids, as well as methods for building team unity.

## Determining Your Team's Style of Play

What style of play do you want your team to use? Should you run or should you slow down the game? Should you play a tough, physical style or a quick, finesse style? Do you need to score a lot of goals or can you keep the score in a game low? These are some of the questions you need to be able to answer in order to succeed as a coach.

If you have the luxury of determining a style of play and then going out to recruit players who fit this style, fantastic. But the more likely scenario is that you're given a team of players, and you have to develop a style of play that fits their individual strengths. For example, you may not have the biggest team around, but you may have the smartest, and your "overpower-them" strategy quickly becomes your "outwit-them" strategy.

If you coach high school or youth lacrosse, you may be able to seek out kids who fit into your system and convince them that lacrosse is a great sport to play!

No matter how you build your team, you still need to determine a style of play so that every player is playing from the same page of your playbook. Here are of the two main offensive styles that you may consider:

- **Transition/aggressive:** These teams rely on fast breaks and getting scoring opportunities off changes of possession, including ground balls and faceoffs. Defensively, they're usually aggressive in checking the opposing stick handler. This style is generally favored by athletic teams that have speed and depth.

- **Deliberate/ball control:** Generally employed by teams that are fundamentally sound but lack speed and depth. Offensively, these teams usually run patient sets that chew time off the clock — sometimes bordering on stalling. Defensively, they often employ zones to make up for their lack of quickness, which could be exploited in a man-to-man set.

Effective coaching comes down to this: Put the players you have into a style of play that brings out the most in all of them so that they're in the best possible position to succeed.

Jeff Brameier, who has won more than 400 games and coached more than 50 all-Americans in 24 years as varsity coach at Darien High School in Connecticut, sums up his coaching philosophy: "Offensively and defensively, we like to consider ourselves multidimensional, meaning we don't like to allow our opponents to be comfortable in knowing exactly what they'll face when they compete against us. Offensively, we like to be very up-tempo and believe that it is important to get your shots. We like to have scoring balance and usually have four or five guys every year that hit the 80-point mark. Defensively, we're quick and aggressive, but we rely a lot on our athleticism and great goaltending. Again, we run a complex offensive and defensive scheme which makes it more difficult to prepare to play us."

# Building Your Team

After you decide the type of system you'd like to try to run, you need to start looking for players who will best fit into that system. Look for players who have the skills necessary to achieve success in your style of play, as well as the game sense to recognize opportunities to both press forward and hold back with that style of play.

Regardless of what style of play your team focuses on, you also need to build a team that has some overall balance. If you're coaching a quick, fast-breaking team, you still need to have a few bigger players who can counteract those opponents who play a tough, hard-hitting, grind-it-out kind of game. If your top goal scorer is a right-handed shooting player, try to add a couple of strong left-handed shooting players so that you can run plays that feature scoring options from both sides of the goal.

When selecting your players, think about building your team in stages. If you're allowed 21 players on your team, decide first — based on your style of play — what skills you must have from your top 7 players, how your middle 7 players will support your best players, and how your last 7 players will contribute:

- **Finding the cream of the crop:** Usually, your top players are going to carry the team offensively. They'll be responsible for most of your scoring and will need to be quick enough to stay away from disruptive checks, wily enough to anticipate defensive tendencies, and have the field vision to spot an open teammate.

- **Finding players who love the dirty work:** Doing the dirty work doesn't (necessarily) mean taking on an opponent physically. Your middle group of players needs to have strong fundamental skills that will support your top players. These players should be able to play well both on offense and on defense. You're looking for solid, if not great, defenders; occasional goal scorers; and players with size and defensive quickness who are willing to take one for the team to get a ground ball or slow down an opponent.

- **Finding the right blend to complement your best:** Based on your team's style of play, you need a few players who have a strong work ethic and positive attitude to encourage your best players to stay within the system. This group is also where you'll place any role players or specialists, such as a player who gives your team the best chance to win any faceoff. Or you may want to use this group to add players who are athletic enough to play any position on the team, giving you a bit of flexibility in case you lose a player or two to injury.

When you're analyzing individual players, look at the following:

✔ **Athletic ability:** You want players who play hard, run hard, and rely on their conditioning. Look for athletic players who have quickness, strength, and endurance. For some players, great athletic potential may outweigh poor stick-handling skills, because you can shape that potential and teach stick handling.

✔ **Lacrosse skills:** Physical talent is relatively easy to spot and is one of the major keys to a team's success. Players who are fundamentally sound in lacrosse skills will succeed on offense, defense, or both.

If a player lacks the sport's specialized skills, he can still be a solid role player who is able to out-hit, out-hustle, and outrun his opponents.

✔ **Intelligence:** Look for players who understand the game, who play focused and alert, who make smart plays, and who seem to be aware of everything that's happening on the field.

# Developing a Game Plan

The goals of any game are very simple: to play as hard and as well as possible, and to try to win the game. Coming up with a plan to achieve those goals, however, takes a bit more time and creativity.

## Understanding your opponent

Find out everything you can about your upcoming opponent. Who are its biggest offensive threats? What are the weaknesses of its defenders? What are the tendencies of its goaltender? By understanding what an opposing team is likely to do during a game, you can build your game plan to match or overcome its strengths.

Take advantage of opportunities to scout an opposing team in action, either in person or on tape. By watching an upcoming opponent play, you can learn a great deal about the team's tendencies. If you have the game on tape, you can watch play after play after play, over and over and over again, and then share the tape with your players.

## Concentrating on defense

All great lacrosse teams win because of their defense. Good, flexible defenses can succeed against any kind of offense: settled, unsettled, or in between.

Defensive skills can be taught more easily than offensive skills. You can teach players how to be physical or how to get in position to dish out a good, clean hit. You can't teach players how to acquire a shooter's touch around the net.

Create an atmosphere on your team that rewards great defensive play. It's natural for players to think that the fun part of lacrosse is scoring goals. By emphasizing solid defense, you help your players see the fun part of the game as stopping an opposing player from scoring goals. Provide incentives for hustling defensive play and hard work, creating quantifiable goals that players can reach, such as number of ground balls recovered.

## Focusing on offense

The great offensive players seem to be born with a "nose for the net." And then there are some players who practice and practice but never get the "touch" around the net to score. So if you have players who have difficulty scoring, you'd better come up with an offensive system that creates open shots, and emphasize that if the shot isn't there, don't shoot.

If you have good offensive players, you have a bit more flexibility in creating an offensive game plan. After establishing your opponent's weaknesses, you can add set plays to your game plan that will take advantage of those weaknesses. If your opposing goalie is a great stick saver, have your shooters focus on the corner of the net that's opposite his stick. And make sure that you have a nice mix of long-ball shooters and inside scorers.

No matter what your team's offensive philosophy is, make sure that your offensive players always know who their defensive backup is — which player goes back on defense when a shot is attempted.

# Coaching Lacrosse to Kids: What You Need to Succeed

When you're coaching lacrosse to kids, you need everything from patience (it's a tough game, after all) to the ability to teach them the game. In the following sections, we outline all the traits that a good kids' lacrosse coach needs.

## Being a good teacher

You can have plenty of knowledge about lacrosse, but your teaching ability will be judged by what your players learn. The most important aspect of teaching is being able to *transfer* knowledge. You may be the most knowledgeable coach in the world, but if your players can't translate that knowledge into action, your expertise means nothing. So in addition to sharing what your players need to *know,* make sure that you're giving them the tools they need to know what to *do.*

Your players will learn more if you follow these basic teaching principles:

- ✔ **Don't just dictate — explain.** Of course, you need to tell players what you want them to do and achieve. But players learn best when they're told what to do, how best to do it, why things need to be done a certain way, and what kind of success will come out of it. Be precise, but also be explicit.

- ✔ **Do as I do, not as I say.** Contrary to the well-known axiom, you *do* want your players to do as you do. So you need to be willing to demonstrate exactly what you're asking your players to do. Use your assistant coaches, other players, or even parents — just make sure that your demonstrations are accompanied by a thorough explanation.

- ✔ **Practice, practice, practice.** Your players have to translate the knowledge they've received from your explanations and demonstrations into action on the field. Be sure to practice enough repetitions so that your players leave the field with confidence in their ability to achieve what you're asking for.

- ✔ **Give feedback.** Make sure to include both positive and negative feedback. You want to reward your players for their successes, as well as give them a chance to learn from their mistakes.

Your attitude about mistakes can help create an environment of support and security. Because mistakes are an important part of the learning process, don't get upset over them. Instead, present your critical feedback with some more positive comments, making sure that players understand that mistakes are there to be learned from. Also, don't compare one player to another player — that only pits them against each other, which is the opposite of what you want to happen.

## Instilling confidence

You need to believe in and see the potential in your players, as well as be able to suffer through your players' growing pains. By doing so, you help your players become more confident, which motivates them to play better. The skills will come with hard work, preparation, practice, and competition. Showing confidence is something that requires your full and constant attention.

## Practicing patience

Setting high standards and having high expectations for your players is great. But you also need to be prepared for disappointment when they don't meet those standards and expectations. In other words, expect a lot, but have patience.

Patience is one of the most important characteristics you need as a coach, because kids make many mistakes when they're learning how to play lacrosse. As a youth coach, you have to be a good role model, and the best way to do so is to keep your cool during practices and games.

## Fostering commitment

If you want to coach a good youth team, your players have to be committed to playing their best and playing with respect for the game and other players.

How do you get commitment? Sometimes the easiest way to foster commitment is to hold fast to the most important rule on the team: *If you miss practice, you don't play.* Make sure that your players expect the consequences of breaking a rule. The first time that you give in and don't enforce the consequences, you guarantee yourself more problems — from that player, from other players, and from all their parents.

When a player returns from a missed practice, make sure that you listen fully to the player's explanation, which could be an honest and legitimate excuse, before handing out a punishment. If it's an excusable mistake, then you can communicate to the rest of the team whether the player is being penalized and why.

# Building Team Unity: All for One, and One for All

One of the most important abilities in coaching is *team building* (the ability to get players to think and act as one). To help create this atmosphere, each team must have a code of conduct that plainly states how the players should view the team and treat each other.

Establish this code of conduct together with your players in a team meeting. These principles get everyone moving in the same direction — together they can accomplish much more than a group of individuals who work on their own.

✔ **Create a "team comes first" attitude.** Teamwork means working together. Team agendas replace individual agendas. When the team comes first, it doesn't matter who scores and it doesn't matter who gets the glory; what matters is the team's success.

✔ **Provide motivation for cohesion.** True motivation comes from a clear sense of shared goals and constantly comparing your team to its goals.

✔ **Have fun together.** Make sure that you and your players do more than practice together. Make your pre-game and pre-practice stretches a required element. Have training-camp breakfast so that players can get to know one another.

✔ **Instill pride.** Foster team unity by creating an atmosphere that suggests "We are the best."

The result of a cohesive team is *synergy* — when the total becomes more than the sum of the parts. Synergy is when you put together 20 disparate players and they end up playing as if there were 30 of them. Working together as a team, a smaller, weaker team can overcome a team that's bigger and stronger. Each player seems to gather strength and energy from his fellow teammates to create this extra strength.

# Recognizing What Gives Your Team the Edge

Many coaching platitudes will tell you that when a team *believes* it will be successful, it can accomplish the impossible. Many teams may approach a season with the attitude that they're going to be successful, but few reach their sport's ultimate pinnacle: a championship.

To have an edge in any sport, you have to work for it. Here are a few practical and tangible tips that you can stress with your team to try to gain that edge:

✔ **Perfect your fundamentals.** Practice basic skills over and over again until your players can execute without thinking.

✔ **Strive for peak conditioning.** Your team's commitment and responsibility to training will require sacrifices, but training also gives the team an edge.

✔ **Go full speed — always.** Whether during a game or a practice, in pre-game stretches or between-game training, give 100 percent.

✔ **Work to improve.** A good work ethic means little if you can't use it to strengthen your weaknesses.

✔ **No pain, no gain.** Sure it's another platitude, but if your players train harder and run faster and farther, even to the point of exhaustion, they'll be giant steps ahead of other teams.

✔ **Accept the hard road.** Players don't cut corners; they don't cheat on laps; they don't cheat by not touching the lines or the boards; they don't leave early on the whistle. That's the easy road to take. Your team takes the *hard* road, and it does so with pride.

# Chapter 14

# Developing Your Coaching Philosophy for the Offense

*In This Chapter*

▶ Deciding your team's style of play

▶ Putting in place an offensive plan

▶ Going up against the zone defense

▶ Penetrating, moving, or running set plays

▶ Running an effective fast-break offense

▶ Looking at offensive tactics for the women's game

*Y*our most important decision as a lacrosse coach is to determine what type of system to run. By *system,* we're referring to a style of play that best fits your offensive and defensive strengths — such as an unsettled, fast-break style of play or a settled, slow-it-down style of play. The decision comes down to either creating a system around the strengths of your players or having your players adapt to the system you have in place. Good coaches adapt their system to their players' talents instead of forcing their players to play their system, though exceptions do exist.

Another option is to have multiple systems. In other words, tailor your offense and defense to the situation or the team you're playing. In some games, you'll want to play an aggressive, fast-break-style offense. In others, you'll want to be more patient. Having this kind of flexibility makes your team difficult for opposing teams to prepare and practice for. But make no mistake: Having multiple systems isn't easy to attain. It requires having coaches who are knowledgeable and flexible enough to master different systems, as well as players who are able to learn and implement them.

This chapter doesn't make the system decision for you, but it does help you understand what your options are.

# Understanding the General Principles of Lacrosse Playing Systems

Good teams have a system they believe in — whether it's an offensive running game or an offensive slow-down game. The most important point is to have a system, instead of allowing your players do whatever they want. Even if your team has a disciplined playing system, you can also be ready to adapt your system to fit the special skills of some of your players or adjust your style of play based on the strengths or weaknesses of the opposition.

## Looking at offensive playing systems

In this section, we run through the basics of the two most popular offensive playing systems for lacrosse — fast-break offense and slow-down offense. Whether you're new to coaching a team and you're looking for the playing system that fits your players, or you have the luxury of going out and finding players to fit the system that works best for you, this information can help guide you.

### Fast-break offense

The goal of this offense is to move the ball upfield as quickly as possible to gain a man advantage. Fast-break offenses thrive in a high-scoring game. They're usually ignited by winning faceoffs, ground balls in the defensive end of the field after an opponent's turnover, or off a quick outlet pass by the goaltender. You may also hear this style of play referred to as a *running* or a *run-and-gun offense*.

The fast-break offense is best suited for players with good speed and quickness who can move up and down the field quickly and efficiently. In addition, it's also important to have players who are able to release their shots quickly in order to execute it effectively.

### Slow-down offense

Quite the opposite from a fast-break offense, a team that runs a slow-down offense is trying to create a game tempo in which players patiently move the ball around before shooting. These offenses usually recognize that they don't have the players to outrun their opponents into their offensive zone, so they focus on taking their time and setting up a play that plays to their strengths.

Players with a good understanding of both positioning and strategy are needed to run an effective slow-down offense. Often, this offense is employed by teams that are not quick afoot and who are consequently not as effective on fast-break opportunities.

## When contrasting styles collide

The 2009 NCAA Division I men's lacrosse final between Syracuse University and Cornell University featured an intriguing matchup of teams with contrasting styles. Syracuse won 10-9 for its second straight national championship on a goal by Cody Jamieson 1:20 into overtime. Cornell dominated the first 56 minutes of the game, but Syracuse, which trailed by three goals late in regulation, rallied to force overtime. Syracuse is a classic example of a "run and gun"–style team. The Orange like to push the ball, push the pace of the game, and fast break because of their athletic and creative players.

How did Cornell, a big underdog entering the game, come within an eyelash of pulling out what would've been its first national title since 1977? By perfectly executing a patient, ball-control offense fueled by the Big Red gaining possession of the ball through excellent play in the faceoff circle and through controlling ground balls. (John Glynn, a senior all-American, won ten faceoffs and came away with nine ground balls.)

Syracuse was able to create a frenetic pace much more to its liking late in regulation, benefiting from turnovers and a failed clear, before rallying to tie it with 4.5 seconds left in the fourth quarter on a wild scramble in front of the net. Syracuse's late comeback showed just how quickly a potent, fast-break offense can decide a game, even though it has been contained or neutralized for the majority of a game.

Teams that employ the "slow-down" offense are, in effect, trying to patiently create and exploit the best matchups that will ultimately result in scoring opportunities. This is known as an *invert offense*. A key aspect of the invert offense is to force the midfielders to play behind the goal and the close defenders to defend above the goal off ball.

## Keeping the system simple

As a coach, try to have a vision, an idea, or a system of exactly how you want your team to play and how you want your team to work within that style of play. Be clear about the system when you're talking to your players. Tell them exactly what you want from them so that they can be successful. Encourage them to voice their opinions, while making it clear that you make the final call.

Your best chance for success is to keep your system simple and organized, and, where possible, to employ a system that reflects your own personality traits, such as competitiveness and stick-to-itiveness. Developing a system that reflects your personality can become a motivational tool for you and your team. When your coaching personality is known and respected, it may also be feared, giving your team a bit of a motivational advantage.

If you're the coach of a varsity team that relies on feeder teams, such as junior varsity squads, implement the same system at those levels as well. This gives players time to get acclimated and adjusted to it before moving up to the team at the higher level. It's extremely advantageous to have continuity in game concepts throughout the levels of a program. A successful high school coach is usually very involved in his youth program.

Study other successful programs and different levels and see what systems they run and how those systems complement the talents of their players. When you decide on a system, your job isn't done. You have to continually look to improve on it by observing how other programs that use the same system have made additions and adjustments to it.

As you continue to study and fine-tune the system you use, you have to keep it simple and readily understandable for players. Simplicity gives players the freedom to focus and stay in the present moment while they perform, giving them the best chance to make big plays. Also, by keeping your system simple, when it comes time to change the game plan, you can tweak things more quickly and easily than you can if you employ complicated schemes.

Organization helps players know where to go and what to look for when seeking guidance about an element of your system. Whether it's in the form of a game or practice plan written out on the locker-room chalkboard or a 2-inch-thick binder complete with set plays for any game situation and tips about what to eat before a game, your players will always know there's a place to look to gets answers to their questions.

Systems help players perform as a team. In a disciplined system, players know where they're supposed to be and what they're supposed to do. The players can anticipate more quickly because they know what's going to happen before it happens.

Here are factors to consider when deciding what type of system to employ:

- **The characteristics of the team as a whole:** Are the players aggressive and physical by nature? Do they rely on their athleticism rather than their stick skills?

- **The characteristics of the team's units:** Is this attack quick and small or big and slow? Is the midfield athletic or not? Is the defense marked more by size or speed? How about that goalie? Is he stronger on perimeter shots or shots from around the crease?

- **Your players' preferences:** Listen to your players: What are their thoughts? Do they think one system takes better advantage of their skills individually and as a unit? If not, why not? Having an open dialogue lets them know that it isn't just *your* system, but the team's, and you're all in it together.

If you believe your system is flexible enough to adjust to athletes of varying skills and abilities, then you can make the decision to stick with a system year in and year out, and put the right players in the right spot to make it all work. If you decide to stick with the same system, allow players time to familiarize themselves with it in practice.

Adjust as needed. Don't become a creature of your system. If it's not working and you've tried hard to fix it without success, change. If it's successful against some teams, but not others, try something different when necessary.

# Setting Up the Offense

The main goal of an offense is to set up a player so that he has a good shot on net with the best chance of scoring. How you go about achieving this goal is the crux of this section.

## Playing to your strengths on offense

You can design offensive set plays and your team can practice them for hours, but the true execution on offense depends more on the players' abilities than on the actual play itself.

As a coach, your first job is to analyze the talents of your players and how they fit into your offensive scheme. Find out about your players' offensive strengths: Look for the shooters, the passers, the players who are best at going one-on-one, the ones who can pick and roll, and even the aggressive players (often the ones who come away with the most ground balls). By knowing your players' strengths, you can create an offense to complement them.

No matter what type of offensive system you run, strive to achieve offensive balance — not only in terms of who scores, but in terms of where they score from on the field.

Your offense can't rely on one or two players. You have six players on offense at any given time — it's vital that they all contribute. Some players will be more naturally gifted shooters; others will be better dodgers; still others will be outstanding passers. Use their strengths and work hard to get contributions from all of them. Emphasize to them that they all contribute equally toward the team's success.

You need players who can go one-on-one, cut, and catch the ball in traffic. Look to fill these roles first before you design a simple offensive scheme; no scheme will be successful without players to fill these roles. Position your players on offense at spots from which you think they're most likely to score. This positioning is usually determined by the players' skills, abilities, size, strength, and quickness.

You need an inside-shooting game, with players who aren't afraid to cut into the middle for a pass and shot, knowing that they'll get hit. You also need a perimeter game to draw the defense out of the middle. Effective shooting from outside can cause the defense to change its alignment and force it to change its game plan.

## Establishing your offensive formation

What kind of offensive alignment do teams set up in?

The most common offensive field formations are the 1-3-2, 1-4-1, 2-3-1, and 2-2-2. In these formations, the first number represents the number of offensive players that are set up behind the crease. The remaining numbers indicate the rest of the offensive players in the attack zone.

Here's a look at each:

- **1-3-2:** The most commonly used formation, the 1-3-2 relies heavily on cutting and rotating. Two attackmen are in the wing position 4 to 6 yards above the goal line on opposite sides. The third attackman is at the X position behind the goal. One midfielder is in the crease area, and the other two middies are up top.

- **1-4-1:** Screening, cutting, and motion are all key aspects of this set, in which one attackman operates behind the cage, two others are in the middle of the box crease area with two midfielders on the wings from 2 to 15 yards above the goal line, and one midfielder up top of the box. It creates great spacing that allows players to see defensive slides.

- **2-3-1:** Two attackmen are stationed behind the net with one in the crease area. The three midfielders umbrella around the top of the box. This formation provides great dodging opportunities for the midfielders against short-stick defenders.

- **2-2-2:** Two attackmen are stationed behind the goal area, about 15 yards or so apart. In the middle of the restraining box, the other attackman is stationed along with a midfielder. The other two midfielders are situated toward each respective corner of the box. This formation is an effective way to get the ball near the net by providing space for dodging in the alleys.

These formations are a starting point. As a coach, you should allow for your players to move out of the area they start in, but your set will enable you to bring organization to the offense.

In box lacrosse, here are your offensive formation choices:

✔ **Strong-side offense:** In this formation, three players are lined up on one side. The strong-side formation is one that works especially well for running offenses. You can create a great deal of player movement off this set, having your three strong-side players alternate in and out of the center of the zone, looking for an opening for a pass or a shot.

✔ **1-2-2:** In this formation, the pointman is at the top of the zone. The 1-2-2 offensive alignment helps your offense maintain floor balance and defensive safety. In the 1-2-2, your pointman determines how much energy the players on the floor have and then decides which side to attack from. At the beginning of a set play in this alignment, the pointman stays at the top of the offense but can move anywhere within the zone when the offense starts.

## *Executing your offensive system*

Some key concepts apply when you're trying to effectively execute an offense — no matter what type of system you employ:

✔ **Find the open man.** Opposing defenses will sometimes double-team and will frequently employ slides, which create plenty of opportunities to find a player who is open for a shot. Players need to react quickly and pass promptly to take advantage of these opportunities.

✔ **Don't try to do too much.** Double teams are part of the game. When they come, players have to recognize them quickly and react accordingly. That means not forcing bad shots or holding onto the ball too long, allowing defenders an opportunity to try to strip the ball away and cause a turnover.

✔ **Know the defense.** Offenses need to adjust to what the defense is doing. So you need to have schemes in place that you can run against whatever you see, whether it be zone, aggressive man-to-man, or specially designed defenses. Specially designed defenses — such as shutting off or variations of the basketball defenses of a box-and-one and triangle-and-two — can be especially troublesome for you if you aren't prepared to counter them.

✔ **Make adjustments.** If a defense is shutting off your high-scoring attackman, be proactive. If he has the necessary speed, put him at midfield so he'll have the ball before the long pole assigned to him can pick him up. This strategy will also allow him to possibly capitalize on fast-break opportunities.

✔ **Take advantage of mismatches.** If you have a balanced offensive attack, there will always be short-stick defenders on one or more of your top scorers. Take advantage by running plays in which they can exploit the opportunity. Do the same if an undersized or slower defense is guarding a larger or quicker offensive player.

✔ **Emphasize balanced scoring.** An offensive with many weapons is much more difficult to defend than one that relies on just one or two players to account for the bulk of the scoring.

✔ **Make sure that players play to their strengths.** Have your strongest shooters in position to take the most shots and from the farthest out. You don't want players with weak shots firing away from the perimeter. Possessions are valuable — don't waste them.

✔ **Take good shots.** It's really pretty simple: If a player is open or going against a short-stick defender and has a shot, he should take it. If he's being double-teamed or isn't in good position to score, he shouldn't. More often than not, the team that takes the most good shots wins the game in matchups of teams with comparable talent.

# Attacking the Zone Defense with a Zone Offense

The reason you run a zone offense is that your opposition is playing a zone defense. Effective techniques against a zone including frequent cutting, as well as overloading one side of the field. Some coaches even run man-up plays against a zone. This helps give players a structured plan of action against what can be a difficult defense to get high-percentage shots off against.

You can use your opponent's choice of defense as a motivating tool for your team. Tell your players that the opposition is playing a zone defense because they can't play you or guard you man-to-man. Now your players will feel good about attacking the zone because they know why they're playing against it.

Because playing a zone offense is more of a reactionary strategy dictated by what the defense gives you, this section starts with a brief look at the strengths and weaknesses of a zone defense.

# Understanding why teams play zone defense

In youth lacrosse, you may decide to run zone defenses much of the time because they're easy to teach. You tell a player to play in a certain area of the field and not to move out of that area. This also helps cover for players whose footwork may not yet be at a level that allows them to backpedal and move quickly enough to keep up with quick and elusive offensive players.

However, coaches also know that opponents don't like to play against zone defenses because they have to attack them a little differently from a man-to-man defense (in which each defender is assigned an offensive player to cover).

Here are a few of the advantages of going with a zone defense:

- ✔ **Zone defenses change the tempo of the game.** Zone defenses are often difficult to attack because they hinder penetration to the crease area. This may result in the offense throwing the ball around because it doesn't feel comfortable taking any of the shots that are available. Conversely, at times, the zone may also result in a team tending to hurry, which can force bad shots.

- ✔ **Defenders in a zone defense are taught to break up the field after an opponent's shot, hoping to set up a fast-break opportunity.** This forces the faster and better offensive players to play at the top of the zone to defend against the breakout.

- ✔ **Some teams play zone defense to hide their weak defenders.** If defenders are assigned to an area of the field rather than to an individual player, their own lack of foot speed, for example, may not be nearly as evident.

- ✔ **In a man-to-man defense, one great offensive player or a solid two-man offensive game stands a better chance of beating you than in a zone defense.** A zone defense forces all six offensive players to work together instead of letting the best players beat their own defenders.

## Recognizing the weaknesses of zone defenses

The major weakness of playing a zone defense is that it doesn't teach young players how to stop an opponent with the ball one-on-one, which is what the higher levels of lacrosse are all about.

Here are a few other strategic weaknesses of the zone defense that you may be able to exploit as an opposing coach:

✔ A zone is set up so that all defenders can see the ball, but they can sometimes get so caught up with watching the ball that they forget about the offensive player in their zone area who can cut and receive a pass and shoot.

✔ Because a zone is usually not active, defenders may play flat-footed, so they don't move as quickly as they would when they're playing on the balls of their feet defending an opponent man-to-man.

✔ Man-to-man defenses are more conducive in allowing defenders to play aggressively, leading to pass interceptions and stripping the ball.

✔ If the zone defensive team gets behind in a game, it's hard for that team to catch up, because its style of play encourages the offensive team to play more deliberately to protect its lead. However, watch out when a zone team gets ahead in a game — the zone team seems to get stronger with every possession of the ball, and offensive teams usually become frustrated and often force bad shots.

✔ Because defenders are assigned to guard areas of the field and not individual players, they don't have the same sense of accountability that they would have if they were given the responsibility of guarding one particular player.

A 3-3 alignment is the most frequently employed zone. In it, the area beyond the goal line in the restraining box is broken up into six zones. Close defensemen cover the three zones closest to the goal, with the midfielders taking care of the remaining zones. Some alignments of this zone station the three midfielders in a line, allowing them to defend horizontally. Other zone alignments include a 2-3-1.

## Grasping zone-offense principles

Running a successful zone offense requires a number of skills, but they all seem to play off the one critical component: patience. Because a good zone defense offers few scoring opportunities per possession, your team needs to show an ability to wait for the best opening to get the best shot. With patience in attacking the zone defense, they'll end up getting a good shot.

In the following sections, we cover some other tips for running a zone offense.

### Moving the ball

By moving the ball from side to side and around the *horn* (the outside of the zone), you stretch the zone from one side to the other. Swinging the ball around the zone quickly creates openings in the zone defense through which players can cut.

Another result of moving the ball around is that when a player receives a pass, he can set up his defender quickly by faking a shot, freezing him, and then going around him for a real shot.

Youth coaches, whose players' stick skills are not as advanced, may want to emphasize moving the ball with fewer passes.

### Aligning in the gaps

Zone offense players have a tendency to stand right beside the zone defender, making it very easy for him to do his job. What a zone offense player should do instead is to align himself in the *gaps* of the zone — that is, between two defenders, to create indecision about who should defend him.

### Moving the players

To be effective against a zone defense, you want to make it move, stretch it out, and make it shift. Defensive players will move, stretch, and shift when they see a great deal of ball and player movement. When offensive players cut through the zone defense, the defensive players have to collapse into the zone to defend those cutters. When those defenders collapse, or shift out of their assigned area, another offensive player can fill that gap and attack the net.

The worst thing your players can do against a zone defense is to remain stationary. If that occurs, nothing will happen and the zone defense will win the battle. When a player cuts, another player should move to the area just vacated by the cutting player. When a player passes, he should cut, giving the receiver another option for the next pass. Cut backdoor (from behind the zone defense) where the defensive players will have a hard time seeing a cut. And cut while running in a circle rotation on one side of the field where you may have two to three players cutting one right after another.

V-cuts are also effective against a zone defense. A *V-cut* is simply a move in which the offensive player turns around and heads back to the position where he started. You don't want the player *looping* back from the center. (That would be a U-cut.) Instead, he should make a sharp redirection, heading back in the general direction of where he came from, creating a V. After the *V-cut*, the player can be an instant threat for a pass or another cut, or he can circle the net. The main thing a V-cut accomplishes is to create movement so that a defensive player is forced to react quickly.

### Making sure the stick handler penetrates

By going one-on-one or penetrating the zone, the stick handler is more likely to draw two defenders. When the stick handler penetrates the gaps, he's trying to make the zone defense shift. If the shift includes two defenders, the stick handler should be able to dish off the ball to an open teammate.

### Attacking from the side of the offense

Because it can be easier to stop the stick handler when the ball is at the top of the offense, attack from the side of the zone defense. You keep the defense moving and reacting to the ball and any moving players, creating openings for attacking the net.

### Being ready to shoot

You never know when an opening in the zone will present itself. The key is to be ready to shoot, or be ready to *create* a shot, such as using a fake shot to freeze the defender and then shoot.

Be extra careful to avoid taking bad shots, because the top zone defenders will break quickly for a breakaway pass.

### Being aggressive

By its very nature, the zone is passive when compared to man-to-man defenses. Zone defenses are designed to make the offense operate passively as well — namely, settling for perimeter shots. Don't fall into that trap. You need to attack the zone aggressively. Have a plan, and be proactive against the zone and not reactive to it.

A goal scored by a good outside shot will often make a team come out of the zone into a man-to-man defense, which it usually doesn't want to play. That doesn't mean you should settle just for outside shots. Take good, open looks when they're available from the perimeter, but remember to continue to work the zone.

### Defending the defenders

On any shot, watch for zone defenders breaking out to take a fast-break pass from the goalie. When a defender takes off, your offensive players at the top of the zone should also take off.

You may be able to take advantage of defenders breaking out by looking to grab long rebounds. Consider keeping a player or two toward the top of the offensive zone in case a missed shot rebounds out there. You may end up with the ball and a couple of overmatched defenders.

BOX LACROSSE

## Box lacrosse zones

Box lacrosse features three basic zone offenses:

✔ **Motion:** This passing-centered type of game gives players the freedom to do whatever they want within your zone offense guidelines. This type of offense allows your players to take what the zone defense gives them.

✔ **Continuity:** This zone offense focuses on running through the same offensive concepts over and over until a seam in the zone defense opens up to create a scoring chance.

✔ **Set plays:** Your zone offense should have a few special set plays that you can run when your normal offense (zone or otherwise) becomes stagnant. The set plays force ball and player movement.

# Running a Penetration Man-to-Man Offense

The penetration offense takes advantage of the skills of your best offensive players. Players take on their defenders one-on-one. The offense runs primarily through the stick handler, who is charged with shooting first, passing second, and asking questions later. Other offensive players have to create their own offensive opportunities by positioning themselves for rebounds, ground balls, or passes when the stick handler is double-teamed.

## Knowing when to go one-on-one

The best time to attempt a one-on-one move is when you have a mismatch against the defense. When no mismatch exists, your offensive players need to rely on fakes and dodges to try to create a mismatch, sending your opponent off balance.

The dodger must be aware of others on the field. He must always dodge to create space. You don't want to make a great move only to run into your teammate or another defender. Space is created by teammates understanding the dodger's strengths and clearing that area for him to dodge.

To beat a defender, you have to be quick. Unless you're setting up a pick, hanging onto the ball while waiting for a chance to beat a defender slows down your offense. If the stick handler beats his defender and another defender helps, your stick handler has a teammate who can take a pass or cut for a close-in shot.

The stick handler must

- Keep his stick moving all the time when he has the ball. This is known as *cradling*. (See Chapter 5 for more on cradling.)

- Protect his stick with his body by turning his body sideways.

- Keep his feet moving, unless he's setting up his defender to take a pick so that he can roll off him.

## Opening up penetration with outside shots

When playing a team that plays a less aggressive defense, your players may find it difficult to beat a defender one-on-one. A less aggressive defender tends to stand back from the stick handler to protect against such one-on-one penetration moves. To combat this style of defense, you need strong perimeter shooters.

Good perimeter scorers complement your best one-on-one moves. When you show the defense that you can score consistently from the outside, they'll play your stick handlers tighter to try to take away the long shot. Their defense becomes more aggressive, and your offense has a better opportunity to beat defenders inside. Conversely, if you show that your stick handlers consistently beat defenders inside, the defense will play more loosely to protect against penetration, opening up space for your outside shooters.

## Running set plays for a penetration offense

Set plays for this offense should create space for your best one-on-one players. You create space by clearing out the five other offensive players. *Clearing out* means positioning the offensive players without the ball to one side so that your stick handler can initiate a one-on-one play from the opposite side of the field or floor.

Mix up your set plays. When teams fall behind during a game, they have a tendency to panic and resort solely to one-on-one plays and nothing else. Make sure to include other set plays so that the defense can't anticipate what your offense will run.

# Mastering the Motion Man-to-Man Offense

The motion offense is just the opposite of the penetration offense. In the motion offense, you look to pass first, and then go one-on-one or shoot second. This offense is designed for passing the ball and cutting.

No matter what offense you run, you must have cutters going through the middle of the field. Some teams are afraid to cut because they may get hit, but the better defensive teams don't let cutters cut across through the middle *without* physical contact.

You can't run a successful offense without any movement; your players will simply just stand outside the defense and look to shoot from the perimeter. You have to cut to collapse the opposition's defense. The offense must dominate the middle of the opposition's defense. But you can pass around the outside of the defense, waiting for a teammate to get open.

## Passing to keep the offense (and defense) in motion

Quality passing is critical to an effective motion offense. The idea behind the offense is to keep the ball moving until you can get it to the offensive player with the most ideal shot at goal or the best matchup to go one-on-one. Encourage your team to take pride in its passing; emphasize simple, unforced passes.

The quality of a player's passing determines the quality of his shots. Remind your players of the following: Before every pass, they should keep their attention on the business at hand — focus on the pass and the target. Before receiving a pass, they should keep their eyes on the ball and be ready for the pass, knowing what they're going to do with the ball before they catch it.

Here are a few other things to keep in mind as you work with your team on passing in the motion offense:

- **Pass early and often.** The qualities that determine a good passing team include players with good passing skills, a team-oriented offensive system (as opposed to one that centers on one or two great players), and players with an unselfish attitude about giving up the ball. By passing early, you're giving the receiver the best chance to do something with the ball; by holding onto the ball too long before passing, you give defenders a chance to anticipate where the ball will go.

✔ **Pass to get the offense going.** Some passes result in a score; other passes get things started. The pass *before* the pass that leads to a score (often informally referred to as the *hockey assist*) is very important. If you start your offense with a bad pass, the next pass will also be bad — a chain reaction that usually leads to your team not having the ball. If a player receives a bad pass, he should pause before throwing the next pass so that your team can regain some purpose and composure in its offensive set.

You also want all your players involved in passing because it makes it harder for the defense to stop you as a team. By moving the ball quickly, and keeping everybody moving, your players are trying to make it hard for the defenders to guard them, which can lead to good things happening offensively.

When you pass the ball, you force the defense to react, usually by moving or shifting in the direction of the ball. Therefore, every pass counts.

The dodge, pass, pass, dodge is a motion play that starts at midfield. After dodging his defender and drawing a double team, the midfielder passes the ball out to the top of the restraining box. The player who receives the pass then throws it to a teammate on the other side of the field. That player then dodges toward the goal before shooting.

The triangle set is an effective way to implement a motion offense. In it, the six players move as one unit, rotating to keep the field balanced. Midfielders form a triangle toward the top of the box. An attackman is stationed in the X area behind the goal. An attackman and midfielder are in front of the net. Players then react to where the ball is passed, with players without the ball making cuts in the middle to draw the defense.

## Moving without the ball

Passing skills are just one element of a good motion offense. The second critical element is your team's ability to move without the ball. You must help your players understand the importance of moving — with or without the ball.

In a motion offense, when your players aren't in the process of passing or receiving the ball, they have the following options:

### Cutting through the middle

Players must cut through the middle with the idea that their defender can't stay with them. They should cut with the stick ready to catch rather than just going through the motions. They can cut to the ball for a give-and-go as well.

One of the ways to measure the toughness of a player is by the number of times he catches the ball cutting through the middle. The toughest battles are getting shots in front of the net or in the middle of the defense. By passing and cutting through the defense, you force the defense to react and move, and start to wear them down.

### Getting open for a pass

Your players need to work hard to get open. Most of a player's time on offense is without the ball, so he should use it wisely. There are many different ways to do this, including

- Setting a pick for the stick handler
- Setting a pick on the off-ball side
- Running off a pick set by his teammate
- Setting a screen for his teammate on their own side of the field
- Running off a screen set by a teammate
- Making a V-cut to get open for a pass
- Staying where he is to stay out of the way of a developing play

When you're running the motion offense, some players play too far outside the defense so that they don't get hit. They may be afraid to cut into the middle and afraid to go one-on-one. Always coach your players to keep moving and working to get open for a pass. In any offensive scheme, but especially in the motion offense, getting open keeps the flow of play moving and increases the team's chances to score.

### Setting picks: Forcing the defense to create openings

Sometimes a defense can help your players get open. If a tough defender overplays your best scorer, call for a pick on the defender. This strategy may force the defender to switch assignments, with your scorer checked by a weaker defender. Or the defense may not switch, choosing to double-team your scorer, leaving a teammate in the clear.

Picks and screens are great ways for your players to help their teammates get in the clear. By getting a stick handler in the clear, you give him an open shot. ***Remember:*** An open shot comes when a player has time to shoot without a defender interfering with the stick.

When setting a pick, make sure that your players set a good solid pick and do so immediately so that the defense can't figure out what play you're running. They need to make body contact with a teammate's defender that may force the defender to switch. When the stick handler passes the picker's shoulder, he should push off on the defender and roll to the net for a soft pass from the stick handler.

In order for a pick to be legal, the picker must be stationary. But when setting the pick, in box lacrosse the picker is allowed to use his body to push off on the defender when he rolls to the net. (Using the body to push off on the defender is illegal in field lacrosse.)

## Running the give-and-go play

This play is the quintessential motion offense set play; it requires crisp passing and quick cutting. It works best when a defender adjusts — even slightly — to the direction of a pass.

In a give-and-go play, an initial stick handler does both the giving and the going. He passes the ball to a teammate, typically in about the same area of the zone, and then cuts toward the goal hoping to take a pass from that same teammate. When it works well, the initial stick handler's defender relaxes or follows the initial pass just enough so that the stick handler can break ahead of his defender toward the net.

When a player passes the ball, his next move is to fake or take one step away from where he threw the ball. When his defender reacts, he should then plant his outside foot and push off explosively and cut sharply to the ball or net. He can ask for the ball by keeping his stick up and out, even shaking his stick hard to indicate that he wants the ball.

When executing the give-and-go, a player has the option of cutting in front of a defender or cutting *backdoor* (going behind the defender). Your players have to anticipate how a defender is going to react and then decide what move to make.

The best option is to cut in front of the defender because your player can receive the pass and still be in a good position to shoot, even if the defender is right beside him. If your player is being overplayed or when the defender tries to cheat to intercept a cross-field pass, the backdoor cut becomes available for a pass and open shot.

## Running the pick-and-roll play

Another game situation that works well in a motion offense, the pick-and-roll is a kind of give-and-go, but with the defender instead of the ball. In its simplest form, an offensive player sets a pick for a teammate before rolling into a passing lane and receiving a pass. It's used in field lacrosse and extensively in box lacrosse.

An offensive player, the *picker,* gets in the way of the stick handler's defender so that the stick handler can create some space for a shot or pass. The picker then rolls to the net for a pass from the stick handler and a close-in shot. In this give-and-go, the stick handler "gives" the defender, and the picker "goes."

The pick-and-roll play creates confusion and indecision for the defense. Plus, it creates a gap for the stick handler, who has three options:

✔ Shooting coming off the pick

✔ Going one-on-one off the pick

✔ Passing to the picker (who could also be called the *roller,* having already set the pick)

When setting a pick, players *will* be checked by the defense. But a player shouldn't let a defender stop him from setting it; if your player gets tied up with the defender, he should stay where he is and let the stick handler read it as a screen and make his cut off the screen. If the defender fires out on the pick at the stick handler, your player can then cut backdoor.

# Running Set Plays in Your Man-to-Man Offense

Running set plays doesn't really work well as an offensive system on its own. Instead, you may call set plays during games in which your better players are not handling the ball as much as you'd like, or your players may be holding onto the ball too long and not moving efficiently enough. The most common set plays in lacrosse involve only two to three players.

No matter the reason for running a set play, you want to maintain some parameters for how your players should execute the play:

✔ A well-executed one-on-one move takes precedence over any set play that you call for.

✔ Players can call a set play on their own during a game. They can either make a real call during action on the field, or they can suggest a play while on the sideline.

✔ If a set play doesn't work, your players should know to return automatically to your regular offensive system.

✔ Consider running two set plays: a real one on the strong side and a decoy play on the off-ball side.

BOX LACROSSE

# Getting set for set plays

The following plays are designed for the strong-side alignment. Each play includes an introduction setting up the play, as well as tips for what you should ask your players to do.

✔ **Up pick-and-roll:** The main player here is at the top of the offensive zone when the creaseman comes up the floor and sets a pick for the stick handler. To make this pick-and-roll work, stress that the stick handler faces his defender or turns sideways and receives a check while he waits for the pick. When coming off the pick, he should look to shoot right away or go one-on-one, and not fade away or look to pass.

✔ **Down screen:** This screen play is designed to create a close-in shot for a shooter. The shooter works off his teammate's screen to try to get to an opening in the defense for a shot. Stress that the picker get his whole body on the pick, not just an arm and shoulder, and then stay with the defender until the stick handler passes his shoulder. And remind him to roll so that he's always facing the ball with his stick ready for a forward pass.

When running set plays, your offensive players need to play alertly and intelligently because you want them to *read* the defense (that is, anticipate what the defense may do so that your players can execute the called play). By reading the defenders, your offensive players can react efficiently when a defender doesn't play the way your set play anticipates. Instead of ending up with a *broken play* (one that doesn't reach its conclusion), you may end up with an improvised play that nevertheless leads to a score.

Teams get scoring chances using a number of offensive weapons. The following plays that help offensive players get in the clear for good shots provide examples:

✔ The outlet pass up the field from the goalie to a breaking player or a player coming from the sideline

✔ Going one-on-one against a player whose team is still in defensive transition

✔ From set plays such as picks, give-and-go, and screens

✔ From a motion-style offense that involves players passing and cutting continuously until someone is open for a shot on goal

# Breaking Out on the Quick: The Fast-Break Offense

A *fast break* is when the stick handler runs the ball up the field before the defense has a chance to get back and set up. A fast-break offense is designed to create odd-man situations and an easy score. But running the fast break is not just frenzied chaos; it's more like organized chaos.

As a defenseman or midfielder brings the ball out of the defensive end, three attackmen and three opposing defensemen are waiting at the midfield line. The most important part of the fast break is for the attackmen to take advantage of whatever lag time exists (a split second usually) between the stick handler and whoever is defending him. This is when the offense can exploit a numbers advantage.

Attackmen must know exactly what to do when their teammates clear the ball and how best to prepare for the incoming players. Attackmen should set up in an L formation with the point attackman stationed on the opposite side of where the ball is being brought down — about 12 to 15 yards in front of the goal. The other two attackmen are positioned about 5 yards outside the crease. Common drills involve running different scenarios over the midfield line — one player bringing the ball up with no one trailing, two players with one trailing, three with two trailing, and so on. These drills help prepare the attackmen to know how to react and the midfielders know how to proceed when charging into the offensive zone.

The fast-break offense works especially well when you can play everyone on your team. The more players that you send out running at full speed, the better your chances of wearing down the opposition. (If you're familiar with football, compare the impact of your fast break on the defense to the impact that a big, strong running back has on a defensive line: After 25 or 30 carries, the defensive line is just too tired to stop the running back.)

You also need to set a team objective to be one of the best-conditioned teams around. Being in proper condition is vital in order to have the stamina and energy you need to be at your best. Achieving it is not easy — it takes a lot of hard work and teammates pushing one another on a daily basis.

To run a fast-break offense, look for players who play with quickness, aggression, and tenacity. You also want players who are daring and aggressive on the defensive end. Because of the pace of play that you want, your fast-break players have to play both ends of the field or floor; aggressive defenders lead to turnovers, ground balls, and more fast breaks.

## The fast break in box

In box lacrosse, you want to break quickly, but in an organized manner, from the defensive end and run down the floor, creating an odd-man situation at the other end from which you can get a good scoring opportunity. When running the ball up the floor, the stick handler should look to attack the net so that he forces a defender to commit to him — that is, to choose to defend the stick handler rather than another offensive player on the fast break — and then he can pass to an open man. If the defender doesn't commit to your stick handler, he may have an open shot on goal or, if another defender has joined the fray, he may just peel off to the side, looking to pass or set up the offense.

Too many fast-breaking teams can get bogged down by the pace of play dictated by a slow-down team, and they end up simply jogging the ball up the floor rather than running full-out. For most teams, slowing down a game is easier than speeding it up. To keep your team focused on running, stress the quick outlet pass by the goalie and the hard and fast breakout by the stick handler. Ideally, your cornerman should start the fast break, either by running the ball up the floor into the offensive end or by passing it to a breaking teammate. He has to protect the ball up the floor at the same time that he's seeing the positioning of his teammates and their defenders.

The fast-break offense places less emphasis on bigger, more physical players, and it has a place for the little guy. When building your fast-break team, look for players with speed rather than size, and then ride, ride, ride. (A *ride* happens when the defensive team tries to prevent the team with possession from advancing the ball from its defensive end to the offensive zone. See Chapter 9 for more on rides.)

Don't limit your fast-break offense to just those few seconds that it takes for the stick handler to run the ball down the field. If your team doesn't score off the fast break, you still want your players to emulate the pressure and intensity of the fast break in its set offense. Constantly attack the net. Keep players moving and cutting, looking for an opening or a breakdown on defense.

# Offensive Principles for the Women's Game

To have an effective offense in women's lacrosse, you need most of the same attributes as you do in the men's game — namely, skill, shooting and passing ability, and good decision-making. Speed and strength are also big pluses. The main goal remains the same — to get as many good shots on net as often as possible, and to convert on as many as possible.

Scoring plays in the women's game are often ignited from the attack wing and third home positions, or midfield in general. Those players are responsible for transitioning the ball from defense to offense. From there, a second home will often look to originate a play. The ball usually moves to the first home, who is stationed in front of the goal and makes numerous cuts toward the goal.

The critical scoring area is located about 15 yards in front of, as well as to each side of, the goal that stretches 9 yards behind the goal, although it is not common for a player to shoot — let alone score — from beyond the 8-meter arc.

Major fouls are called within the 8-meter semicircular area in front of the goal. Similar to lane violations in basketball, a defender can't remain in the 8-meter arc for more than 3 seconds unless she's within a stick's length of the opposing player.

Offensive players are awarded free-position shots after major defensive fouls. The fouled offensive player is placed on a hash mark somewhere along the 8-meter arc, while the defender who committed the foul is placed 4 yards behind. All other defenders must clear out of the 8-meter area, either to an adjacent hash mark in preparation of defending the free-position shot, or if taken, somewhere else outside the 8-meter arc with both feet and sticks outside of the arc. When the whistle sounds, that player may shoot, pass, or run with the ball.

Following minor fouls called in the 12-meter fan after play resumes, a player may pass or run with the ball but may not shoot until someone has played the ball. The 12-meter fan is a semicircle located in front of the goal.

Just as in the men's game, catching, cradling, and cutting are all crucial in setting up shots in the women's game, as is dodging. Because sticks in women's lacrosse don't have deep pockets, cradling is much more difficult than it is in the men's game. It requires a special skill set that the men don't have to employ. Cradling is taught and necessary as a specific skill in the women's game because of the lack of a pocket in the stick. As a result, stick handlers often don't hold onto the ball as long as they do in the men's game. However, this also results in a finesse game, because the women rely on smart, well-placed passes to advance the ball, instead of just running with it. Women don't rely heavily on physical or lengthy one-on-one opportunities. Instead, they often employ one or two moves or dodges with a quick release on a shot. The women's game is less gritty because it can't rely on excessive physical play because of the rules and mechanics of the skills. In addition, longer passes are possible, but not overly used because catching is more difficult without deep pockets.

There's also a difference in the method of shooting. In the women's game, the shooter can release the ball more quickly and easily because there is no pocket in the stick. Men's players can drop their sticks further back when winding up to release the ball from the deep pockets.

Here are a few effective offensive plays for the women's game:

- ✔ **Going back door:** One of the attack players sets a pick while another attacker has possession near the goal. Meanwhile, a third attacker cuts toward the front of the goal where she receives a pass from the second attacker near the goal. This play works effectively when the initial stick handler draws the defense toward her, usually by pretending to drive to the goal. After her own defender and any adjacent defenders step or slide to the stick handler, there is room and a free player to pass to in a back-door position.

- ✔ **Using the trailer:** An attacker breaking toward the goal must use the *trailer* (the player who is directly behind). This doesn't necessarily mean passing to the trailer, but it's important to try to deceive the defense into *thinking* that it will or could be happening at any moment.

- ✔ **Give and go:** After passing off to the trailer, the lead player breaks to the goal for a pass after the defenders shift over to the trailer.

- ✔ **Stack set:** Here, the attack players form a line in front of the goal at the top of the fan while the first home holds the ball behind the net. When the first home calls for a break, the attackers move in various directions while a wing cuts in front of the goal. This play works well when the cutters are organized, yet unpredictable. The more you move the defense and make them adjust, the more likely that someone will be open for a pass and/or shot.

# Chapter 15

# Coaching Defensively

## In This Chapter

▶ Focusing on a defensive system

▶ Defending one player at a time: the man-to-man defense

▶ Blanketing the offensive zone with a zone defense

▶ Shutting off a top scorer

The main objective for any defense is to stop the opposition from scoring, or at least to force it to take as many bad shots as possible. And whether it's a stay-in-your-area zone or an aggressive and pressuring man-to-man, another objective for the defense is to create a change of possession so that its own offensive team can get the ball and score.

Playing effective defense involves being physical and aggressive, but that doesn't mean that defenses should be designed to find out who can give the biggest hit or who can intimidate the opposing team the most.

You want to develop a defense that's physical and tough but also smart enough to avoid bad penalties from over-aggressive play, such as tripping, pushing, or slashing a player.

This chapter focuses on the two primary defenses that you'll likely use in youth lacrosse: the man-to-man defense and the zone defense. We also share a few drills that you can use to develop your team's defensive philosophy.

## Choosing Your Defensive Playing System

Defense wins championships. So in order to achieve success, it's crucial you find — and employ — the right defensive system for your team. Here's a look at the two most frequently employed systems:

✔ **Man-to-man defense:** A man-to-man defense is an aggressive system that is constantly trying to create turnovers. Defenders are usually looking for stick handlers to hit or short sticks to slap at, trying to get their opponents to lose possession or make a bad pass or shot. This defense is prone to giving up goals when their aggressive play leads to overplaying mistakes, or it may create a number of goals when the offense becomes frustrated with the physical nature of play. The aggressive defense can also lead to penalties and man-up opportunities for the opposing team.

✔ **Zone defense:** Most teams that employ zone defenses also use more patient offenses. The zone defense can be effective at setting the pace of the game and creating lower scoring results.

The main difference between a man-to-man defense and a zone defense is that, in a man-to-man defense, defenders are assigned to specific offensive players. In a zone defense, they're assigned to guard areas of the field (and whatever players enter them), rather than specific players.

Regardless of which playing system you choose, keep in mind the following tips when plotting your defensive strategy:

✔ **Know your players and adjust accordingly.** Are your players quick and athletic or good-sized but lacking speed? If the players have the foot speed and other intangibles, then a man-to-man defense may be the best fit for your team. Conversely, if your players are solid fundamentally but perhaps lacking in foot speed, think about employing a zone.

✔ **Desire makes a difference.** Whatever your players' attributes may be, you should always remember, and emphasize the fact, that there's no substitute for desire. You don't have to be the biggest, strongest, or fastest player to be great on defense, but you must be a hard worker. Good defensive play, more often than not, is the byproduct of hard work.

✔ **It takes more than defensemen.** It's all about six-on-six. Yes, the three close defensemen get the toughest assignments, but the midfielders have to play just as hard and with as much purpose.

✔ **Players have to communicate.** They have to know what their teammates are doing and where they're going at all times. The man playing the ball should yell, "Ball, ball, ball" or "I got ball."

✔ **Footwork is fundamental.** Hard hits and slick body checks may get the most attention in the stands, but nothing is more important than strong footwork when playing defense. Body positioning is also critical — a player should always keep his body between the offensive player and his own goal. It's also important that players don't cross their feet at any point while playing defense. Doing so prevents them from having the mobility to make quick movements in relation to where the offense has the ball.

# Going Head to Head: Playing a Man-to-Man Defense

In lacrosse, the unsung heroes are the standout defenders who either shut down the offensive stars or make it tough for the stars to score. If you don't have a strong defense, you won't be successful in lacrosse — plain and simple. No matter what league, the top teams generally boast the lowest goals-against average, but not necessarily the best goals-scored stats. The common perception is true: Offense may win games, but defense wins championships.

Your defense should be the cornerstone of your team. With a solid defense, your team can be competitive game in and game out, no matter how your offense performs.

There's no quicker way to put together a competitive team from scratch than by emphasizing strong defensive play and working hard in practice and in games to achieve it. A solid defense starts with solid defenders, the kind of players who can take on offensive players on their own and have some measure of success in preventing them from scoring. These defenders are the foundation you need for a successful man-to-man defense.

## Recognizing the types of man-to-man defenses

In a man-to-man defense, you assign individual defenders to cover specific offensive players by following them around wherever they go.

You can play a man-to-man defense in a variety of ways, centering on the ball or on individual players, or some combination of both. We cover these three types of man-to-man defense in the following sections.

### Ball-oriented man-to-man defense

There's no questioning the fact that in order to play great team defense, each defensive player must know where the ball is at all times. If you're a ball-oriented defensive team, your players focus more on where the ball is rather than where their opponents are.

However, defenders still have to keep track of the players they're defending, which presents the primary challenge with this type of man-to-man defense: With the great ball movement and skills of today's players, it's hard to focus on the ball and also follow your man.

To play this style of man-to-man defense, you have to stress maintaining an open stance, looking down the field, and keeping your eyes on both your off-ball man and the ball by looking between them so that you can see both of them at the same time.

In order for this defense to be effective, you need good pressure on the ball, which admittedly is hard to do with the ball moving so quickly and accurately. But without pressure on the ball, your defenders who are playing the off-ball opponent are susceptible to cross-field passes to the player they're defending for a quick shot, or quick cuts by the offensive player to the ball.

### Man-oriented man-to-man defense

If you're a man-oriented defensive team, you must stress a closed stance — belly-to-belly — to keep your eyes on the opponent even to the point where you stay with him more than helping out. In this system, players don't always know where the ball is, and they're susceptible to picks and screens, so they end up trailing the play rather than anticipating and staying with the play. If the stick handler beats his defender, his defensive teammates aren't looking for the ball and aren't in position to help him.

### Combination man-to-man

A combination type of defense gives the ball and the opponent equal importance. When a player defends an off-ball opponent, he should play in a closed stance, staying with him while looking slightly over his shoulder to find out where the ball is.

When your players know both where the ball is and where their opponents are, they're better able to anticipate the next offensive move: Which offensive player will make a cut? Who will set a pick for a teammate? Who will receive a pick? Who will stay and wait for a return pass?

Anticipating an offensive player's next move is half the battle on defense.

The difference in this defensive scheme is that, although a player defends one person, as does each of his teammates, they're still looking to help. No matter what defensive systems you play, if you have defenders who play strong on-the-ball defense, you're going to be in great shape every game.

The combination man-to-man defense is the primary one played in the National Lacrosse League (NLL).

## "I have 6!"

The easiest way for a player to know his defensive assignment is to have him call out his opponent's number and point a stick at him. This simple practice helps keep everybody mentally in the game and removes indecision about who's covering whom.

However, most of the time in the man-to-man defense, assignments will be determined prior to the game. In fact, defenders will have the advantage of knowing who they're going to guard while offensive players are left wondering who will be assigned to cover them. This also allows defensive players more time to plan and prepare for the opposing players they'll be covering.

In addition to knowing who's defending whom, each player must know who has the ball. Get your players on the sideline to yell out to their teammates who has the ball. The hidden-ball trick is not just a baseball move.

## Playing both ways in the man-to-man defense

A team needs offensive defenders and defensive defenders on its defense. To be successful, a team needs to score goals from its six-on-six offense, from its fast breaks, and from its defense. When your defensive players can run down the field and score rather than just run down the field and pass off, you're in a great position.

Midfielders must be active and aggressive on defense. No six-on-six defensive unit can be effective without getting strong efforts from its midfielders. It can't just rely on the efforts of the long-stick defensive players.

You want to build a man-to-man defense that can initiate an instant offense from steals, ground balls, forced turnovers, and missed shots. These situations can lead to easy fast-break goals, and they take a great deal of pressure off your six-on-six offense.

Players who can play both ways — offense and defense — are a tremendous asset on any team.

## Applying pressure in the man-to-man defense

The man-to-man defense is a very aggressive, pressuring defense. Most man-to-man teams want to put the opposition under continuous pressure by aggressively checking the stick handler. But where should you start applying this pressure?

The obvious answer is to start applying pressure when the stick handler enters the attacking zone. But when the stick handler isn't in a scoring area, he can still pass the ball to a teammate who is in a prime scoring area. Now you have to defend a stick handler who's a threat to both score *and* pass.

So the obvious answer may not always be the best answer, meaning that you have to rely on your players to decide how to play a stick handler, based on what they know about his offensive strengths and weaknesses. Scary? Yes, but that's where your preparation as a coach comes in handy. By attending other games, watching game films, and doing research on your opposition, you can tell your players exactly what the opponent's strengths and weaknesses are.

Continue to encourage your players to check the stick handler to slow him down, or to try to steal the ball from him. Aggressive checking can often pressure the offense into making mistakes and turnovers. However, if your players try to force a turnover, they risk enabling the stick handler to dash past his flailing defender on the way to the net. But if you don't put pressure on the ball, the opposition will pick you apart with their passing. It's a fine line. Knowing the risks of both options helps players and coaches decide what course of action to take.

## Forcing defensive action to get an offensive reaction

Players in a man-to-man defensive system are daring and aggressive. They'll take calculated risks and instigate action by attacking on defense. They don't play conservatively or cautiously. They're dictating the pace of play.

This type of defense doesn't want to react to the offense by guessing where the play is going or waiting to find out what the offense is going to do. The man-to-man defense attacks the offense before it has a chance to attack the net. For example, when the stick handler is at the top of the offense, the defenders should try to force him toward the sidelines.

This defense wants to make the offense do something by taking it out of its comfort zone. When the offense reacts to the defense's aggressiveness, the defense is in a better position to anticipate and out-think what the offense is going to do before they do it.

When coaching an aggressive and pressuring man-to-man defense, you can compare your team to a small boxer taking on a big boxer in the ring. Size won't help them knock anybody out, so they have to keep moving and jabbing to wear down the bigger opponent. In an aggressive man-to-man defense, you want to apply relentless pressure throughout the whole game to wear down the opposition. You'll wear them down physically and mentally and force them into mistakes with your constant defensive pressure. If you're fortunate enough to have a defensive team that includes both quick *and* big players, you can add explosive hitting to your repertoire. Your players will be quick enough to recover when they take themselves out of position to deliver a hit.

## Concentrating on getting the job done

How many times have you seen a defensive player fall asleep for just a split second only to have a non–stick handler cut for a wide-open pass and shot with the defender trailing behind him? Or a stick handler faking one way and then going the other way when the defender bites on the fake? An alert defender can avoid these situations.

One of the qualities that great defenders all have in common is that they seldom get caught off-guard. Certainly, defensive players who play on the off-ball side may have a tough time staying alert when they have to concentrate on both their man and the ball. But the best defenders have a great ability to focus on the two things at once. And defending the stick handler means concentrating on more than just the stick handler. Your defender has to be aware of players picking him or the stick handler coming off a screen.

You may want to stress to your players that no stick handler should be allowed to go directly to the net without a defender attacking him to try to force a pass instead of a shot. In other words, don't let a stick handler take an uncontested shot.

Defensive help can come from the interior or adjacent areas. Determine where the help should come from based on the quickness of your defensive team on the field.

## Helping: Slides and rotations

A man-to-man defense is not successful if only individual defenders keep their own *man* from scoring. The defense has to keep the other *team* from scoring. Helping out is critical to a man-to-man defense because a good one-on-one offensive player can often beat a good defender — the offensive player knows where he's going. Man-to-man defense works best when defenders help each other.

*Sliding* is simply helping out a teammate who has been beaten by the offensive player he's covering. You need to decide how and under what situation you want your defense to slide.

In box lacrosse, slides are referred to as rotations. You can also use some planned rotation, where any or all of your defenders can rotate to play the ball or the moving offensive players.

Players need to be sure to use proper sliding technique: The defender closest to the defender who gets beat picks him up on the slide. Defenders must slide where the offensive player is *going* to be, not where he already is. The defender must veer toward the stick handler's shooting hand on slides.

Where does the beaten defender go after a teammate has helped him? The typical move is for the defender to rotate opposite the direction in which the stick handler passes.

## Using the man-to-man defense in game situations

The rest of this section about the man-to-man defense suggests a few ways in which this style of defensive play can help your team against certain offensive situations.

### Defending the off-ball pick-and-roll

Most teams switch defenders when the offense executes an off-ball pick or screen. To prevent a pick or screen, however, off-ball defenders must play between their man and the ball, not between their man and the net, which is a perfect setup for a down screen.

If an offensive player cuts and tries to get the inside position on his defender so that he can set a screen, the defender must not let this happen because he won't be in a position to switch to help his teammate being screened. The defender should instead move down with the screener evenly, staying between his man and the ball.

BOX LACROSSE

# Rotating against a motion offense

In box lacrosse, a total full rotation — with all five defensive players rotating — happens only in the ball-oriented type defense, because your players are following the ball as it moves around the offensive end of the floor. In a man-oriented or a combination-type defense, rotation occurs generally in a helping situation. Ideally, your defense will have such great defenders that they'll never get beaten, and you won't need any rotation at all.

Here is a sample rotating progression in box lacrosse against a motion offense, one that passes the ball around the zone:

1. **Rotate when the stick-handler from top corner cuts inside.**

   If a defender in the top area of the floor is beaten by the stick handler into the middle of the floor, help comes from the off-ball top defender sliding over. If the stick handler sees the defensive pressure coming across, he may pass to a cornerman on the side of the floor where the help came from.

2. **Rotate on pass across to the cornerman.**

   To help his teammate who rotated across, the bottom off-ball defender may leave his check to come up and pressure the new stick handler, who now may pass down to the creaseman on his side of the floor.

3. **Rotate on pass down to the creaseman.**

   The off-ball bottom defender now rotates across the floor to check the creaseman who just received the pass.

4. **Rotate on pass across to the creaseman.**

   And to make the rotation complete, the offensive creaseman, on seeing the bottom defender coming across, may pass to the other creaseman, but one of the off-ball top defenders has now rotated down to pressure the creaseman on his side of the floor.

## Defending a player standing in the middle of the field

Some offensive players love to stand in the middle of the attacking zone, waiting to receive a pass and then take a shot. A good offensive player can lean and relax on the checker to neutralize the defender, receive a pass, turn, and get a shot off.

To counter a player who stands in front of the net looking for a pass, a defensive player just has to stand beside him, playing between him and the ball, and playing his stick by clamping his stick over the opponent's stick. Now the defender is in a position to help a teammate if a screener tries to rub him out of the play.

## Defending the give-and-go play

The give-and-go is one of the best plays in lacrosse. It's simple to execute because all the player does is pass the ball and cut. Ideally, the cutter wants to beat his defender by a step so that he gets into the clear for a pass and shot. Or he can cut in front of his check and lean into him as he receives a pass and while he gets his shot off.

To defend this play, the defender shouldn't wait to find out what a passer does after passing. Instead, when the stick handler passes the ball, the defender drops to the direction of the pass and toward the middle.

The defender is trying to maintain his position between his opponent and the ball. He doesn't want to end up behind or beside the offensive player when he cuts. By stepping in the direction of the pass, the defender has a good chance of getting in front of the cutter, getting the inside position, forcing the cutter to go backdoor, and then reacting by playing his stick hard. If the cutter does get inside position on the defender, stress that the defender should just check his stick hard, assuming that a pass is coming.

### Defending the odd-man break situation

At some point during a game, probably even at several points during a game, in both box and field lacrosse, your defenders are going to be outnumbered by attacking offensive players. These situations occur mainly in transition, or *breaks*.

Here are a couple coaching tips for defending these odd-man situations in a man-to-man defense:

- **Defending the 4-on-3:** The three back defenders play a triangle zone defense. The keys are to pressure the ball and rotate in the opposite direction to where the pass goes.
- **Defending the 5-on-4:** The four defenders play a box zone defense and rotate as against the 3-on-2.

## Defending penetration by the stick handler

The standard man-to-man reaction to offensive penetration in box lacrosse is called help and recover. It's a two-man game in which a defensive player helps a teammate who has been beaten while staying in position to *recover* should his own opponent end up with the ball. On the recovery back to his opponent, the defender has to close out quickly.

Closing out is running back to the new stick handler (the helper's previous check), staying down in a defensive stance, shuffling the last two steps, and coming at an angle to force him to the boards and stop him from going to the net or from taking a long shot.

Stress to your defenders to cross-check the stick handler when they go to help, rather than stick-check, especially when closing out on great offensive players. If they gamble for the ball by stick-checking, they'll come up out of their defensive stance and will become vulnerable to getting beaten.

# Defending the Zone

A zone defense places your defenders in assigned areas that they're responsible for covering. So instead of being assigned to defend against specific offensive players, they're entrusted with defending specific areas of the field.

The most commonly employed zone defense in field lacrosse is a 3-3. In this alignment, the close defense is assigned to cover the lower three zones, and the midfielders are assigned to the top three zones. The 3-3 is made up of four long sticks and two short sticks. The two short sticks play either up top or near the crease.

Playing near the crease is best against players who are more prone to dodging.

In a 2-3-1 zone, the defenders match up the positions of the players on offense with two players up top, three in the middle, and one down low.

Two basic types of zone defense are employed in box lacrosse. The only differences between these two alignments are how they start out and match up against the offensive alignment.

- ✔ **1-2-2:** If the offense starts with an offensive player at the top of the offense, the zone defensive team plays a 1-2-2 zone defense, with the "1" player of the 1-2-2 matching up against the top offensive player.

- ✔ **2-1-2:** If the offensive team overloads one side of the floor (the strong-side alignment), the zone defensive team plays a 2-1-2 zone defense, with the "1" player staying in the middle of the zone. Except for this distinction, the guidelines for playing these defensive systems are the same, so the balance of this section applies to both alignments.

Some teams like to change to a zone defense just to change up the defense and give the offense a different look and try to change the tempo. Other teams change defenses each time down the floor to create some confusion and hesitancy with the offense.

## Understanding the zone defense philosophy

The zone defense is designed to take away the opposition's inside game and force outside shots, which are easier for the goalie to handle. This defense works best against offensive teams that haven't yet developed as a team, that aren't great at passing, or that have players who prefer to go on one-on-one and don't want to give the ball up.

Here are some critical elements to any successful zone defense. Work with your players on these actions in the defensive zone:

- **Adjust.** When playing a zone defense, defenders must remember to adjust. The defenders have to constantly change and make adjustments during an offensive set, depending on the position of the ball.

- **Talk.** Defenders must communicate with each other. The close defenders (closest to the goal) are usually designated as field generals because they can see most of the defensive zone.

- **Pressure the ball.** The closest defender to the location of the ball must pressure the ball to stop the offense from moving it around easily. This strategy also helps keep all your defenders alert and in the game, because they always have a task to do as soon as the ball enters their area of the zone.

- **Stop any penetration.** Nobody penetrates between two or more defenders. This rule is important for helping out between defenders.

- **Move with every pass.** On every pass, all six defenders must move, even if it's only a quarter-turn of the body to get a better view of the ball without losing sight of the offensive player in that area of the zone. By stressing universal movement on *every* pass, your defense will be in better position before the offense adjusts to the new ball position.

- **Follow the cutter.** If an offensive player cuts, the defender goes with the cutter until the cutter crosses over to another defender's area of the zone. On the cut, make sure to cross-check the cutter (if you're playing box lacrosse) or deny him a pass.

The 1-2-2 box lacrosse zone defense looks especially like a man-to-man defense — at least until the first pass when the top defender drops into the middle to plug up any gaps. The four perimeter players are responsible for an area of the floor rather than for an offensive player, so the defense divides the floor into quarters. In this setup, when an offensive player goes from one area to another in the zone, the defender in the vacated area doesn't follow.

If the new defender doesn't pick up the cutter, you can't leave him alone to wait for a pass and an open shot. The initial defender should stay with the cutter, with an eye to any activity in his own area of the zone, until the new defender finally picks up the cutter.

- **Protect the net in the middle.** The middle defender always stays between the ball and the net. Even when the ball goes back to the top of the offense, the middle defender remains between the ball and the net while playing one of the top offensive players.

✔ **Protect the middle against a strong-side offensive set.** When the ball is on the *strong side* (the side with the most offensive players), and the stick handler is in the middle of the other offensive players, the top ball-side defender must play him. If you play the middle defender in this situation, you're leaving the middle vulnerable to an open shot by a cutter.

✔ **Back up the middle against the weak-side offense.** If the ball is with a player on the *weak side* (the side with fewer offensive players), the defenders on that side match up with each of them. The middle defender acts as a backup in this situation, protecting the middle from any cutters.

## Containing the stick handler with a double-team

The one thing you don't want to happen as a coach is to have one player beat you. So you should have a few wrinkles that will make it difficult for a great player to play against your team.

One way is to double-team him and force him to give up the ball. Although you can double-team an offensive player in any defensive set (including man-to-man), the double-team is essentially a zone-like defensive play. On the *double-team,* two defenders double the stick handler — that is, they both defend the stick handler at the same time — while the other defenders form a zone, ready to help and rotate if the stick handler breaks through the double-team. Because one offensive player will always be open during a double-team, the defender furthest from the ball plays between the two offensive players closest to his area of the zone.

Here are some game situations in which coaches often like to call for the double-team:

✔ When the stick handler turns his back to the rest of his teammates

✔ When the stick handler is a weak stick handler who's less likely to handle the pressure, making him panic and turn the ball over

✔ To force the opposition's best player to pass the ball to a less talented teammate

## Executing the double team

The *double-teamer* — the player who leaves his own offensive assignment to join another defender — should usually come from the strong side of the defense, the side with three defenders on it.

If the stick handler is on the strong side of the defense, the defender beside the defender checking the stick handler leaves his man to double-team. If the stick handler is on the weak side of the defense, the top defender on the strong side leaves his check and comes across to double-team the ball.

If the stick handler is on the weak side, but is with the creaseman, the top defender on the weak side drops down while the top defender on the strong side comes across. The other three defenders form a triangle ready to slide or rotate.

The defender creating the double-team should stick-check the stick handler rather than cross-check. If the ball is passed out of the double-team, the double-teamer rotates or drops opposite to the pass.

# Defense in the Women's Game

Just as in men's lacrosse, the two basic defenses in women's lacrosse are man-to-man (sometimes referred to as *person-to-person*) and zone. In man-to-man, the defender is assigned one specific player, and it's her responsibility to guard her, try to prevent her from scoring, and deny her passes. In zone, the defender's main purpose is to keep herself between the offensive player and the goal, and guard an area of the field rather than a specific pre-assigned player.

## Emphasizing body positioning and footwork

Because checking and contact to the body with the stick are not allowed in women's lacrosse, the main concepts to emphasize with players are body positioning and footwork. Defenders can't use their bodies to physically lead an offensive player to veer in one direction or another, so positioning and footwork are especially important. Your players have to move their feet quickly to keep pace with the offensive players they're guarding, as well as remain balanced so they can react quickly to shifts from the opponent. Your players' sticks should follow (or mirror) the position of the attacking players' sticks, which are usually in the air.

Teaching techniques for stick checking (for the players marking "on ball") is also important. Because women's lacrosse sticks don't have deep pockets and because body checking isn't allowed, the skill level of the players needs to be at a high level. (Checking is not allowed at the modified level, according to US Lacrosse rules.)

An opportunity to check presents itself only when a player has done everything else she can to use good defensive body positioning to slow down, contain, or direct the offensive player to her disadvantage. When the offensive player makes a wrong move and fails to protect her stick, a defender can check in a quick, controlled motion that moves down and away from the body of the player with the ball. A check must also have a *release,* where the defender retracts her stick — she can't hold her stick against the player's with the ball. A check must be assessed as controlled, safe, and away from the body; otherwise a referee must call a foul in order to maintain safe play. Therefore, a check in the women's game requires much skill, patience, eye-hand coordination, and timing.

At the heart of any successful defense — whether men's or women's — is good communication. This means that players must actively call out slides they'll be making or those that their teammates should make. Instruct your players to call out in advance occasions in which your team will be double on the ball. They should keep the instructions clear and concise, because a split second can make the difference in whether a goal is scored. Have them use both general terms such as "I'm hot" (the player saying that is the first slide) and other terminology or words for strategy specific to your team.

Major or minor fouls result in a "free position." Defenders are situated 4 meters behind the offensive player taking the free position on major fouls. Those called for minor fouls are placed 4 meters in the area where she approached the offensive player prior to the foul. If the minor foul occurs in the critical scoring area, an indirect free position is awarded to the player with the ball. The 3-second rule requires defenders to stay outside the arc unless they're following an attacker.

Defensive players must get low when going after ground balls. Make sure your players choke up on their sticks and bend their knees. This will help allow for clean pickups rather than swatting after the ball. Many players make the mistake of attempting to get ground balls while staying upright — make sure your players stay low. And moving through the ball while in stride (using a consistent motion involving your hips as well as your arms), as opposed to scooping while standing still, is crucial; it aids players not only in gaining possession of the ball, but also in evading any opponents competing for the ball and generating an offensive run.

## Everyone's a defender

All players on the field need to realize that, at some juncture in the game, all players are defenders. When a turnover happens in the attacking zone, players who just seconds earlier were on offense have to become defensive players. So every player on the field must be mindful of proper defensive strategies and techniques.

Emphasize to your players that a big part of defense comes down to effort and energy. Hustling after ground balls and working hard to follow the ball are essential — especially in the women's game, where contact isn't allowed.

Playing as a team is vital. Everyone must realize what her main mission is — namely, to prevent the other team from scoring. When your team prevents the opponent from scoring, their next priority is to shift from defense to offense and help create scoring opportunities.

# Part IV
# Following Lacrosse: The Fan's Point of View

The 5th Wave                    By Rich Tennant

©RICHTENNANT

"Just how much do you think you can embarrass me? If you think I'm going to the lacrosse game with you wearing those ridiculous socks, you're sadly mistaken!"

## In this part . . .

1f you're a lacrosse fan, one of the things that drew you to the sport is likely its similarities to other popular sports. In fact, in some respects, you can say lacrosse is hockey and basketball, with a little football and wrestling, all rolled into one. It's also hard hitting, high scoring, and fast moving. Those are some of the reasons the sport is more popular now than it's even been before — with participation and fan interest growing at jaw-dropping rates. This part offers a look at all that and more. Here, we discuss what to watch for in games, take a look at some premier programs at the high school and college levels, and give an overview of the two professional lacrosse leagues.

# Chapter 16

# How to Watch Lacrosse

## In This Chapter

▶ Identifying how lacrosse is similar to other sports

▶ Knowing what to look for at a lacrosse game

▶ Finding lacrosse on TV

*W*hen you see the game of lacrosse for the first time, you may be a bit taken aback. What the heck is going on? Players run around at one end, and then they run up to one part of the field and right back to the other end. Some run back and forth to the sideline, while others don't run from the playing surface at all. Players hit everything that moves and then, in turn, they're hit. And just try following that little ball around — off a pass, off the turf, off the goalie, and off anything else that gets in its way.

As a fan, that last point is the key. Most of lacrosse action follows the ball — following ground balls, following shots on goal, following cross-field passes, following fast-break passes, or following where the ball goes on a faceoff.

This chapter offers some advice about watching the game of lacrosse from a fan's perspective. Whatever the game — high school, college, pro, or your community's youth lacrosse league — this chapter helps you follow all the action.

## It All Looks a Little Familiar . . .

Fast breaks. Man-to-man defenses. Zone defenses. Outlet passes. Basketball? Sure. But lacrosse, too.

Man-up opportunities. Stick checks. Goalies coming up with big saves. Hockey? Yes, of course. But it's also lacrosse.

Box lacrosse especially may seem familiar to you. You're in an arena. If you're at a National Lacrosse League (NLL) game, you're probably in a pretty large arena — perhaps even one that you've been in before for a concert or a truck show or maybe a hockey or basketball game.

You'll notice a host of similarities between ice hockey and box lacrosse — from the rink to the lines and rules to the way the game moves. Partly because they share an out-of-bounds factor, basketball and field lacrosse are quite similar as well. But all these sports are intertwined by a common flow to the game: Fast breaks are spliced into the action, but most of the games are dictated by half-court offenses and defenses. The offense works the ball around in an effort to get the defense out of position and create a scoring opportunity.

Two-man plays such as the pick-and-roll work in lacrosse as well as in both basketball and hockey. And knowing how to push the ball, how to play a numbers advantage or disadvantage, and when to slow things down are as important in lacrosse as they are in hockey and basketball.

In the following sections, we outline the specific similarities that lacrosse has to hockey and to basketball, as well as some differences between the sports.

## Recognizing the game's similarities to hockey

Like hockey, lacrosse is a very fast game. The two sports are also very physical; go to a pro hockey or a pro box lacrosse event, and you're as likely as not to see a fight break out. And they're both exciting games to watch as well as to play. Though there are many similarities between hockey and field lacrosse, there are even more similarities between hockey and box lacrosse.

Here are a few other similarities between hockey and lacrosse:

- A faceoff begins play at the start of each game, at the start of each quarter or period, and after a scored goal.
- In both hockey and lacrosse, a crease area around the net is a protected area for the goalie.
- Like hockey players, lacrosse players are legally allowed to hit an opponent with the body or stick.
- Both hockey and lacrosse players wear heavily padded equipment, such as kidney pads, gloves, and helmets.
- Like hockey, lacrosse uses different lines and shifts, so matching up players is crucial.

There are also a few specific similarities between hockey and box lacrosse:

- Each team has a goalie and five players on the playing surface.
- Each game is played in an arena 200 feet long and 85 feet wide.
- Each game has two- and five-minute penalties.
- That old hockey joke works for lacrosse, too: Went to a fight the other night and a lacrosse game broke out.

But the games aren't completely alike. Here are a few important differences between hockey and lacrosse:

- Hockey is played on ice; field lacrosse is played on grass or turf and box lacrosse is played on AstroTurf.
- Hockey players wear skates; lacrosse players wear running shoes.
- The dimensions of the goals are different. A hockey goal is 4 feet high and 6 feet wide; a field lacrosse goal is 6 feet high and 6 feet wide, and a box lacrosse goal is 4 feet high and 4 feet wide.
- Box and pro lacrosse have shot clocks during which a team must get off a shot on goal in a designated amount of time or lose possession of the ball. Hockey has no shot clock.

## Recognizing the game's similarities to basketball

Lacrosse is similar to hockey because of all the hitting and physical play, but it's even more like basketball because of the passing and ball control. In hockey, a team doesn't always have complete possession of the puck because of the nature of the game — the puck takes weird and unexpected bounces and ricochets.

However, as in basketball, when a lacrosse team has possession of the ball, it can control the game and possession time. It's pretty hard to get the ball away from a good stick handler. For this reason, winning a faceoff and getting ground balls are crucial in the game of lacrosse. After a team takes possession of the ball, it can control the tempo of the game.

Youth lacrosse coaches coming from the hockey world may have a tendency to play their players like hockey forwards and defensemen — keeping the defensemen back toward the center of the field when in their own offensive zone, for example. But lacrosse is more like basketball when it comes to what players do on each end of the field. When a team has possession of the ball, everybody has an active role on the offense. When a team doesn't have the ball, just about everybody plays defense.

Here are some other similarities between lacrosse and basketball:

✔ Although you won't see any teams scoring 100 points in a game, lacrosse is a bit more like basketball in that it has many more legitimate scoring opportunities than hockey does.

✔ The lacrosse equivalent of a jump ball is the faceoff, which takes place at the start of each game, at the start of each subsequent quarter and any overtime periods, and after each goal is scored.

✔ In basketball and box lacrosse, each sport has a shot clock to regulate offensive play and help speed up the action. The shot clock in Major League Lacrosse (MLL) is 60 seconds; the NLL's shot clock is 30 seconds; and the National Basketball Association has a 24-second shot clock.

✔ The three options of a basketball player with the ball are pass, shoot, or try to fake out the defender — and that's the same in lacrosse.

✔ The cuts and movement of off-ball play are crucial in creating space and opening opportunities in both basketball and lacrosse.

✔ In both basketball and lacrosse, *vision* (that knack of seeing peripherally and being able to play with your head up) is essential. It's what allows a player to follow his teammates and know where they'll be.

✔ When an attack player in lacrosse backs into a defender while attacking the crease area, it's similar to the way a forward posts up in basketball.

✔ Lacrosse involves both zone and man-to-man defensive play, just as basketball does. In fact, individual and team defense are virtually identical in basketball and lacrosse.

The footwork, lateral movement, and bent knee translate from one sport to the other. The communication, sliding/shifting, double teams, and cover schemes characterize team defense in both games.

Though there are similarities, lacrosse and basketball have some distinct differences as well:

✔ Most notably, basketball is primarily played indoors; field lacrosse is played outdoors.

✔ There are twice as many players on the field in lacrosse as there are in basketball (with ten players in lacrosse and five in basketball).

✔ Every player on the court in basketball must continuously play defense, whereas, in lacrosse, there are long stretches where players, especially attackmen, don't have to play defense at all.

✔ Basketball players wear little gear aside from their uniforms. The physical nature of lacrosse, however, makes helmets, gloves, shoulder pads, elbow pads, and mouth guards necessities.

# Knowing What to Watch For

You've made it to the game in time to buy a program or pick up a lineup so that you know who the players are. If you're already a fan, you probably know the home team's players. If you're new to the game, you'll want to read up on both teams.

You should be able to find out who the outstanding players are on both teams — the ones to watch during the game — based on matchups. Teams usually match up their best defensive player with the opponent's best offensive player, so you're sure to see at least one classic struggle.

Another great way to get information about either team is to ask the fans sitting around you. Most fans love to share information and advice on who to watch, what to watch for, and what other exciting things to anticipate during the game, such as a player who may be approaching a scoring record or a team battling to earn a playoff spot.

Lacrosse is different from some other sports in that there is a community-type atmosphere. As a result, fans are usually eager to interact in the stands — even with fans from the opposing team. One of the reasons for this is that so many fans in stands are new to the game. Unlike sports such as football and basketball, in which most fans have grown up with the games and know the rules, lacrosse is still a new phenomenon to many. So their neighboring fans are always quick to pitch in with info and insights.

Don't worry about trying to figure out the rules of the game. Even those who have followed the game for decades are still trying to figure some of them out. For example, box lacrosse players are allowed to slash another player's stick, but they can also be penalized for slashing. If you really want to learn more about the rules of the game, check out Chapter 4 of this book. At the game, it may be helpful to remember some of the referee's signals (also discussed in Chapter 4) so that you have some idea of what has happened to cause a play stoppage.

The balance of this section offers some suggestions about what game action to watch for. You'll probably concentrate on what your favorite team is doing during the game, so these tips are written from that perspective.

Of course, if your team is playing against a team known for its defensive prowess, for example, you may want to pay closer attention to that team's defense when your team has the ball.

## Watching the offense

When your team has the ball, it's obviously looking for ways to score. As a fan, you want to try to figure out its style of play or what type of play it's running that will give the team the best chance to score. In the following sections, we cover what to look for.

### Getting open

Following the ball doesn't always take you to the most action. Often, the most exciting thing to watch is how the offensive team gets its better players open or away from the best defenders.

Look for offensive players off the ball who set picks for their teammates. A *pick* occurs when an offensive player positions himself in front of a defensive player defending one of his offensive teammates so that his teammate can have an opening to receive a pass or take a shot.

The player setting the pick has to be stationary; a moving pick is illegal. When it's done correctly, picking off a defender can be the most exciting event in an offensive set; fans (and players) love it when a defender is picked right off his feet.

### Executing plays

Most teams have a tendency to run similar plays all the time. They rely on a particular play because of the type of players they have on offense. For example, you may see offensive players habitually taking on a defender one-on-one, or you may see a lot of pick-and-roll plays.

*Motion offenses* are those in which players are constantly cutting and passing. Or a team's offense may simply run through the player who has the hot hand during a particular game.

### Controlling the tempo

Is your team dictating the pace of play? If you're familiar with the style of play that your team prefers, you may be able to tell whether it's controlling the tempo of the game. For example, if your team is loaded with smaller players, it probably has to play a fast-paced running game to be successful.

If its opponent is a bigger team that tends to run a more deliberate, patient offense, then two distinct styles of play are colliding. In this case, if both teams are scoring a lot of goals, then your team is probably controlling the tempo. If it's a low-scoring game, then your team is likely losing the tempo battle — and probably the game.

Besides watching for a fast or slow tempo, you may spot another kind of tempo in a game: a *scoring run*. This is when a team scores consecutive multiple goals over a short period of time, also known as *going on a run*.

Momentum shifts swiftly in a lacrosse game. If your team quickly finds itself down by four or five goals, don't worry: A scoring run could be right around the corner to get those four or five goals back. These scoring runs tend to come from playing good aggressive defense that forces a lot of turnovers, leading to transition opportunities. Winning several consecutive faceoffs also leads to scoring runs.

### Pressing on the man-up

When the opposition takes a penalty, it gives the offense a man-up advantage. How does your team take advantage of the situation? Some teams have a series of set plays that they save for those man-up situations. Other teams prefer to stay back and pass around the zone until the defense allows an opportunity for a cutter or an open shot.

Man-up opportunities allow some of the best offensive players to have a chance to really show off their skills, taking on a defender one-on-one because eventually his opponent will run out of help and a teammate will be open.

## Watching the defense

Are the teams playing man-to-man or zone defense? How is one team defending the great offensive players of the opposition? Does the defense pressure the stick handler or just sit back and let the offense take shots from long distance? These are a few things to look for on the defensive side of the ball. However, defense is also where you see most of the activity that results in turnovers or ground balls.

In the following sections, we tell you what to look for on defense.

### Forcing turnovers

A *turnover* is when possession of the ball changes teams. Turnovers can be the result of careless offensive play (a bad pass, a dropped or missed pass, or an offensive penalty) or aggressive defensive play (a stolen pass, the ball stripped from the stick handler, or an offensive penalty).

But the action doesn't stop after the ball has been turned over. Good teams look to score off turnovers, creating scoring-run opportunities (see the "Controlling the tempo" section, earlier in this chapter). Aggressive play that forces turnovers can turn a game around, making the opposition pay the price for dropping the ball.

### Forcing missed shots

A missed shot can technically be considered a turnover, but a missed shot can also be thought of as part of the natural flow of the game. No matter how you look at them though, missed shots are often the result of good solid defensive play.

From the offense, look for examples of

- Long-distance shots through a phalanx of other players
- Awkward, off-balance shots from poor angles toward the goal
- Arcing, slow-moving shots from players who've been hit as they shot

These poor shots are all the result of a good aggressive defense forcing low-percentage shots.

### Going after ground balls

Ground balls should not be taken for granted. Whoever controls the ground balls, usually controls the game. Watch what happens after most of the ground balls are picked up.

If players are constantly running down to the other end of the field after a ground ball, chances are, you're watching a good defense control the game. Also, you're likely to see one or two players who just seem to have a nose for the ball and are always in the middle of a pile, fighting for that ground ball.

In box lacrosse, ground balls are known as *loose balls*.

## Watching the goalie

The goalie is the backbone of the team. Watching a great goalie perform is a bit like watching a great artist at work. The best goalies rely not only on fundamental skills but also on their shot-saving creativity in goal.

In the following sections, we cover some things to look for in the goalie.

### Playing the angles

Goalies who play the angles move around in goal more than you may expect. They're looking to cut off any angle that an offensive player may have at a shot.

You'll often see angle goalies reaching back to feel where they are in relation to the net — they try to keep themselves centered between the posts. And because they've usually cut off a shooter's angle when they make a save, you'll see a lot of body saves from angle goalies.

### Relying on reflexes

Reflex-oriented goalies will make more stick, leg, or glove saves than body saves. That's because they're depending on their reflexes for seeing the ball as it approaches the net.

Reflex goalies still try to play the angles (see the preceding section), but they also tend to take more risks than angle goalies, thinking that their quick reflexes can save them from poor positioning.

### Releasing the ball

After every stop, goalies have an opportunity to start the offense with a well-timed and well-thrown pass. Scoring runs, for example, can be extended with a quick and accurate pass from a goalie to a fast-breaking offensive player.

## Watching the game action

Any activity on the field or floor is relevant to the outcome of a lacrosse game, even if the clock isn't ticking. In the following sections, we tell you what to watch for.

### Winning the faceoff

Watch the faceoff strategy between the two teams. Some teams may place three players back on defense to defend against losing the faceoff. Other teams may place just two players on the defensive end, playing to win the faceoff and get an offensive start.

How they line up around the circle usually gives you a pretty good idea about whether a team is trying to score off the faceoff or just trying to get possession of the ball (or not let the other team get possession of it). You'll also notice that teams have specific players who play the draw in almost every faceoff.

### Noting substitution patterns

Most coaches do have a specific substitution strategy for their players, but often that strategy is dismissed because of line changes made by the opposing team.

Teams try to match up their best defenders against the opposition's best offensive players. So you're bound to see a cat-and-mouse game between the two coaches as each tries to run players on and off the field or floor to get a matchup that's in his favor. You can also keep track of which players play on both the offensive and defensive ends or which coaches operate an offense-defense strategy.

### Monitoring injuries

Because of the physical nature of the game, players do suffer injuries. When a player leaves a game, make note of it and consider how his absence may influence the remainder of the game.

### Spying on the fans

Lacrosse has passionate, loyal, and diehard fans. They dress with their home-team sweaters, hats, buttons, and colors. They get into the game, and anybody who hurts their team will hear about it, especially the referee.

Fans love to harass a referee about any little thing that may hurt the home team, no matter how legitimate the complaint may happen to be. You *should* get involved in the game — be a part of cheers and chants, wear the team colors — but maintain respect for the opposition and for the officials.

## Closing out the game

In the last five minutes of a close game, hang onto your seat. Every possession could turn out to make the difference in the game. At this point in the game, you should be able to figure out who the real stars on each team are. With the game on the line, the best players — offensive and defensive — step up to challenge the opposition and find out who blinks first.

Look for the offensive player who handles the ball on every possession. He's likely to be the one who wants the ball in that situation, the one who plays with composure and doesn't panic. And he's likely to score the game-winning goal.

## Calling it a night

Stick around after a game is over because you'll see some interesting things. First, the players from both teams line up and shake hands. Now, these warriors have just beaten up on each other for four quarters, but like true athletes, they shake hands to thank their opponents for the game.

In the NLL, the league also has a post-game tradition in which the players run around the

arena and wave to the fans to thank them for their support.

If you're willing to hang around after a pro game, you may be able to get an autograph from your favorite player. In fact, your favorite player may be your teacher or your neighborhood policeman or fireman — most players in the MLL and NLL work at another career.

But that star player needs help. He probably has a teammate who will sacrifice a little pain to set him up for that game-winning goal, stepping in front of the opposition's best defender to set a crushing pick.

At the end of a close game, you're almost guaranteed to see a one-on-one matchup between the best players on each team. Look for the little things that may give one player an edge over the other on that particular night, such as who looks more tired and who looks more alert at this stage of the game.

And then just sit back and enjoy. These one-on-one battles are what the game is all about — a healthy confrontation between a top scorer and a top defender to determine who's the best.

# Following Lacrosse on Television

Watching lacrosse on TV is a good way to keep up with your team's rivals, in addition to watching your favorite team. But a televised game can't match the entertainment value and intensity of watching a game in person. Plus, the ball moves so quickly that television cameras are often playing catch-up just to keep pace (though TV crews are getting better as more games are broadcast).

If you can't get to the field and the big game is coming up, however, catch it at home. Televised lacrosse is fairly widely available, especially in lacrosse-crazy areas of North America. And as with any sport, increased television coverage is monumentally crucial to the growth of lacrosse.

## Field lacrosse hits Xbox LIVE

Madden NFL. Tiger Woods PGA Tour. MLB 2K9. NHL. NBA Live. Grand Slam Tennis. Fight Night. NCAA Football. . . . There have been video games for NASCAR and even pool. But field lacrosse didn't join the fray until late November 2009 when Inside Lacrosse College Lacrosse 2010 made its debut on Xbox LIVE's Indie Games channel. You can choose from 60 teams or create your own team, make a schedule of games, and even pick the jersey color. The game also features stat tracking. For more information on College Lacrosse 2010, go to www.collegelacrosse2010.com.

## *Professional lacrosse*

Major League Lacrosse, the pro lacrosse's outdoor league, has a game of the week broadcast on ESPN2 and ESPN360.com. Select Toronto Nationals games appear on TSN2.

The National Lacrosse League, the indoor pro league, has national coverage in Canada and the United States on various outlets, including for the following teams:

- ✔ **Calgary Roughnecks:** Shaw TV
- ✔ **Colorado Mammoth:** Altitude
- ✔ **Minnesota Swarm:** KSTC
- ✔ **Philadelphia Wings:** Comcast SportsNet
- ✔ **Rochester Nighthawks:** Time Warner SportsNet
- ✔ **Toronto Rock:** Rogers Sportsnet Ontario

In addition, all NLL games are available as broadband broadcasts through B2 Networks at www.nll.com on game nights. The cost to watch is $7 per game.

## *NCAA lacrosse*

Both ESPNU and CBS College Sports broadcast games on a weekly basis during the regular season and playoffs. ESPN owns the rights to broadcast the lacrosse version of the Final Four — the Division I national semifinals and final — both on Memorial Day weekend. The semifinals air the Saturday of Memorial Day weekend on ESPN2. The national championship game follows on Memorial Day.

## New ways to bring you the action

With advents in technology, lacrosse broadcasts have evolved quite a bit the last few years and now include several new elements.

For example, the MSG Network in New York regularly attaches a portable microphone to high school players and coaches during games, and shows condensed highlights of what transpires during the subsequent week on its highlight show. The interaction between coach and player and coach and official is often very interesting.

Also interesting are the behind-the-scenes storylines that occur in lacrosse. During the 2009 season, New Balance followed the Canandaigua, New York, varsity boys team from its first game to its last. The Braves' final game was a 10-5 win against previously unbeaten Niskayuna in the Class B state championship game in Rochester. Marshall Johnson, a freshman (as of this writing) at Fairfield University, was followed extensively during the series. He had three goals and won 14 of 19 faceoffs in the state final. You can't script things much better than that.

CBS College Sports broadcasts the Division II and Division III championship games — and the Division I women's national title game — which are also played over Memorial Day weekend.

Regular-season NCAA men's and women's games are broadcast live in select markets, with a game televised every spring week on WMAR in Baltimore.

## *High school lacrosse*

Select varsity games are shown in some parts of the United States on cable TV and on the Internet. Perhaps the most extensive coverage of high school lacrosse is provided in the New York City area by the MSG Network. A weekly game of the week is shown on the MSG Network. In addition, MSG broadcasts a weekly lacrosse highlight show during the season called *The Lax Report*. Additional games are broadcast each week on the MSG Varsity channel, which launched in September 2009.

# Chapter 17

# Getting in the Game

• • • • • • • • • • • • • • • • • • • • • • • • • • • • • • • • • • • • • • • • • • • • • • • •

## In This Chapter

▶ Looking at the increasing popularity of high school and college lacrosse

▶ Noting the dramatic increase in attendance at the NCAA championships

▶ Getting acquainted with minor-league box lacrosse in Canada

• • • • • • • • • • • • • • • • • • • • • • • • • • • • • • • • • • • • • • • • • • • • • • • •

The popularity of lacrosse continues to grow, so it makes sense that the number of participants and programs at the high school level has also surged. This increase at the high school level has transferred to colleges as well, where the number of college programs is up around the country.

What this means for you is, whether you're a kid who's interested in playing lacrosse yourself in high school, college, or beyond, or you're a fan of the sport, you have plenty of opportunities in front of you. In this chapter, we fill you in on the growth of the sport at the high school and college levels, and give you some information on minor-league box lacrosse and the World Lacrosse Championship as well. (For information on the pros, check out Chapter 18.)

## High School Highlights

High school lacrosse participation has experienced a massive amount of growth since 2000. According to the National Federation of High Schools, there were 74,225 high school boys and girls lacrosse players in 2000; by 2008, according to US Lacrosse, the number had reached 218,823 players. As a result, the number of high schools offering the sport has also grown significantly. The State High School Association reports that lacrosse is the second-fastest growing sport in this decade. (Bowling is number one.)

Although lacrosse was traditionally popular in certain regions of the country — such as Long Island, Baltimore, and New York's Hudson Valley — its popularity at the high school level (and beyond) has spread nationwide. The sport has caught on big time in states such as California, Colorado, Florida, Minnesota, North Carolina, Ohio, South Carolina, and Texas.

# Ten tradition-rich high school boys' lacrosse programs

Here's a look at ten high school boys' programs that are synonymous with success:

- **Gilman School (Baltimore, Maryland):** The Baltimore-based Greyhounds began and ended the 2009 season ranked number one in the final Under Armour/Inside Lacrosse 2009 national rankings.

- **West Genesee High School (West Genesee, New York):** The Wildcats' streak of seven straight state title-game appearances ended in 2009.

- **Ward Melville High School (East Setauket, New York):** The Patriots have played in the state championship game nine times, winning seven titles.

- **Yorktown (Yorktown Heights, New York):** Located in the lacrosse hotbed of the Hudson Valley, Yorktown has one of the most impressive streaks in the nation, with 28 sectional championships since 1980 (as of this writing).

- **Manhasset (Manhasset, New York):** The alma mater of the legendary Jim Brown, there is no program with as long and rich a history as that of the Indians.

- **Wilton (Wilton, Connecticut):** The Warriors have won (as of this writing) a jaw-dropping 20 state titles and 13 Fairfield County Interscholastic Athletic Conference championships.

- **Darien (Darien, Connecticut):** The Blue Wave won its fifth straight Class M state title in 2009 — a season in which coach Jeff Brameier picked up his 400th career win.

- **West Islip (West Islip, New York):** The Lions defeated Orchard Park 10-5 in the 2009 Class A championship game for its third state title in four years.

- **Garden City (Garden City, New York):** Garden City fell to Manhasset in the 2009 Woodstick Classic, the longest running continuous boys high school lacrosse rivalry in the nation. The Trojans had won 11 of 12 meetings in the series, which dates back to 1935.

- **McDonogh (Owings Mills, Maryland):** The Maryland Interscholastic Athletic Association is a power-packed league that includes Gilman as well as McDonogh.

Many of the top boys' programs also have exceptional girls programs as well, including McDonogh, Darien, West Genesee, Yorktown, and Garden City, to name a few.

The following states officially sanction lacrosse as a championship sport at the high school varsity level: California, Connecticut, Delaware, Florida, Georgia, Maryland, Massachusetts, Michigan, Minnesota, New Hampshire, New Jersey, New York, North Carolina, Ohio, Pennsylvania, South Carolina, Tennessee, and Texas.

# College Corner

Though the traditional strength of U.S. collegiate lacrosse has been in the northeastern states and along the eastern seaboard, lacrosse has now found its way into the Midwest and into the West, with the programs at Ohio State, Notre Dame, Denver, and Air Force gaining prominence.

About 600 schools at the division I, II, III and junior-college levels field men's and women's lacrosse teams. The majority of men's college programs — a total of 130 — compete at the Division III level. There are 35 Division II programs.

The Division I level, with 59 men's teams in 2009, features the best talent and attracts the most attention from fans and media, thanks primarily to scholarships and much bigger budgets. Though Division I schools such as Michigan State University, the University of New Hampshire, and Boston College have recently dropped men's lacrosse, other new programs such as Bellarmine University, the University of Detroit Mercy, Mercer University, and Jacksonville University have helped keep the number of teams at a steady level.

The level of parity in NCAA lacrosse has increased dramatically the last decade. Although the tradition-rich programs such as Johns Hopkins, Syracuse, Princeton, and Virginia remain in the national title chase, more programs than ever are in the hunt for postseason glory.

The most growth in collegiate lacrosse can be found on the women's side, where there are now more than 300 programs — three times the number there were in 1990. As of this writing, more than 50 new Division III teams have been added since 1997.

The number of college lacrosse players increased 5.4 percent in 2008, according to US Lacrosse. There were a total of 29,822 players — 18,148 male and 11,674 female.

College lacrosse starts its official season in late February and culminates with the Division I men's championship game on Memorial Day in late May. Teams play an average of about 15 regular-season games each spring, mostly on Saturday afternoons.

The culmination of every college lacrosse season is the Final Four, played on Memorial Day weekend and traditionally broadcast live on ESPN and ESPN2. The Division I men's semifinals take place on Saturday; the Division II and III championships, on Sunday; and the Division I final, on Monday.

# Talented players from far and wide

Most of the NCAA's stars come from traditional hot-bed locations. For example, Syracuse stars Ryan, Casey, and Mike Powell grew up in upstate New York; Johns Hopkins legend Dave Pietramala came from Long Island; Princeton's Jesse Hubbard played his prep lacrosse around Washington, D.C.; and Johns Hopkins's Paul Rabil grew up playing in Maryland.

Plenty of Canadians have also made a large impact on the NCAA and that influence seems to be increasing as more players in

Ontario and British Columbia are looking for scholarships at U.S. colleges. Legends such as Gary and Paul Gait and Tom Marechek (all three of whom went to Syracuse from British Columbia), Gavin Prout (who went from Ontario to Loyola College), and John Grant, Jr. (from Ontario to the University of Delaware), dominated college lacrosse during their tenures.

Colleges have also been tapping into overseas talent from such locations as Australia and England.

In the Division I tournament bracket, 16 teams compete for the title. Four teams make the Division II playoffs, and 22 teams vie for the Division III championship.

Since 2003, the Division I men's final four has been regularly played at NFL stadiums, including Baltimore's M & T Bank Stadium and Gillette Stadium in Foxborough, Massachusetts. It has grown into a massive event that now regularly draws crowds of more than 40,000 people.

The NCAA added a national championship for women's lacrosse in 1982 with a Division I title game. (The men's started awarding championships in 1971 at the D-I level.) A title game was added for Division III in 1985 and for Division II in 2001. Maryland has a Division I–leading nine national titles, including seven in a row from 1995 to 2001. A crowd of 6,515 attended Northwestern's 21-7 win over North Carolina in the 2009 NCAA D-I championship game at Towson University.

The NCAA isn't the only place to play lacrosse at the college level. The Men's Collegiate Lacrosse Association (MCLA) is made up of 213 men's teams in two divisions in the United States and Canada. The Women's Collegiate Lacrosse League (WCLL) has been in existence since 1994 and is made up of 40 teams; all told, there are 200 teams competing in the US Lacrosse Women's Division I Intercollegiate Associates (WDIA), and the WCLL is just one of the leagues.

## Tradition-rich college programs

Here's a look at some men's collegiate programs that are synonymous with success:

✔ **Johns Hopkins:** Perhaps no college is as synonymous with a sport as Hopkins is with lacrosse. After all, at Hopkins — unlike most of the other top programs — lacrosse is the clear number-one sport. The Blue Jays have won nine NCAA championships.

✔ **Syracuse:** The roots of the Orange program date back to 1916, and its 11 national championships (as of this writing) are the most of any program in history. The list of legendary players who have worn Syracuse uniforms may also put SU at number one.

✔ **Princeton:** The Tigers appeared in eight Division I championship games from 1992 to 2002, winning six times.

✔ **Virginia:** The Cavaliers have won three national titles since 1999 (as of this writing).

✔ **Cornell:** As of this writing, the Big Red have been to the NCAA title game seven times.

Few — if any — programs in any sport have risen to dominance in NCAA history faster than Northwestern University's women's program. After resuming play at the NCAA level in 2002 (following nine years as a club team), the Wildcats have, as of this writing, won five national titles and enjoyed two undefeated seasons.

# Introducing Minor-Level Box Lacrosse in Canada

Canadian box lacrosse at the minor level features three age levels, each with additional divisions, according to age or according to the quality of players:

✔ **Minor lacrosse:** A variety of leagues for players between the ages of 7 and 20.

✔ **Junior A and B leagues:** For players ages 17 through 21. The A league features the better players.

✔ **Major A and B leagues (also called Senior):** For players over 21 years of age. These leagues also have the more highly skilled players at the A level.

BOX LACROSSE

# Other Canadian national trophies

Canadian lacrosse players have numerous national trophies to aim for. The following trophies are also highly coveted by players, coaches, and fans at other competitive levels:

✔ **The Minto Cup:** This trophy goes to the Canadian Lacrosse Association's junior men's league champion.

✔ **The Mann Cup:** This trophy goes to Canada's senior men's league champion.

✔ **The President's Cup:** For the national box lacrosse champions at the Senior B level, this trophy was first awarded in 1964. Past champions have included the usual array of teams from Ontario and British Columbia, as well as three teams from Alberta — including

the Edmonton Outlaws in 2002 — and a team from Tuscarora, New York, in 1994.

✔ **The Founders Trophy:** Since 1972, this trophy has been awarded to the national box lacrosse champions at the Junior B level. Nearly all past champions have come from the Province of Ontario.

✔ **P. D. Ross Cup and Victory Trophy:** Two divisions of senior men's field lacrosse teams vie for these prizes, both first awarded in 1984.

✔ **First Nations Trophy:** Junior men's field organizations compete for this championship, first awarded in 1985.

With levels such as Tyke (ages 7 and 8), PeeWee (ages 11 and 12), and Midget (ages 15 and 16), minor-level lacrosse offers the greatest opportunity for young players to play the game. You can find minor leagues around Canada, called *house leagues;* they're usually affiliated with a community's arena. Teams typically are formed at the youngest ages, with the more successful teams staying together through the duration of their players' minor careers. And the best of these teams — called *rep teams* — represent the community in national tournaments. At age 17, the best players from these house leagues reach the next level in a player draft conducted by teams in the Junior A and Junior B leagues.

The Junior and Senior leagues operate somewhat like professional or university competitive leagues. They're made up of teams from communities primarily in Ontario, British Columbia, and Alberta who draw on the best players in their particular house leagues. The teams then compete during the regular season for the right to participate in playoffs that can lead to a national championship series.

TECHNICAL STUFF

Because teams — franchises, almost — are responsible for fielding players, coaches, equipment managers, and so on, as well as for the fees required to maintain membership in a league, the number of teams participating may vary from year to year. In 2003, for example, three teams were added to the Junior B league of the Ontario Lacrosse Association, increasing the number of franchises from 22 in 2002 to 25 in 2003.

## Taking on the world: The World Lacrosse Championship

The pride of wearing your home country's sweater in competitive lacrosse started in 1967, the year of Canada's centennial celebration. Canada invited the United States, England, and Australia to compete in an international amateur field lacrosse tournament, the beginning of the World Lacrosse Championship, now held every four years and sponsored by the Federation of International Lacrosse. Nations compete in a weighted round-robin tournament during which higher-ranked teams play an easier schedule based on their record in the previous World Lacrosse Championship. Since the first tournament, the games have been held in Melbourne, Australia; Stockport, England; Baltimore, Maryland; Perth, Australia; Manchester, England; and London, Ontario.

The champions of Junior A leagues from the Ontario Lacrosse Association (OLA) and the British Columbia Lacrosse Association (BCLA) compete for the Minto Cup. The championship is a best-of-seven series. The Junior A playoff participants are determined by a regular-season schedule. Between April and July, teams in the BCLA play a 24-game schedule. The OLA starts the season a little later (in May), and plays a 20-game schedule through July.

# Chapter 18

# Keeping Up with the Pros

*In This Chapter*

▶ Watching the pros play indoors and out

▶ Looking at the differences between the two professional leagues

▶ Getting to know the top pro players

**S**ure, lacrosse's popularity has surged at the youth, high school, and college levels throughout the United States. But as a lacrosse fan, you're not limited to watching amateurs play. Whether you're a fan of field lacrosse or box, you can get your fill of the best that lacrosse has to offer in Major League Lacrosse (MLL) and the National Lacrosse League (NLL).

In this chapter, we fill you in on both leagues, and let you know which teams are in each league, how long each league's season lasts, what the teams play for, and what the playoff structure is like.

## Everything You Need to Know about Major League Lacrosse

The genesis of Major League Lacrosse came when fitness guru Jake Steinfeld read a 1998 *Spin* magazine story documenting the surge in popularity of lacrosse. Steinfeld discussed the idea of forming a pro field lacrosse league with one of the story's contributors, Warrior Lacrosse president Dave Morrow. Tim Robertson, the former CEO of the Family Channel, teamed up with Steinfeld and Morrow to launch the league, which made its debut with Summer Showcase exhibition games at six sites in 2000. The league began play in 2001, giving field lacrosse a professional league of its own. (For more on the history of the MLL, check out the nearby sidebar, "Major League Lacrosse: The early years.")

In the following sections, we fill you in on the MLL itself, as well as some of the best players to ever play in the league.

# Major League Lacrosse: The early years

Here's a look at some key dates in the formation and introduction of Major League Lacrosse:

✔ **February 1999:** Jake Steinfeld, Dave Morrow, and Tim Robertson partner up to form the league.

✔ **July–August 2000:** Summer Showcase exhibition games are played at six sites.

✔ **January 13, 2001:** Goaltender Sal LoCascio is selected by Bridgeport as the number-one choice in the inaugural MLL draft.

✔ **March 8, 2001:** The league unveils names and logos for its teams at a press conference in New York City.

✔ **June 7, 2001:** Baltimore beats Long Island 16-13 in the first game in MLL history. Chris Turner of Baltimore holds the distinction of being the first player to score a goal in the history of the league.

✔ **August 2, 2001**: Mark Millon of Baltimore has three goals and four assists and is named MVP in the league's first all-star game, called the MLL LacrosseStar Game. It was played at the Ballpark at Harbor Yard in Bridgeport, Connecticut.

✔ **September 1, 2001:** The first Major League Lacrosse playoff games are played as Long Island beats Rochester and Baltimore defeats Boston in the semifinals at Kennedy Stadium in Bridgeport, Connecticut.

✔ **September 3, 2001:** Paul Gait of Long Island scores seven goals to earn MVP honors as Long Island beats Baltimore 15-11 in the inaugural MLL championship game.

✔ **June 6, 2002**: The MLL meets the NFL when the league plays a game at an NFL stadium for the first time as the Baltimore Bayhawks defeat the Rochester Rattlers 13-10 at Ravens Stadium.

✔ **July 21, 2002:** The league's orange "grippy" ball debuts in the second annual all-star game, which is played at Prince George's Stadium in Bowie, Maryland. The fluorescent orange ball has been the MLL's official game ball ever since.

✔ **September 1, 2002:** Baltimore beats Long Island 21-13 at the second annual MLL championship game, which was played at Crew Stadium in Columbus, Ohio. Mark Millon has five goals and two assists for the Bayhawks.

✔ **August 24, 2003:** The Long Island Lizards win their second MLL title in three years, beating Baltimore 15-14 in overtime at Villanova Stadium in Villanova, Pennsylvania.

✔ **May 22, 2004:** The MLL meets the West Coast for the first time as the league game between Baltimore and Rochester is played at Seahawks Stadium in Seattle, Washington. Baltimore wins 24-18.

## League basics

In an effort to create more scoring and more excitement, the MLL made some dramatic changes to field lacrosse rules, including eliminating the restraining box, adding a 60-second shot clock, and adding a 2-point goal line for shots from 16 yards out from the goal.

Up until the 2009 season, the league limited the number of long-stick defensemen on the field to three (from the traditional four). The change to four long poles makes the MLL more consistent with the collegiate and high school levels.

As of this writing, there are now six teams in Major League Lacrosse:

- ✔ Boston Cannons
- ✔ Chicago Machine
- ✔ Denver Outlaws
- ✔ Long Island Lizards
- ✔ Toronto Nationals
- ✔ Washington Bayhawks (formerly of Baltimore)

The Cannons, Lizards, and Bayhawks all started play when the league made its debut in 2001. The Machine and Outlaws launched in 2006 as the league expanded to the western part of the United States. The MLL went beyond the U.S. border prior to the 2009 season with the addition of the Nationals.

Five MLL teams ceased operations after the 2008 season because of financial reasons. The Toronto Nationals were formed after they bought the rights to the Rochester Rattlers, assuming the Rattlers' staff and player personnel.

One of those five defunct teams, the Philadelphia Barrage, won a league-leading three MLL championships.

Each MLL team plays a 12-game regular season that totals 36 games among the teams. The regular season begins in mid-May and lasts until early August.

The top teams in each of the MLL's two divisions advance to the semifinals. The teams with the best records regardless of division also make the semifinals. The MLL championship is played in late August over the course of one weekend, with the two semifinals on Saturday and the championship, called the Steinfeld Cup, on Sunday.

MLL teams are made up of 19 players per team during games, most of whom were former NCAA Division I stars. The majority of the players in the league are from the United States, but a growing number are from Canada. (For more on the top MLL players, check out the next section.)

## *The top players*

Major League Lacrosse has a long list of players familiar to fans of the college game. Here's a look at 25 of the best:

- ✔ **Matt Bocklet:** A ground-ball machine for Johns Hopkins, Bocklet, one of three brothers who went on to play at the Division I level, is now starring for the Denver Outlaws after playing his inaugural MLL season with the Washington Bayhawks.

- ✔ **Ryan Boyle:** The four-time all-American at Princeton was a new arrival in Boston for the 2009 season. Boyle was a key member of the Philadelphia Barrage's MLL title teams in 2006 and 2007. Also a standout in the NLL, he was NLL rookie of the year in 2005 with the New York Titans.

- ✔ **Steven Brooks:** An all-American midfielder for Syracuse University, the 6'2", 192-pound Brooks has been a handful for opposing defenders while playing for the Chicago Machine.

- ✔ **Joe Cinosky:** A team captain at the University of Maryland, Cinosky, at 6'3" and 225 pounds, brings size and strength to the Toronto Nationals' defense.

- ✔ **Matt Danowski:** The former four-time Duke all-American and NCAA career-points leader is a fan favorite for the Long Island Lizards. He grew up in Farmingdale, Long Island.

- ✔ **Jake Deane:** Known as "Jake the Snake," the former University of Massachusetts star is a defenseman for the Chicago Machine. The 6'3", 200-pound native of Annapolis, Maryland, was nicknamed "The Terminator" while in college.

- ✔ **Kyle Dixon:** The Washington Bayhawks midfielder is a former star for the University of Virginia, where he helped the Cavaliers win two national championships.

- ✔ **Brian "Doc" Dougherty:** The three-time MLL goaltender of the year was the MVP of the 1995 NCAA Championships for the University of Maryland.

- ✔ **Spencer Ford:** Ford, who led the nation with an average of more than four assists per game as a senior at Towson in 1999, has been getting his point(s) across for the Long Island Lizards.

- ✔ **John Grant, Jr.:** Grant has been an impact player in the league since it started play in 2001, when he starred for Rochester. (He took a two-year hiatus from the league from 2002 through 2004, but he's been unstoppable since.) Grant, who is also an NLL star, won MLL MVP honors in both 2007 and 2008.

- ✔ **Zack Greer:** After a storied career at Duke University in which he became the NCAA's all-time leading goal scorer, and one season at Bryant University under former Duke coach Mike Pressler, the attackman made an immediate impact with the Long Island Lizards for the 2009 season, his first in the professional ranks. Greer's brother, Bill, plays for the NLL's New York Titans.

✔ **Kevin Huntley:** The former Johns Hopkins star wasted little time showing his abilities at the pro level, earning 2008 rookie of the year honors. He joined the Washington Bayhawks in 2009 after playing the previous season for the Los Angeles Riptide.

✔ **Kevin Leveille:** An attackman for the Chicago Machine, the former University of Massachusetts all-American was named the MLL's most improved player in 2005 and was among the leading candidates for MLL MVP in 2008.

✔ **Sean Lindsay:** An all-American at Syracuse University, he has made a big impact for several MLL teams. Most recently, the midfielder is starring for the Denver Outlaws.

✔ **Ryan McClay:** A four-time all-American at Cornell who played on the U.S. team at the World Games, he is one of the MLL's top defenders and also one of the league's premier ground-ball specialists.

✔ **Brodie Merrill:** The Ontario native and former Georgetown University star who plays for the Toronto Nationals won the league's defensive player of the year award from 2006 through 2008.

✔ **Sean Morris:** The former University of Massachusetts star has stayed close to his old college campus in the professional ranks, playing for the MLL's Boston Cannons and NLL's Boston Blazers.

✔ **Brett Queener:** After a standout 2008 rookie year with the Rochester Rattlers, the former University at Albany star goaltender joined the Toronto Nationals for the 2009 season.

✔ **Paul Rabil:** The former Johns Hopkins midfielder extraordinaire, who has been a professional player for just two years, plays for the Boston Cannons. He has the size, speed, and shooting ability to be a perennial MLL star.

✔ **Jesse Schwartzman:** A two-time Johns Hopkins University all-American and a member of the Denver Outlaws, Schwartzman is one of the league's top goaltenders.

✔ **Alex Smith:** After shattering faceoff marks for the University of Delaware, Smith did the very same thing during the 2008 season for Rochester, winning 249 of them.

✔ **Kyle Sweeney:** A three-time all-American long-stick midfielder for Georgetown, Sweeney has emerged as an MLL mainstay.

✔ **Merrick Thomson:** The Toronto attackman and former University at Albany star had played for the New Jersey Pride, one of the MLL franchises that folded. He was named the MLL's most improved player for 2008.

> ✔ **Joe Walters:** A Jack Turnbull winner as attackman of the year, Atlantic Coast Conference player of the year, and four-time all-American at the University of Maryland, Walters is scoring big for the Toronto Nationals.
>
> ✔ **Jeff Zywicki:** The Ottawa, Ontario, native and former University of Massachusetts star, who plays for Toronto, has emerged as one of the MLL's top scorers.

# Everything You Need to Know about the National Lacrosse League

The National Lacrosse League is an 11-team indoor league that is played during the winter months. Its origins are in Canada, where it still holds the bulk of its popularity. (For more on the NLL's history, see the nearby sidebar "Building on history: Professional lacrosse through the decades.")

In the following sections, we fill you in on the NLL itself, as well as some of the best players to ever play in the league.

## League basics

The National Lacrosse League (NLL) fields 11 teams, divided into two divisions (Eastern and Western):

| *Eastern Division* | *Western Division* |
|---|---|
| Boston Blazers | Calgary Roughnecks |
| Buffalo Bandits | Colorado Mammoth |
| New York Titans | Edmonton Rush |
| Philadelphia Wings | Minnesota Swarm |
| Rochester Knighthawks | San Jose Stealth |
| Toronto Rock | |

BOX LACROSSE

# Building on history: Professional lacrosse through the decades

In 1931, a group of hockey promoters came up with the idea to create a professional box lacrosse league. They wanted their hockey arenas to be in use during the summer, and they wanted to keep their players in shape for hockey during the winter. The Canadian Professional Indoor Lacrosse League formed with four teams — the Montreal Canadians, the Montreal Maroons, the Toronto Maple Leafs, and the Cornwall Colts — using players from their hockey teams. Although the league enjoyed a successful first season, it closed down in 1932, but not before introducing the lacrosse world to a new game. Though several modifications to the field game were made, the indoor lacrosse game was basically the field game played in an enclosed space.

The number of players was reduced from 12 to 7 (and then down to 6 in the 1950s). From the wide-open field game, lacrosse was transformed to a hard-checking game when cross-checking was introduced, and games were played in a restricted boarded area. This new lacrosse came to be known as box lacrosse, or *boxla*.

In 1968, the National Lacrosse Association began play in eight cities in Canada and the United States. The teams were the Montreal Canadians, the Toronto Maple Leafs, the Detroit Olympics, the Peterborough Lakers, the Vancouver Carlings, the Victoria Shamrocks, the New Westminster Salmonbellies, and the Portland (Oregon) Adanacs. This league introduced the 30-second clock to speed up the game, but the league only lasted until 1969.

An earlier incarnation of the National Lacrosse League made a go of it in 1974 and 1975. Again, teams were based in both the United States and Canada, but the league wasn't successful. Over the two years of play, the league fielded teams in Baltimore, Boston, Long Island, Montreal, Philadelphia, Quebec, Rochester, Syracuse, and Toronto.

Then came the National Lacrosse League, which started play in 1987 as the Eagle Pro Box Lacrosse League, with four teams playing a six-game schedule. In 1988, the league upped the schedule to eight games, and in 1989, the league became the Major Indoor Lacrosse League (MILL), with six teams playing an eight-game schedule. Just before the 1998 season, the MILL abandoned its single-entity ownership strategy — that is, teams were operated by the league itself — in favor of franchise ownership by individuals, and renamed the reorganized league the National Lacrosse League.

During a season that runs from early January through late April, each team plays 16 regular-season games: 8 at home and 8 away. Each team plays both home and away games with every other team in its division. Most games are played on Fridays, Saturdays, and Sundays.

While some professional athletes may claim that they play "for the love of the game," this cliché is a way of life for players in the NLL, who are effectively moonlighters in a profession that they love. Because the maximum player salary in the league is $23,000, players have to report to their regular (if not necessarily first-love) jobs during the week.

Eight teams — the top four from both divisions — earn playoff berths. First-round matchups pit each division champ against the fourth-place finisher in their divisions in the semifinals. The number-two and number-three seeds in each division meet in the other semifinal. The higher-seeded teams host the games. The winners of those games then meet in the Eastern and Western division championship finals. The winners of the divisional finals series meet for the NLL Championship Game.

Each NLL team can dress 18 players and 2 goalies for each game; a team carries 23 players on its roster with 3 practice players. The league draws players from all over North America, whether the sources are NCAA field lacrosse or Canadian junior and senior associations. The team rosters are still primarily filled by Canadian players. Approximately 70 percent of players are from Canada. That statistic represents the prevalence of box lacrosse as the preferred style of play in Canada.

Still, the number of NCAA players in the league is moving upward. Some of the NLL's top players had no box lacrosse experience when they entered the league, coming out of NCAA field-lacrosse traditions. These top players (and the U.S. universities where they played) include

- ✔ Jake Bergey (Salisbury State University)
- ✔ Paul Cantabene (Loyola College)
- ✔ Roy Colsey (Syracuse University)
- ✔ Hugh Donovan (Bucknell University)
- ✔ Jamie Hanford (Loyola College)
- ✔ Mike Law (Denver University)
- ✔ Brian Reese (University of Maryland)
- ✔ Mike Regan (Butler University)
- ✔ Tom Ryan (Bowdoin College)
- ✔ Tim Soudan (University of Massachusetts)

# Growing pains

The professional sports world is littered with failed franchises and leagues, from the American Basketball Association of the late 1960s and 1970s (remember the red, white, and blue basketballs?) to the United States Football League of the mid-1980s (at least no red, white, and blue footballs) to the North American Soccer League (which operated from 1967 through 1984 and gave North American soccer fans an opportunity to see the remarkable Pelé in action).

The National Lacrosse League has had its share of disappointments as well (but signs of steady growth exist, including plans to expand even further to perhaps as many as 24 teams). The following franchises have been forced to pull the plug during the league's history:

- Albany Attack, 2000–2004 (relocated to become San Jose Stealth)
- Anaheim Storm, 2004–2005
- Arizona Sting, 2004–2007
- Baltimore Thunder, 1987–1999 (relocated to become Pittsburgh CrosseFire)
- Boston/New England Blazers, 1989–1998
- Charlotte Cobras, 1996
- Chicago Shamrox, 2007–2008
- Columbus Landsharks, 2001–2003 (relocated to become Arizona Sting)
- Detroit Turbos, 1989–1994
- Montreal Express, 2001–2002
- New Jersey Saints, 1987–1988 (relocated to become New York Saints)
- New Jersey Storm, 2002–2003 (relocated to become Anaheim Storm)
- New York Saints, 1989–2003
- Ontario Raiders, 1998 (relocated to become Toronto Rock)
- Ottawa Rebel, 2001–2003
- Pittsburgh Bulls, 1990–1993
- Pittsburgh CrosseFire, 2000 (relocated to become Washington Power)
- Syracuse Smash, 1999–2000 (relocated to become Ottawa Rebel)
- Vancouver Ravens, 2002–2004
- Washington Power, 2001–2002 (relocated to become Colorado Mammoth)
- Washington Wave, 1987–1989

When attending an NLL game, check out each team's roster for players from your hometown (or nearby). Especially if you come from Ontario or British Columbia, or from the northeastern United States, you're likely to find someone on a team to watch.

## The top players

The National Lacrosse League has been filled with phenomenal players, but here's a look at 25 of the best:

- **Anthony Cosmo:** The Boston Blazer is a three-time NLL all-star goaltender who was the league's 2007 goalie of the year. He launched his pro career in 2001 with Toronto.

- **Dan Dawson:** An effective feeder and finisher for the Boston Blazers, Dawson, an Ontario native, combines exceptional stick skills with good size at 6'2" and 220 pounds.

- **Dane Dobbie:** Though small at 5'8" and 160 pounds, the Calgary Roughnecks standout is an accomplished scorer known for his left-handed shooting ability — including strong outside shooting — and a strong, well-rounded game.

- **Colin Doyle:** Known as "Popeye," Doyle has been an NLL star since he joined the league in 1998. Now with the San Jose Stealth, he's the first player in league history to be named playoff MVP three times (in 1999, 2002, and 2005). He was also named league MVP in 2005.

- **Rhys Duch:** Duch, the NLL rookie of the year for the 2009 season, set the league record for points by a first-year player with 89 (with 35 goals and 54 assists). The former Stony Brook University standout helped the San Jose Stealth make the 2009 Western Division final.

- **Scott Evans:** The fifth overall selected in the 2003 NLL draft, he went on to make the league's all-rookie team and continued to star for the Rochester Knighthawks for the next four seasons before suffering a torn anterior cruciate ligament, which sidelined him for the 2009 season.

- **Shawn Evans:** The younger brother of fellow Rochester Knighthawks star Scott Evans and Chicago Shamrocks assistant coach Stephen Evans, Shawn had four goals and six assists in a 15-14 win over the Buffalo Bandits in March 2009.

- **Athan Iannucci:** A first-round draft choice (eighth overall) by the Philadelphia Wings out of Hofstra, Iannucci hasn't disappointed. He broke Gary Gait's NLL record for goals in a season by scoring his 61st in April 2008 in just his second year of pro lacrosse. Earlier in the year, he became the first NLL player in 12 years to be named the league's player of the month for back-to-back months.

- **Tracey Kelusky:** After making his NLL debut in 2000, Kelusky led the Calgary Roughnecks to the 2004 NLL Championship. The next season, he was named MVP of the NLL's all-star game.

✔ **Brian Langtry:** He will always be fondly remember by fans of the Colorado Mammoth as the player who scored the first goal in franchise history — a 13-12 double-overtime victory against the Toronto Rock in 2003. Five years later, the native of Massapequa, New York, enjoyed another unforgettable outing, scoring nine goals to go along with four assists in a loss to the Portland LumberJax. Langtry also plays in the MLL as a member of the Denver Outlaws.

✔ **Ken Montour:** In his third tour of duty with the Buffalo Bandits, Montour was the 2009 NLL goaltender of the year. Named to play in the 2009 NLL all-star game, Montour led the league with a goals-against average of 9.57 (making him the only starting goalie to average fewer than ten goals allowed per game) and a save percentage of 81.3.

✔ **Bruce Murray:** The Colorado Mammoth's two-time all-star leads what is considered to be the premier defense in the NLL.

✔ **Sean Pollock:** Known for scoring clutch goals, the forward joined the Minnesota Swarm during its 2005 expansion season after playing as a rookie in 2004 with the Arizona Sting.

✔ **Casey Powell:** The first overall choice in the 1998 NLL draft, Powell started his pro career with the Rochester Knighthawks. Most recently, the Syracuse University legend has starred for the New York Titans, an expansion team that joined the league in 2006. He earned a spot in the all-star game for the 2007, 2008, and 2009 seasons.

✔ **Lewis Ratcliff:** The Toronto Rock standout, a native of London, England, was named MVP of the 2006 all-star game, when he scored four goals, including the winner with 4 seconds remaining.

✔ **Josh Sanderson:** Known simply as "Shooter," the Calgary Roughneck has been named to the NLL's all-pro team six teams. He shared the NLL's single-season assist mark of 74 with Dan Dawson. Sanderson has a pair of cousins — Phil and Nate — who also play in the NLL.

✔ **Mark Steenhuis:** Despite the fact that he didn't start playing lacrosse until he was 17 years old, Steenhuis has made a major impact. The Buffalo Bandits star is known as much for his bright orange shoes and long, curly, blond hair as he is for his exploits on the field. That's not to say he's not one of the premier players in pro lacrosse, though: He's the first player in league history to be named MVP in multiple all-star games, earning the award in 2004, 2007, and 2009. Plus, he set the NLL single-game mark for points (17) and assists (13) in February 2009.

✔ **John Tavares:** The Toronto native is the NLL's all-time leader in career points, goals, and assists. He has played his entire NLL career with the Buffalo Bandits, since the team's 1992 debut.

- **Mike Thompson:** He teams with Ken Montour (see earlier in this list) to give the Bandits perhaps the best goalie tandem in pro lacrosse. The duo teamed up to lead the Bandits to the 2008 NLL title; Thompson, a native of Akwesasne, Ontario, made 39 saves in the Champion's Cup.

- **Kaleb Toth:** The second overall pick in the 1999 NLL draft, Toth, a Calgary native, has played with the Calgary Roughnecks since 2001. The 6'1", 205-pound right-hander is known for having one of the hardest shots in the league.

- **Daryl Veltman:** The left-handed shooting attackman for the Boston Blazers was the first pick overall in the 2008 NLL draft. Veltman's uncle, Jim Veltman, a former Toronto Rock captain, is the NLL's all-time leader in loose balls.

- **Drew Westervelt:** One of the leading scorers in the NCAA during his career at the University of Maryland–Baltimore County, the Philadelphia Wings attackman earned a spot in the 2009 NLL all-star game.

- **Luke Wiles:** The Toronto Rock forward, who was named to the 2006 NLL all-rookie team, has quickly emerged as one of the league's rising talents. He was given the nickname "The Show" when he was in high school.

- **Shawn Williams:** A six-time NLL all-star, the Rochester Knighthawks forward, a left-hander, is equally adept at scoring and dishing out assists.

- **Jeff Zywicki:** A former University of Massachusetts star, Zywicki scored a combined 88 goals and 160 points for the San Jose Stealth in the 2008 and 2009 seasons. He and Colin Doyle (see earlier in this list) combine to form one of the most potent one-two scoring combos in pro lacrosse.

# Part V
# The Part of Tens

The 5th Wave    By Rich Tennant

"This is great! It even comes with a jar of tooth-black for that 'just checked' look."

# *In this part . . .*

**R**eady to have some fun — and start a few spirited discussions? Then you're ready to dive into this part. We start off with a list of the greatest men's and women's lacrosse players who've played the game. Is it a definitive list? Of course not. Be sure to discuss it with fans and friends and see what other names you think should be added — or even subtracted.

We also tell you the aspects of the game that give you the most reason to get excited about lacrosse. We share some interesting facts surrounding the oldest team sport in North America.

Finally, we end this part with a glossary of lacrosse terms and an appendix of resources you can turn to if you want even more information on lacrosse.

# Chapter 19

# Ten of the Greatest Men's and Women's Lacrosse Players

## In This Chapter

▶ Looking at the legends of the game

▶ Reading up on some others who almost made the cut

**M**ost of these top ten men's and women's players are well-known. Others have made significant accomplishments despite flying under the radar just a bit. All have had major impacts on the game.

## Jen Adams

This southern Australia native is regarded as the best player in the history of women's lacrosse. A 2001 University of Maryland graduate, Adams is a three-time national player of the year, starred on four teams that won national titles, and finished her career as the all-time NCAA leader in career points (445) and assists (178). She also led Australia to its first world title in nearly 20 years when it won the 2005 World Cup. A natural right-hander who also frequently used her left hand, Adams was known for her strong stick skills and deceptive moves to the goal.

## Kelly Amonte Hiller

Amonte Hiller is known today as a championship coach who built the Northwestern women's team into a perennial national champion, but she was equally accomplished as a player. She was a four-time all-American at Maryland, where she is the school's all-time leader in goals (187), assists (132), and points (319). She led the Terrapins to national titles in 1995 and 1996, earning national player of the year honors both seasons. She was named to the All-World team at the 2005 World Cup.

# Jim Brown

Best known for his football exploits, Brown once said, "I'd rather play lacrosse six days a week and football on the seventh." The three-time All-State star for Manhasset High School enjoyed a groundbreaking career at Syracuse University, where he was a two-time all-American. With no professional lacrosse opportunities available, he wound up becoming a National Football League Hall-of-Famer with the Cleveland Browns.

# Roy Colsey

Few players in the game's history have had the combination of Colsey's strength, stamina, and one-on-one scoring ability. A prototypical two-way midfielder, Colsey was a first-team all-American for Syracuse University in 1993, 1994, and 1995, and was Division I midfielder of the year in 1995. He enjoyed similar success at the professional level, as a four-time Major League Lacrosse (MLL) all-star. He also played for four National Lacrosse League (NLL) teams and was a member of the 2006 U.S. men's national team.

# Gary Gait

No matter what the level of lacrosse, Gait made a monumental impact, starting with his days at Syracuse University, where he was a three-time, first-team all-American and two-time NCAA player of the year while starring alongside his twin brother, Paul (see the next section). Gait made an impact right from the start of his NLL career in 1991, when he began setting records and winning awards, including rookie of the year in his first season with the Detroit Turbos. Known as a strong one-on-one player who could score from anywhere on the floor, Gait retired from the NLL in 2005 after being a perennial all-star. He also coached in the league (with the Colorado Mammoth). Gait has also had a distinguished player career in the MLL, including a four-year stint as player/coach of the Baltimore Bayhawks. He is now the head coach of Syracuse University's women's team.

# Paul Gait

Like his identical twin (see the preceding section), Paul was a strong one-on-one player who could score consistently from inside and outside. Just like Gary, Paul enjoyed a star-studded career at Syracuse University and was named the most outstanding player of the 1989 NCAA tournament. He played in the NLL for 12 years and was selected to ten all-star teams. A chronically bad back prevented him from reaching even greater heights, and he retired from competitive play after the 2002 season, a season that saw him earn his first most valuable player award. Paul has won three NLL championships: Detroit in 1991, Philadelphia in 1994, and Rochester in 1997. Out of their 12 years in the league, Paul and Gary played together for seven seasons. And like Gary, Paul is making his mark in coaching: He now guides the NLL's Rochester Knighthawks.

# Tom Marechek

Known for his wizardry with the stick and behind-the-back shots, this British Columbia native has been an impact player on championship teams in the collegiate ranks and in both the MLL and NLL. After forming an incomparable triumvirate at Syracuse University with Gary and Paul Gait, Marechek, who was a four-time all-American for the Orange, started his pro career in 1994.

# Dave Pietramala

There may be no more high-profile position in the lacrosse world than that of head coach of the Johns Hopkins University men's team. Pietramala has thrived in that position for the last ten years, guiding the Blue Jays to national titles and national prominence. That's a role he had already served in to perfection as a player. The 1990 Hopkins graduate distinguished himself as one of the greatest defensemen in the history of the game, earning first-team all-American honors three times. A native of Hicksville, New York, Pietramala was twice named the nation's most outstanding defenseman.

# Casey Powell

After a groundbreaking career at Syracuse University in which he was a four-time all-American (making the first team three times), Powell has starred at the professional level in both the MLL and NLL. The 6'1" attackman, who was a Division I Most Outstanding Player twice, is the oldest of the Powell brothers — a trio that includes former Syracuse stars Ryan and Mikey.

# Mikey Powell

The most highly decorated recruit in Syracuse University history, Powell didn't disappoint. He became the first player ever to win the Turnbull Award (as the top attackman in Division I) four times and was a four-time, first-team all-American at Syracuse. In 2001, he became the first freshman all-American in Syracuse history. As a high school star in Carthage, New York, he shattered state records for points (194) and assists (120) in a season and points in a game (15).

# More Lacrosse Greats

From Jack Turnbull, who starred at Johns Hopkins in the 1930s, to Paul Rabil, who did the same for the Blue Jays through 2008, scores of impact players have helped shape the game. Among the more noteworthy of late, in addition to Rabil, are Jake Berey; Rick Beardsley; Ted Dowling; Kevin Finneran; John Grant, Jr.; Kyle Harrison; Duane Jacobs; Mark Millon; Matt Panetta; Ryan Powell; Alex Smith; John Tavares; Frank Urso; and Jim Veltman.

# Chapter 20

# Ten Reasons to Get Excited about Lacrosse

*In This Chapter*

▶ Focusing on the play

▶ Appreciating the atmosphere

▶ Taking part in the camaraderie

*L*acrosse is an exciting game, played in an exciting atmosphere by men and women and boys and girls who love and respect the game. Here are ten of the many reasons for you to get excited about the fastest game on two feet.

## Lacrosse Is a Magical Game to Watch

You'll be amazed at the wizardry that players work with a stick, especially those at the professional level. From the best stick handlers, you'll see fakes with the stick, behind-the-back shots and passes, pinpoint passes, no-look passes, and perfect simple passes.

They even dazzle their opponents and the game's fans with such plays as the hidden ball trick, in which one player fake-flips the ball to a teammate and hangs onto the ball. This trick still works against even the most experienced players — anyone can be fooled when he's not paying attention to what's happening in the game.

Players and fans alike appreciate all this stick work, because they recognize how long and how hard players have practiced to refine and execute these skills. These players have a seemingly innate ability to perform magic with the stick and ball. Most of us could practice for hours and hours every day and never come close to what these great players can do.

# Lacrosse Is Simple to Play but Hard to Learn

If you've never played the game, but you appreciate lacrosse as a fan, get your hands on a stick and find out how hard and frustrating it is to pass or shoot the ball and hit a target. After a number of futile attempts, you'll have an even greater appreciation for the skills of passing and shooting.

After you've mastered the skills of the game so that you don't have to think too much about what you're doing, but instead can just execute a game plan, lacrosse becomes easy — relatively speaking, of course. All you have to do is shoot the ball and put it into the opposition's goal. And if you don't have the ball, you just try to stop the opposition from scoring. Although you can still learn a variety of methods to achieve those two simple goals, the game always comes down to scoring and preventing your opponent from scoring.

# Lacrosse Is Fast Paced

The tempo of the game makes lacrosse exciting. It offers constant up-and-down action. Players are running around all over the place. The ball is being fired quickly around the playing surface and at the goalie. The goalie gets in the action by passing the ball up the field or floor to a breaking teammate, quickening the pace of the game even more. And offenses use plays such as the pick and roll or the screen to free up players so that they can attack the goal quickly. It's organized chaos.

# Lacrosse Is High Scoring

The ultimate rarity in sports may be a shutout in lacrosse. Shutouts almost never happen. In fact, games that don't reach double figures in goals are the exception rather than the rule. Lacrosse arguably has the perfect amount of scoring — not too much (like, say, basketball) or too little (like, oh, soccer). The average lacrosse game has a good amount of goals to be sure, but not so many that they lose significance.

Because lacrosse is high scoring, a team is almost never out of it — unless the game is a blowout. A string of faceoff wins and quick goals can easily pull a team back into the game. A recent example: Syracuse's 10-9 overtime win over Cornell in the 2009 NCAA Division I men's championship game. The Orange, who fell behind 9-6 with 5:37 remaining in the fourth quarter, tied it on a goal by Kenny Nims with 4.5 seconds left in regulation before winning it on a goal by Cody Jamieson in overtime.

# Lacrosse Has a Great Feel — Literally

One of the real reasons that players love to play lacrosse is because of the tremendous feeling you get just throwing the ball and having it go where you want. Players experience great exhilaration when the ball hits the twine of the net in goal. Male lacrosse players like to deliver a good, clean hit that stops a stick handler from getting by. (Contact is not permitted in the women's game.) Goalies relish the challenge of stopping a player one-on-one. And players take great satisfaction in absorbing a hit yet still rolling past the player who's trying his hardest not to get beaten. These one-on-one battles really get the competitive juices flowing and provide a feeling of satisfaction when you win the battle.

# Lacrosse Is a Fair-Weather Friend

In box lacrosse, the weather is always fine. You go to the arena on a rainy day and walk past soccer players getting drenched in the rain or baseball players shivering from the cold and think to yourself, "Boy, am I glad to be playing inside tonight."

Field lacrosse has its great-weather moments as well. There's not much to beat the atmosphere of the well-played contest on the soft green grass on a crisp, sunny day in spring. The enormous increase in the number of turf surfaces has vastly improved playing conditions on the field during wet weather. In fact, except for when there's thunder or lightning, a field lacrosse game is rarely canceled or postponed.

The college game can be a different story. Because the championships must be concluded by Memorial Day weekend, the season starts in mid to late February, which can be problematic in the Northeast — especially for those colleges that don't have turf fields, which are more equipped when it comes to clearing off snow.

# Lacrosse Is a Community Game

In small towns, lacrosse is a lot like a family gathering: Everyone involved in lacrosse pretty much knows everyone else. And when someone in the lacrosse community needs help, the lacrosse family pulls together and provides it.

Plus, you can relate easily to the players because they're as likely as not to live right next door. For example, MLL and NLL players often work in your community as teachers, police officers, stockbrokers . . . you name it. And they make themselves available to the fans before and after games.

# Lacrosse Welcomes New Players

The lacrosse community is always willing to rally around newcomers, especially when it comes to helping them become involved in the sport. Want to know where to buy a good lacrosse stick? Lacrosse people will point you in the right direction. Want to know how to work on your faceoff technique? Lacrosse people will give you direction and advice on what to do.

# Lacrosse Breeds Respect

The true lacrosse player and fan holds the game in high regard. And this respect transfers to the players on the field or floor. Players respect each other because they know how tough you have to be to play this great game. No lacrosse fan is ever surprised to see players who are bruised up, bleeding, exhausted, sore, and fatigued from the game, still take the time to shake hands with their opponents after the game. Grudges never last long after a lacrosse game — maybe because, if a player hits you hard, you know you'll have a chance to return the favor in the next game.

# Lacrosse Creates Atmosphere

College or pro players can often be seen running around after the game, waving and greeting the fans. They're also very accommodating in signing autographs. The players' accessibility at the higher levels of the game is just one of the many things that makes for an excellent atmosphere.

So, too, does the camaraderie among fans. Did something just happen in the game that you don't quite understand? No problem. If the person next to you in the stands can't help out with an explanation, just ask anyone else within earshot. Even total strangers are like longtime friends when they're watching a lacrosse game.

# Chapter 21

# Ten Interesting Facts about Lacrosse

*In This Chapter*

▶ Finding out about the history and growth of lacrosse

▶ Identifying famous folks involved in the game

▶ Focusing on some of the sport's other intricacies

*L*acrosse is a fun game to play! It has lots of high-paced action, scoring, and exciting plays. Lacrosse is also a fun game to learn about. All sorts of fascinating facts surround the game's history and its growth. In this chapter, we take a look at some of them.

## Lacrosse Is the Oldest Team Sport in North America

Lacrosse has a proud history filled with fascinating facts. For starters, the name *lacrosse* itself came from French-Canadians who started playing the game in the 1800s and thought the stick resembled the crosse of a bishop's crosier, or *la crosse.* The sport itself was first played by Native Americans as a way to train for battle. It was known as *baggataway,* or "little brother of war." Many teams numbered in the hundreds and competitions lasted for days. Participants often were seriously injured during play; some even died.

# "The Father of Lacrosse" Was a Dentist

The first written set of rules for the game was put together in 1867 by the Montreal Lacrosse Club's George Beers, who named the positions and limited the number of players to — at that time — 12 per side. Beers, who was a dentist, is rightfully referred to as the "father of lacrosse." The rules he put in place were quickly employed by the Canada Lacrosse Association, which started using a rubber ball and newly designed sticks. The sport as we know it today was first played in the United States in the mid-1870s, shortly after it was introduced in the United Kingdom.

# The First Women to Play Lacrosse Were Scottish

Women's lacrosse was born in the spring of 1890 when the first game was played at a girls prep school in St. Leonard's, Scotland. In September 1884, the school's headmistress, Louisa Lumsden, traveled to Canada where she witnessed a game between the Montreal Lacrosse Club and the Canghuwaya Indians, who were led by their chief, "White Eagle." Impressed by the beauty and grace of the game, she decided to introduce it at St. Leonard's.

The first girls game in the United States was played in 1926 in Baltimore, Maryland, at the Bryn Mawr School.

# New York University Fielded the First College Lacrosse Team

Collegiate play began in the United States in 1877 when New York University fielded the first men's team. Harvard and Columbia soon had squads of their own. Within a couple of years, Princeton and Yale also launched lacrosse teams. Harvard and Princeton were the most successful teams during the early years of collegiate lacrosse. But the sport experienced growing pains. Despite its success, Princeton dropped the sport because of conflicts with the use of its fields with other sports, but it reinstated the sport in 1921.

# Lacrosse Made Its Olympic Debut in 1904

Lacrosse made its Olympic debut at the 1904 games in St. Louis. It was played again in 1908 in London. Canada won the gold medals both times, and every team medaled, because only three nations — including the United States and England — fielded teams.

Since then lacrosse has been either a demonstration or exhibition sport four times — in 1928, 1932, 1948, and 1984.

# Body Contact Wasn't Allowed in Men's Lacrosse until the 1930s

Neither men's nor women's teams playing lacrosse in the United States used protective equipment when the sport was first introduced. But that all changed in the mid-1930s when men's rules were changed to allow body contact.

# The Mann Cup Was Originally Awarded to Field Lacrosse Teams

Box lacrosse joined the fray around 1932 as an activity that could be played at hockey arenas when they weren't in use. The six-man game quickly caught on and, by the end of the decade, the Mann Cup, which was first awarded in 1910 to Canada's top amateur field team, had been transferred over to box. Though field lacrosse is still played in Canada, box lacrosse is far more popular.

# Lacrosse Didn't Go Pro until the 1980s

Professional lacrosse debuted in the mid-1980s when the six-team Major Indoor Lacrosse League (MILL) began playing box lacrosse in 1987, after evolving from the Eagle Pro Box Lacrosse League, which began a year earlier. The MILL merged into the National Lacrosse League in 1998. The professional outdoor game, Major League Lacrosse, launched in 2001.

# A Super Bowl Coach Has Roots in Lacrosse

Bill Belichick, who has (as of this writing) coached the New England Patriots to three Super Bowl victories, played lacrosse throughout his youth, including stops at Annapolis High School in Maryland; Phillips Academy in Andover, Massachusetts; and Wesleyan University in Middletown, Connecticut.

Belichick, a regular at NCAA lacrosse final fours, was actively involved in bringing the 2008 and 2009 men's championships to Gillette Stadium in Foxborough, Massachusetts. He also coached the sport to three of his children, including son Stephen, who is, as of this writing, a defenseman at Rutgers University in New Jersey.

# Lacrosse Is a Hit in Movies and on TV

Lacrosse has been featured in several popular major motion pictures, including the 1999 box-office smash hit teen comedy, *American Pie*.

The sport is also featured prominently in the new version of the popular TV show *90210,* about teenagers growing up in Beverly Hills, California.

Actor Robby Benson received a Golden Globe nomination for best actor for his 1975 portrayal of 17-year-old prep-school lacrosse player Johnny Gunther, who died of a brain tumor in a made-for-television adaptation of the book *Death Be Not Proud,* by Gunther's father, John.

# Glossary

**all left:** An offensive player who relies on his dominant left hand. The term is often shouted to defenders by coaches and teammates so they can overplay that hand.

**all right:** An offensive player who relies on his dominant right hand. The term is often shouted by coaches and teammates to defenders so they can overplay that hand.

**alley:** The area between the sideline and the side of the restraining box. See *sideline* and *restraining lines*.

**assist:** When a player passes the ball to a teammate who scores a goal.

**attack wings:** The players in women's lacrosse responsible for finishing a fast break.

**attackman:** The primary offensive player. Attackmen generally play behind or right around the goal and provide most of a team's offense. Three attackmen stay in their own offensive half of the field at all times.

**backdoor cut:** When a player cuts behind a defender for a pass.

**behind-the-back pass or shot:** When the stick handler brings the stick up behind his back and passes or shoots the ball. Also called *over-the-shoulder pass or shot*.

**block:** When a defender in women's lacrosse moves into an offensive player's path without providing space for that player to change direction or stop.

**box lacrosse:** The indoor version of the game that bears a strong similarity to hockey and that is played mainly in Canada.

**breakaway:** When a defensive player breaks out from his own end. Also, in box lacrosse, when an offensive player runs out of the bench door and gets behind the new defenders.

**breakout:** When a player gets the ball out of the defensive end either by running it or by passing it up the floor in box lacrosse.

**bull dodge:** An offensive move in which a player leans into a defender while cradling the stick on the opposite side and using his own size and strength to create room to pass or shoot.

**butt end:** The extreme lowest portion of the handle of a stick.

**cage:** See *goal.*

**can opener:** See *poke check.*

**centerman:** The position name for the player who takes the faceoff in indoor lacrosse.

**chest protector:** A heavy padding that protects the goalie's chest.

**circle:** When, on offense in box lacrosse, the team just keeps cutting over and over again from the off-ball side. Also known as the *cycle.*

**clamp:** Probably the most popular faceoff grip, in which the player places the back of the head of the stick over the ball before trying to pull it back toward him.

**clear:** When the ball moves from the defensive half of the field into the offensive zone.

**cornerman:** The player who plays behind the creaseman on the creaseman's side and is usually a good long-ball shooter in box lacrosse.

**cradle:** When a player swings the stick in a sweeping arc, locking the ball into the middle of the pocket and setting it up for a quick shot, dodge, or pass.

**crank shot:** Any hard shot in which the shooter winds up from a set position or fully extends while shooting on the run.

**crease:** A full circle surrounding the goal with a 9-foot radius. An offensive player is not allowed in the crease. In box lacrosse, the crease is the semicircular area in front of the net.

**creaseman:** A position on the offensive floor in box lacrosse. The creaseman plays at the front of any fast break and usually starts his offense low in the corner area. Most of his scoring is around the crease. In field lacrosse, a player who primarily scores from this area is referred to as a "crease attackman."

**critical scoring area:** The 15-meter area located to the front and on each side of the goal and extending 9 meters behind the goal in women's lacrosse.

**cross-check:** A defensive tactic to stop a stick handler from scoring by keeping both hands on the stick, a shoulder's-width apart, and thrusting the arms out to jar or hit the stick handler. This tactic is illegal in field lacrosse.

**crosse:** The stick.

**cut:** When an offensive player breaks toward the goal in an attempt to receive a pass.

**cycle:** See *circle*.

**delayed penalty:** When the defensive team gets a penalty while the offensive team has possession of the ball.

**deuces:** A 2-2-2 offensive set.

**dodge:** An offensive move in which a player jukes a defender.

**double over:** A faceoff method in which both hands face downward (allowing for more power) and are positioned high on the stick. Also known as a *motorcycle grip*.

**draw:** The women's lacrosse equivalent of a faceoff, in which the ball is drawn upward after it's put between the sticks of two standing players. See also *faceoff*.

**draw method:** A method of winning the faceoff by drawing the ball straight back while clamping the ball.

**EMO:** See *extra-man opportunity*.

**extra-man opportunity:** A situation in men's lacrosse when a team has an extra player on the field as a result of a penalty against its opponent. Also known as *man-up opportunity*.

**face dodge:** An offensive move in field lacrosse in which the player runs at a defender and pulls his stick across his face to the opposite side of the body while running by.

**faceoff:** When two players place their sticks back-to-back to fight for possession of the ball by directing the ball to a teammate or by picking it up.

**faceoff X:** The area in the center of the field where faceoffs are held.

**fake:** A move in which an offensive player pretends to go one way and then goes the other way in order to beat his defender. This move can be executed with or without the ball.

**fast break:** When the defensive team gets possession of the ball and quickly tries to get the ball up the field or floor, either by running it or by passing it up to a breaking teammate off the bench.

**feeder:** A player who is adept at setting up teammates with assists. See also *assist.*

**finisher:** A player who is adept at scoring goals off assists. See also *assist.*

**5-minute major penalty:** In indoor lacrosse, given for spearing and butt-ending, both using the stick; kicking; boarding; checking from behind; and fighting.

**free position:** After a minor or major foul in women's lacrosse, all players are required to move 4 meters from the offensive player of the team that drew the penalty. After play resumes, the player may run, shoot, or pass.

**give and go:** When the stick handler passes the ball to a teammate and then cuts to get a return pass back for a scoring opportunity.

**GLE:** See *goal-line extended.*

**goal:** The net on each end of the field in which points are scored when the ball crosses the goal line at the front of the goal. Also called the *cage.*

**goalie:** See *goaltender.*

**goal-line extended:** The area adjacent to the goal line from sideline to sideline.

**goaltender:** The player whose main job is to keep the ball from entering the net. He carries the stick with the biggest pocket. Also known as the *goalie.*

**ground ball:** In field lacrosse, a loose ball that is picked up from the field. See also *loose ball.*

**hand ball:** When a player touches the ball with his hand. The player's team loses possession of the ball when this happens. This rule is the first and oldest in lacrosse.

**hold:** When a player wraps his arms around an opponent or grabs an opponent's sweater to impede his progress. This results in a holding penalty.

**home positions:** Attackers in women's lacrosse with distinct responsibilities for each specific position — first home, second home, and third home.

**hot:** A defenseman is "hot" if he's the number-one slide. After the goaltender or another defensive player yells out, "Who's hot?" the player will call out, "I'm hot."

**jump:** A faceoff method in which the ball is trapped with the face of the head, rather than the back. It's basically a reverse clamp.

**long stick:** A stick held by defensive players. Long sticks can measure up to 72 inches long.

**loose ball:** In box lacrosse, a ball of which neither team has possession. Loose balls are the real battles in lacrosse. Balls can become loose off a shot, off the faceoff, or off a bad pass. See also *ground ball*.

**Major League Lacrosse (MLL):** The professional field lacrosse league, featuring a schedule of games played mainly in the summer. It's comprised of six teams: five in the United States and one in Canada. The MLL's inaugural season was 2001.

**man-down:** When a team gets a penalty and plays only five defensive players against six offensive players. This applies to both box lacrosse and field lacrosse, because in field lacrosse, there are six offensive players and six defensive players (or six-on-six) in the attacking zone at any given time.

**man-short:** When a box lacrosse team gets a penalty and plays only four players against its opponent's five players.

**man-to-man defense:** A type of defense in which each player is responsible for guarding one player on the opposing team.

**man-to-man offense:** A type of offense that is run when the defensive team plays man-to-man defense. See also *man-to-man defense*.

**man-up:** The offense that faces a penalized defense with a one-player advantage.

**man-up opportunity:** See *extra-man opportunity*.

**match penalty:** In box lacrosse, a penalty given when a deliberate intent to injure is involved — examples include biting, spitting, pulling hair, and so on. This is the most severe of all penalties; players are ejected from the game, and a subsequent hearing decides how many games they are suspended from participating in. Players may also be ejected from field lacrosse games for such offenses as fighting and unsportsmanlike conduct.

**middie:** See *midfielder.*

**midfielder:** A player who plays both ends of the field, offensively and defensively. Midfielders are crucial in transition play. They're also called *middies.*

**misconduct penalty:** A 10-minute penalty for unsportsmanlike behavior or becoming the third man in a fight in box lacrosse.

**motion offense:** When all players pass and cut, looking for the open man in the best scoring position.

**motorcycle grip:** See *double over.*

**National Lacrosse League (NLL):** The leading professional box lacrosse league, comprised of 11 teams — 8 in the United States and 3 in Canada. Games are played in the winter. The NLL's inaugural season was 1987.

**neutral zone:** The central area of the lacrosse field or floor that lies between the two restraining lines.

**no-look pass:** An attempted pass in which the passer deliberately does not make eye contact with his intended receiver.

**non-releasable penalty:** A penalty that does not end when the offense scores. This penalty is most frequently seen when a team is penalized for the use of an illegal stick.

**outlet pass:** The pass that triggers the fast break. On the breakout, the goalie makes a short pass to a teammate waiting around one side of the faceoff circle.

**overhand pass or shot:** A pass or shot where the stick is held straight up and down and follows through straight ahead.

**over-the-shoulder pass or shot:** See *behind-the-back pass or shot.*

**penalty:** The result of an infraction of the rules by a player, resulting in the removal of the offending player for a specified time — such as 30 seconds, 1 minute, or 3 minutes in field lacrosse, and 2 minutes, 5 minutes, or 10 minutes in box lacrosse.

**penalty area:** Where the penalized player sits for the duration of a penalty.

**pick and roll:** An offensive play in which a player blocks or interferes with his teammate's defender to free him for a shot or pass. The picker then rolls to the net for a lob pass.

**plunger:** A faceoff method in which the back of the head goes over the ball. The player then lifts his backhand while putting pressure on the front hand, pinching the ball with the head to allow him to control the ball and pull it around his opponent, often leading to a fast break.

**pocket:** The mesh area inside the frame of the lacrosse stick head. The pocket should be about the depth of a lacrosse ball.

**pointman:** The offensive player who plays either on the strong side or at the top and in the middle of the offense in box lacrosse.

**poke check:** A checking technique in which the defender tries to get his stick in between the opponent's stick and his body to pry the ball loose or at least make him take a hand off the stick so that he isn't a threat to score. Also called a *can opener.*

**power play:** In box lacrosse, when a team has more players on the floor than the opposition has, because of a penalty against the opposing team.

**push:** When a player pushes the stick head forward as the top sidewall is facing toward him so that the ball moves forward, behind the opposing faceoff player so it can be scooped up by either the player or a wingman, often leading to a fast break.

**quick stick:** A quick pass or shot in which the player doesn't hesitate after the catch — the ball is in and out of the pocket.

**rake:** A faceoff method in which the player sweeps his stick like a rake to get the ball to one of his wing players.

**restraining lines:** In field lacrosse, the two lines, 35 yards from each end line, that separate the field into thirds. In box lacrosse, they're the lines that run across the width of the floor on either side of the center circle. These lines determine one end of the offensive and defensive zones.

**ride:** A play that aims to prevent the team with the ball from advancing it from its defensive end to the offensive zone.

**rip:** An informal term for a shot on goal, usually one that's hard and accurate.

**screen:** An offensive tactic in which a player blocks his defender from switching to defend the stick handler.

**settled:** A slower, more deliberate pace to a game. (The opposite of *unsettled.*)

**set play:** An offensive strategy that usually involves a series of predetermined moves in which each player has an assigned task.

**shin guards:** Leg guards to protect the goalie's legs and used for stopping shots.

**shooting strings:** The strings stretched from the two widest parts of the head. Most sticks have between one and four shooting strings, and most are either nylon or hockey laces — or a combination of the two. They're used to create a smoother release of the ball from the pocket.

**sidearm pass or shot:** A type of pass or shot in which the arm and stick movement is parallel to the field.

**sideline:** The two lines that run along either side of the field or floor and mark its limits.

**slashing:** A form of defense to stop or dislodge the ball that is more prevalent in the game today because of the use of the plastic stick.

**slashing penalty:** This penalty occurs when a player gets carried away with violent hitting of the stick on another player.

**slide:** When a defenseman leaves the man he is guarding to guard another player.

**slough:** A defensive strategy in which defenders play off their man to move further toward the goal area.

**specialty teams:** A group of players used in specific situations, such as man-down, man-up, and faceoff.

**sphere:** In women's lacrosse, no stick checks in the direction of the head are allowed to break this 7-inch area that surrounds the attacking player's head.

**split dodge:** This offensive move in field lacrosse involves running at a defender and switching the stick from one hand to the other and running by.

**stall:** A strategy in which the offensive team runs time off the clock by passing the ball frequently and not shooting on goal.

**stick check:** When a player tries to check his opponent's stick with his own stick to try to dislodge the ball.

**stick fake:** When the stick handler fakes a pass or shot to get a reaction out of the defender and to try to beat him.

**switch:** When two defenders exchange opponents. A pick is set and the defender on the stick handler gets blocked out of the play, so the back defender calls "switch," and the two defenders exchange opponents.

**Tewaaraton Award:** The national College Player of the Year for men's and women's lacrosse earns this honor.

**3-second rule:** The women's lacrosse rule in which defenders may not stay in the arc for more than 3 seconds without guarding an offensive player.

**30-second rule:** The box lacrosse offensive team must take a shot on net within 30 seconds or lose possession of the ball.

**30-second shot clock:** A clock that counts down the 30 seconds allotted to a box lacrosse offense to attempt a shot. With the exception of the 60-second clock in Major League Lacrosse, the outdoor professional league, field lacrosse has no shot clock.

**transition:** The change a team undergoes when it switches from defense to offense or vice versa.

**trip:** When a player uses his leg to cause an opponent to fall.

**turnover:** When a team loses possession of the ball without taking a shot, such as off a bad pass, when checked off the ball, or when committing a violation.

**two-point goal:** In Major League Lacrosse, the play in which a team is awarded two points for a successful shot from 16 yards or more out.

**underhand pass or shot:** A type of pass or shot in which the arm and stick movement comes from near the field or floor.

**unsettled:** Situations that occur after a team gains possession after a faceoff or turnover and often has a transition opportunity.

**violation:** An action that causes a team to lose possession of the ball.

**warding off:** An act of pushing off the defender with the arm when a player has possession of the ball. If it's called, the stick handler loses possession.

**wings:** The two lines parallel to the sidelines where one player from each team stands during faceoffs. They are 20 yards from the faceoff X.

**wrap check:** This is used when the defender has to go around the player's body to get to his stick.

**zone defense:** In a zone defense, defenders are stationed to defend against an area of the field rather than one specific player, as they do in man-to-man. Lacrosse features two common zone defenses: 2-1-2 and 1-2-2. Teams play zone to change the pace of the game, to hide a weaker defensive player, or to enable players to be in position to break away on a shot.

**zone offense:** An offense that's run when the opposition is playing a zone defense.

# Appendix

# Resources

. . . . . . . . . . . . . . . . . . . . . . . . . . . . . . . . . . . . . . . . . . . . . . . . . . .

**C**ombine the growing interest in lacrosse at all levels with the growth of the Internet, and what do you get? More sources of information for coverage of the sport than ever before. But the Web is not the only place where lacrosse's increasing popularity is evident. In 2009, a record 63 collegiate men's and women's games were televised nationally on CBS College Sports and ESPN's family of networks.

All this is good news if you're looking for more information on lacrosse. In this appendix, we provide all kinds of resources you can turn to when you've read every last syllable in this book and still want more lacrosse.

## *Magazines*

*Inside Lacrosse:* Founded in 1996, *Inside Lacrosse* magazine has quickly become a staple in the lacrosse world. Known for its vibrant design, action-packed color photos, and glossy pages, it's simply a must-read for anyone devoted to the sport. *Inside Lacrosse* publishes 11 issues per year, including popular issues on recruiting and previewing the collegiate season. Bob Carpenter, a former Duke University player who founded the company, serves as publisher. John Jiloty, a Syracuse University graduate, is vice president and editor-in-chief. As of this writing, subscriptions cost $34.95 for one year in the United States ($44 in Canada and Mexico, $88 elsewhere). To order, go to www.insidelacrosse.com or call 866-724-7334.

*Lacrosse Magazine:* Published by US Lacrosse, the magazine is distributed to the organization's more than 300,000 members, with 12 issues published per year. Useful standing features include a camp directory. Edited by Paul Krome, the magazine is the most tradition-rich lacrosse magazine on the market — it's been published for more than 30 years. To receive the magazine, you need to join US Lacrosse, which, as of this writing, costs $50 for adults, $35 for high school students, and $25 for kids. To join, go to www.uslacrosse.com/membership or call 410-235-6882, ext. 102.

# *Web Sites*

**Canadian Lacrosse Association** (www.lacrosse.ca): The governing body for lacrosse in Canada, the origins of which date back to 1925, oversees tournaments for both men's and women's field and box lacrosse. Content is available in both English and French.

**e-Lacrosse** (www.e-lacrosse.com): Timely news, features, and videos make this site one worth visiting.

**Inside Lacrosse** (www.insidelacrosse.com): A popular Web site has helped Inside Lacrosse, an ESPN affiliate, become the sport's leading media presence. The site has strong content, including video highlights and interviews, staff blogs, and a thriving forum with threads on the pro and college games, as well as women's and high school lacrosse and recruiting, coaching, officiating, and training.

**The Intercollegiate Women's Lacrosse Coaches Association** (www.iwlca.org): This site includes news and information about women's lacrosse.

*Lacrosse Magazine* (www.laxmagazine.com): In addition to coverage of pro, college, and high school lacrosse, the site also provides daily news updates on the sport. It lacks the reader interaction found in other leading Web sites.

**LaxLessons.com** (www.laxlessons.com): The newly designed site, which originally debuted in 2002, was relaunched in March 2009, and now features up-to-date and useful instructional information for coaches, including virtual practice plans and playbooks, as well as news and information for players and fans, with video highlights and interviews. (Full disclosure: The coauthor of this book, Joe Lombardi, provides editorial and video content for the site.)

**LaxLinks.com** (www.laxlinks.com): As the name suggests, this site offers links aplenty — including for camps, clubs, colleges, pros, high schools, and youth leagues.

**LaxPower** (www.laxpower.com): If you're looking for glitz and glamour, this isn't the place for you. On the other hand, if in-depth and comprehensive content is what you're after, you've come to the right place. LaxPower is a portal for information on the college and high school ranks. It also has live-action game reports and forums on every lacrosse-related topic under the sun. Its database of recruiting commitments for current high school players is especially noteworthy.

**LaxTips.com** (www.laxtips.com): Players, coaches, officials, and even trainers offer useful info and pointers on this site.

**Major League Lacrosse (www.majorleaguelacrosse.com):** News, statistics, team info — you name it. You can find whatever you need to know about the MLL right here.

**Men's Collegiate Lacrosse Association (www.mcla.us):** The official Web site of the Men's Collegiate Lacrosse Association includes scores, stats, and standings for the men's club teams in the United States.

**National Lacrosse League (www.nll.com):** The National Lacrosse League's official Web site has the latest news and all related info on the league.

**United States Intercollegiate Lacrosse Association (www.usila.org):** The official site of the United State Intercollegiate Lacrosse Association includes news, awards, and coaches' polls.

**US Lacrosse (www.uslacrosse.org):** US Lacrosse is the national governing body for men's and women's lacrosse. You can find membership and program information on the US Lacrosse Web site.

# *Television*

**CBS College Sports:** The network broadcasts games on a weekly basis during the regular season and playoffs. It broadcasts the Division II and Division III men's championship games, and the Division I women's national title game, which are played over Memorial Day weekend.

**ESPN:** ESPN broadcasts the Division I men's championship game on Memorial Day Weekend. Dave Ryan handles the play-by-play and former Johns Hopkins goaltender Quint Kessenich is analyst.

**ESPN2:** The network broadcasts Major League Lacrosse games. In addition, it airs the NCAA Division I men's semifinals each Saturday of Memorial Day weekend as well as *Inside Lacrosse TV,* biannual hour-long shows that precede and follow the men's college lacrosse season.

**ESPNU:** The ESPN companion network that focuses on college sports broadcasts games on a weekly basis during the regular season and playoffs. In addition, it also broadcasts selected other lacrosse games, such as the 2009 Under Armour All-America Senior Classic, featuring 44 of the nation's top high school seniors, from Towson University in Maryland.

**Altitude:** The regional sports and entertainment network broadcasts select Colorado Mammoth NLL games each season.

**Comcast SportsNet:** The cable network broadcasts select Philadelphia Wings NLL games each season.

**Fox Sports Net Bay Area, Comcast SportsNet West:** The cable networks broadcast select San Jose Stealth NLL games each season.

**KSTC-TV:** The Minneapolis–St. Paul ABC affiliate broadcasts select Minnesota Swarm NLL games each season.

**MSG Network:** A weekly game of the week is shown on the New York–based MSG Network. Jimmy Cavallo is the play-by-play announcer. Former Syracuse University star Paul Carcaterra provides the color commentary. In addition, MSG broadcasts a weekly lacrosse highlight show during the season called *The Lax Report,* hosted by Mike Quick. In the fall of 2009, MSG launched a new channel, MSG Varsity, which airs a weekly package of games and also has a daily high school sports highlight show. (Full disclosure: The co-author of this book, Joe Lombardi, is a member of the MSG Varsity staff.)

**Rogers Sportsnet:** The Ontario-based cable network broadcasts select Toronto Rock NLL games each season.

**Shaw TV:** The Western Canada network airs several Calgary Roughnecks NLL games each season.

**Time Warner SportsNet:** The cable network broadcasts select Rochester Nighthawks NLL games each season.

**TSN2:** The Canadian network broadcasts select Toronto Nationals MLL games.

**WMAR-TV:** The Baltimore-based ABC affiliate broadcasts roughly 12 collegiate games each season.

# *Organizations*

**US Lacrosse:** Founded in 1998 when several existing organizations merged, the Baltimore, Maryland–based organization serves as the sport's governing body. Its headquarters are located alongside the Lacrosse Museum and National Hall of Fame. Its mission is to promote the responsible development of the game. US Lacrosse has more than 300,000 members in 62 chapters located in 38 states. To find out more about US Lacrosse, go to www.uslacrosse.org.

**Canadian Lacrosse Association:** The Ottawa-based association is the governing body for box lacrosse as well as men's and women's field lacrosse in Canada. For more on the Canadian Lacrosse Association, go to www. lacrosse.ca.

**Intercollegiate Women's Lacrosse Coaches Association:** This organization assists coaches at all levels of women's lacrosse. For more information, go to www.iwlca.org.

**United States Intercollegiate Lacrosse Association:** Founded in 1885, the USILA is an association of the member institutions that field varsity lacrosse programs at all levels of National Collegiate Athletic Association competition: Divisions I, II, and III. For more information on the USILA, go to www.usila.org.

**Federation of International Lacrosse:** Established in 2008, when the men's and women's international lacrosse organizations merged, the federation oversees such events as the men's and women's Under-19 World Lacrosse Championships, the World Indoor Championship, the Women's Lacrosse World Cup, and the Men's World Lacrosse Championship. For more information on the FIL, go to http://76.163.49.139/index.htm.

# Index

................................................................

## • *Numerics* •

1-2-2 formation, 213, 241
1-3-2 formation, 146, 212
1-4-1 formation, 212
1-4-1 set play, 162–163
1-handed cradle (field lacrosse), 67
1-on-0 drills, 75, 83
1-on-1, going. *See* beating a defender
1-on-1 drills
  beating a defender, 86–87
  bump, 84
  charging defender, 85
  circle (protecting the ball in the stick), 84
  defending against stick handler, 110–111
  defending other offensive players, 112–113
  equalize pressure, 85
  game, 87
  live half-field, 86–87
  man-in-the-middle, 85
  off the bench, 87
  offense from stationary start with
    a cross-field pass, 86
  offensive-move progression, 86
  taking a check, 84–85
1-on-2 circle drill, 84
2-1-2 formation, 169, 241
2-2-2 formation, 146, 212
2-2-2 set play, 164, 166
2-3-1 formation, 212, 241
2-line shooting drills, 98–99
2-minute penalties, 60–61
2-on-0 drills, 76–77, 83–84, 100
2-on-1 drills, 111–112, 155, 182
2-on-2 screen on the ball drill, 148
2-point goal, 305
2-way midfielders, 30
3-3 camouflage play, 164, 166
3-3 set with a screen, 162, 163
3-on-2 defensive drills, 156
3-on-3 offense drills (box lacrosse), 148
3-second rule, 44, 229, 305
4-on-4 defensive drills, 156

5-minute penalties, 61, 300
5-on-0 run, pass, and shoot drill, 182
5-on-5 pointman double drill, 148
5-second count, 45, 58, 59
6-on-5 situation, 167
10-minute penalties, 61
10-second count, 46
20-second count, 45, 58, 59
30-second rule, 305
30-second shot clock, 53, 305
60-second shot clock, 46, 53

## • *A* •

abdomen and groin stretches, 176
Adams, Jen (player), 285
aggression. *See also* checking
  attacking in offense, 144–145
  attitude for defense, 152
  defensive, 105
  double-teaming, 102, 243–244
  in man-to-man defense, 232, 236–237
  in picking up ground balls, 134
  pressuring the stick handler, 150–151,
    236, 237, 240, 243–244
  in rides, 136
  style of play, 198
  in zone offense, 218
agility and quickness. *See also* footwork
  defensemen needing, 30
  defensive drills for, 184–185
  drills, 109
  offensive drills for, 183–184
Air Gate, 45
all left, 297
all right, 297
alley, 297
Altitude network, 260, 309
Amonte Hiller, Kelly (player), 285
angle goalies, 257
angle saves, 42, 121, 124
arc, 3-second rule for, 44, 229, 305
arm guards, 23

assist, 297
attack positions (women's lacrosse), 29
attack wings (women's lacrosse), 142, 297
attackmen (field lacrosse)
  crease attackmen, 140
  defined, 297
  in fast break, 227
  feeders, 29, 140, 300
  finishers, 29, 140, 300
  overview, 29
  role of, 140
  traits of, 139–140
attitude
  for defense, 152
  for relaxing, 190
  "team comes first," 204
automatics, 94

• *B* •

back over, 58, 59
back stretches, 174
backdoor cut, 297
ball, about, 10, 18
ball handling. *See* stick handling
ball-side defending, 108
Bartomioli, Michael (player), 126
basketball, lacrosse compared to, 250,
    251–253
Beardsley, Ric (player), 110, 153, 154
beating a defender
  by cornermen, 34
  drills, 86–87
  keys to, 80
  by pointman, 36
  shooting after, 88
Beers, George (father of lacrosse),
    18, 51, 294
beginners, tips for, 66, 67, 76. *See also* kids
behind-the-back pass or shot, 74, 297
Belichick, Bill (player), 296
bench play, 167
block (women's lacrosse), 297
boarding, 61
Bocklet, Matt (player), 274
body fakes, 81, 88
body position. *See* stance or body position
bombing, 92
bounce passes, 74, 77

box lacrosse. *See also* field lacrosse;
    women's lacrosse
  30-second rule, 305
  in box lacrosse, 238, 239, 240
  broadcast games, 260
  closing out, 240
  defensive drills, 156
  defined, 297
  double-teaming in, 244
  faceoffs in, 130
  fast break in, 228
  gloves for, 23
  goal size, 10–11
  goalie penalties in, 48
  goaltenders in, 31, 36, 118
  hockey compared to, 35, 249–251
  icon indicating information about, 5
  as indoor game, 2
  loose balls in, 133
  maintaining floor position, 155
  man-short defense in, 159, 169, 301
  man-to-man defense in, 238, 239, 240
  match penalty, 301
  minor-level, 267–269
  number of players, 10, 52
  offense, 141
  offensive formations, 213
  overview, 10–11
  penalties, 60–61
  players, 32–37
  playing surface layout, 48–50
  playing surface size, 10, 48–49
  playing the proper side of the floor, 33
  pocket width for, 19
  positioning in, 105
  power plays, 159, 161, 165, 167
  set plays in, 165, 167, 219, 226
  stick length for, 20
  times for penalties, 58, 157
  zone defense in, 241, 242, 244
box-and-one defense, 168
Boyle, Ryan (player), 274
Brameier, Jeff (coach), 198
brawl situations, 56
breakaways, 97, 118, 122, 297
breakout, 297
breathing, deep, 190
British bulldog game, 85
Brooks, Steven (player), 274

Brown, Jim (player), 286
bull dodge, 81, 82, 298
bull-oriented man-to-man defense, 233–234
butt end, 66, 298
butt-ending, 61

# • C •

can opener (poke check), 105, 107, 303
Canadian Lacrosse Association, 308, 311
Carcaterra, Paul (TV analyst), 94, 142
catching
  basics of, 38
  body position for, 69
  drills, 76–78, 83–84
  dropping due to thinking ahead, 74
  giving on the catch, 70, 71, 75
  grip for beginners, 66
  hand-thrown balls for practice, 76
  moving around after, 73
  swapping hands after, 70
  in women's lacrosse, 70
CBS College Sports network, 261, 309
centerman, 298
centers, 35
change area (box lacrosse), 49
charging, 61
checking. *See also* taking a check
  from behind, 60
  boarding, 61
  cross-checking, 41, 47, 60, 106, 240, 299
  field lacrosse rules for, 47
  free-hand check, 58, 59
  goaltenders, rules for, 48
  illegal body check, 60
  introduction of, 295
  large cradle for taking a check, 68, 69
  in man-to-man defense, 236
  not allowed in women's lacrosse, 10, 12, 28, 47
  poke check, 105, 107, 303
  positioning during, 104
  relaxing during, 82
  sphere (women's lacrosse), 304
  stick-checking, 41, 104, 105, 304
  tripping, 59, 305
  use of hands in, 107
  wraparound check, 105, 151, 305
chest protector, 298

children. *See* kids
Cinosky, Joe (player), 274
circle, 298
clamp grip, 129, 298
clears, 125, 137–138, 151
close defensemen (field lacrosse), 30, 227
close-in shots, 96–97, 99–100
closing out (box lacrosse), 240
coaching
  building team unity, 203–204
  building your team, 199–200
  challenges of, 15
  defensive coach, 52
  determining the style of play, 197–198, 207
  game plan development, 200–201
  giving your team the edge, 204–205
  head coach, 52
  informing parents of equipment needed, 25
  to kids, 201–203
  offensive coach, 52
  overview, 15
  understanding your opponent, 200
coaching defense
  man-to-man defense, 232, 233–240
  overview, 201
  playing systems, 231–232
  tips for, 232
  in women's lacrosse, 244–246
  zone defense, 240–242
coaching offense
  executing your system, 213–214
  fast-break offense, 227–228
  formations, 212–213
  man-to-man offense, 219–220, 225–226
  motion offense, 221–225
  overview, 201
  playing systems, 208–211
  playing to your strengths, 211–212
  set plays, 225–226
  in women's lacrosse, 228–230
  zone offense, 214–219
cocking the stick, 93
college lacrosse
  broadcast games, 260–261
  first team, 294
  first women's game, 11
  overview, 265–266

college lacrosse *(continued)*
  times for halves (women), 44
  times for quarters (men), 44
  tradition-rich programs, 267
Colsey, Roy (player), 286
combination man-to-man defense, 234
Comcast SportsNet, 260, 310
Comcast SportsNet West, 310
communication
  defensive, 30, 101–102, 116, 149–150
  by goaltenders, 117, 122–123
  in man-to-man defense, 235
  in zone defense, 242
community, 253, 291
conditioning. *See* physical conditioning
contact. *See* checking
continuity zone offense (box lacrosse), 219
cornermen (box lacrosse), 34–35, 141, 298
Cosmo, Anthony (player), 280
cradling
  for beginners, 67
  defined, 38, 66, 298
  goals of, 38
  grip for, 67
  individual drills, 82
  large cradle, 68, 69
  medium cradle, 67, 68
  one-handed (field lacrosse), 67
  small cradle, 67, 68
  in women's lacrosse, 67
crank shot, 298
crease area
  in box lacrosse versus field lacrosse, 49
  defined, 298
  goaltender outside, 48
  use by creasemen, 33
crease attackmen, 140
crease pass and shoot play, 161–162
crease violation, 44–45, 58, 59
creasemen (box lacrosse), 33–34, 141, 298
critical scoring area, 298
cross-checking
  defined, 47, 60, 299
  in man-to-man defense, 240
  penalties for, 47
  stick-checking versus, 41
  technique for, 106
crosse. *See* sticks

cuts. *See also* moving without the ball
  defensive communication about, 102
  defined, 299
  mistakes in, 144
cutter play, 165
cycle, 298

**• D •**

Dalton, Brian (player), 135
Danowski, Matt (player), 274
Dawson, Dan (player), 280
Deane, Jake (player), 274
deep breathing, 190
defense. *See also* checking
  attitude for, 152
  box-and-one, 168
  communication for, 149–150
  cornermen on, 35
  creasemen on, 33
  diamond man-short formation, 168, 169
  drills, 155–156, 170
  establishing your position, 40
  five-man zone, 159
  force of personalities in, 149
  forcing the ball, 152–153
  importance of, 231
  maintaining floor position, 155
  man-down, 168–169, 170
  man-to-man, 232, 233–240, 301
  man-up, 167
  mistakes in, 150
  against picks, 153–154
  players, 37
  pressuring the stick handler, 150–151
  ride, 303
  slashing, 105, 304
  sliding, 151, 304
  slough, 304
  stick length for, 20
  switching on, 153–154, 305
  watching lacrosse, 255–256
  in women's lacrosse, 244–246
  zone, 232, 240–244, 306
defense positions (women's lacrosse), 29
defensemen (field lacrosse), 30, 227
defensive clear-out, 45
defensive coach's role, 52

defensive players
  keys for, 40–41
  overview, 37
defensive skills. *See also* goaltending
  ball-side, 108
  coaching, 201
  communication, 101–102
  defending the field of play, 105, 107
  drills, 109–113, 184–185
  footwork, 102–103
  off-ball-side, 107–108
  overview, 13
  playing hard with heart, 105
  playing with your head, 103–104
  positioning, 104–105, 107–108
  against stick handler, 101–107, 110–112
  stopping the player, 107–108
delayed penalty, 57, 299
deliberate/ball control style of play, 198
deuces, 299
diagonal pass to crease play, 165
diagonal play, 165
diamond man-short formation, 168, 169
diet, 188
disallowed goal signal, 57
dive, 45
Dixon, Kyle (player), 274
Dobbie, Dane (player), 280
dodging
  bull dodge, 81, 298
  defined, 299
  face dodge, 80, 299
  keys to, 79
  in motion offense, 222
  question-mark dodge, 81
  roll dodge, 80
  split dodge, 80, 304
double over grip, 129, 299
double-teaming, 102, 243–244
Dougherty, Brian "Doc" (player), 274
down screen play, 226
Doyle, Colin (player), 280
draw method, 299
draws (women's lacrosse), 28, 46, 53, 127,
    299. *See also* faceoffs
drills
  beating a defender, 86–87
  conditioning, 181–183

cradling, individual, 83
defensive skills, 109–113
games, 85, 87, 99
for goaltenders, 120, 121–122, 124
improving quickness and agility, 183–185
man-down, 170
passing, 75
passing, individual, 75
passing, partner, 76–77
passing, team, 77–78
picking up ground balls, 134
protecting the ball in the stick, 84
shooting, close-in, 99–100
shooting, guidelines for goalies, 100
shooting, long, 98–99
stick-handling with partner, 83–84
taking a check, 84–85
team defense (box lacrosse), 156
team defense (field lacrosse), 155–156
team offense (box lacrosse), 148
team offense (field lacrosse), 146–147
drinking fluids, 188
drop step, 102
Duch, Rhys (player), 280

# • E •

eating and drinking, 188
ejection of players, 59, 301
e-Lacrosse site, 308
elbow pads, 23
emotional control, 192
endurance training, 178–179, 180
energizing yourself for a game, 193–194
equipment
  arm guards, 23
  ball, 10, 18
  elbow pads, 23
  for field lacrosse, 22
  fully-equipped player, illustrated, 21
  gloves, 23
  for goaltenders, 22
  helmets, 24
  importance of, 21
  league requirements for, 25
  "less is more" philosophy, 21
  mouth guards, 24
  rib or kidney pads, 23

equipment *(continued)*
  running shoes, 24
  shoulder pads, 23
  sticks, 12, 18–20
  for women's lacrosse, 22
  for youth levels, 24–25
ESPN, ESPN2, and ESPNU networks, 260, 309
Evans, Scott (player), 280
Evans, Shawn (player), 280
extra-man opportunities (EMOs)
  aligning players on, 159
  in box lacrosse, 159, 161, 165, 167, 169
  called man-up (field lacrosse), 14, 59, 301
  called power plays (box lacrosse),
    14, 59, 303
  defined, 14, 299
  five-man zone defense, 159
  fundamental principles for, 159–160
  man-down defense, 168–169
  man-down drills, 170
  man-down offense, 170
  man-up defense, 167
  man-up offense, 157–167
  man-up set plays, 160–166
  passing in, 158, 160
  patience for, 157, 158
  release of penalized players, 59
  shooting in, 159, 160, 161
  six-on-five situation, 167
  specialty teams for, 14, 157, 304
  success rate for, 47
  traits of good players for, 159
  watching lacrosse, 255

**• F •**

face dodge, 80, 299
face off, get off (FOGOs), 126
faceoff X, 125, 126, 299
faceoffs. *See also* draws (women's lacrosse)
  body position for, 126, 128
  in box lacrosse, 130
  clamp grip, 129, 298
  defined, 299
  described, 46, 126
  double over grip, 129, 299
  draw method, 299

goal of, 129
jump method, 129, 301
in NLL, 130
plunger method, 129, 303
push method, 129
rake method, 129, 303
signal for, 57
specialty players for, 126
sticks for, 128
techniques for, 128–129, 130–131
times when held, 126
watching lacrosse, 257
wings' role in, 128
faking. *See also* faking shots
  body fakes, 81, 88
  defined, 300
  drills, 183
  inside-fake move, 81
  outside-fake move, 81
  passes, close-in, 96
  passes, practicing, 76
  split dodge for, 80
  stick fake, 92, 304
faking shots
  1-on-0 drill, 83
  after beating a defender, 88
  fakes for different situations, 96
  freezing the defender, 81
  goaltender's protection against, 122
  long shots, 92
  practicing, 76
fans, 16, 258. *See also* watching lacrosse
fast break, 208, 218, 227–228, 300
fast pace of lacrosse, 290
Federation of International Lacrosse, 311
feeders (field lacrosse), 29, 140, 300
field. *See* playing surface
field lacrosse. *See also* box lacrosse;
    women's lacrosse
  cross-check illegal in, 106, 299
  defensive clear-out, 45
  as either indoor or outdoor game, 2
  equipment for, 22
  five-second count, 45
  goal size, 10, 44
  goalie penalties in, 48
  goaltenders in, 31–32, 118
  number of players, 10, 27, 51

offensive formations, 212–213
origins of, 11, 293
overview, 10
penalties, 46–48
personal fouls, 59–60
players, 27–32
playing surface layout, 44–45
playing surface size, 10, 44
pocket width for, 19
positioning in, 104
restraining lines, 303
split field in, 27
stick length for, 20
substituting players, 46
ten-second count, 46
times for halves (women), 44
times for penalties, 58, 157
times for quarters (men), 44
field vision, 40
fighting, 56, 61
finishers (field lacrosse), 29, 300
five-minute penalties, 61, 300
5-on-0 run, pass, and shoot drill, 182
5-on-5 pointman double drill, 148
five-second count, 45, 58, 59
floor. *See* playing surface
focusing on the game, 192–193
FOGOs (face off, get off), 126
follow-through in shooting, 94
footwork
  defensemen needing skills in, 30
  defensive, 102–103, 106
  drills for agility, 109, 184
  drop step, 102
  for faceoffs, 131
  hop-step for shooting, 93
  shuffle step, 103, 106
  slide steps, 109
  for stick-checking, 41
  in women's lacrosse defense, 244–245
forcing the ball, 152–153
Ford, Spencer (player), 274
4-on-4 defensive drills, 156
Fox Sports Net Bay Area, 310
free position shot (women's lacrosse), 47, 59, 300
free-hand check, 58, 59

• *G* •

Gait, Gary (player), 45, 286
Gait, Paul (player), 287
game plan development, 200–201
games (drills), 85, 87, 99
give-and-go play, 224, 230, 239–240, 300
gloves, 23
go play, 81
goal disallowed signal, 57
goal scored signal, 57
goal-crease violation, 44–45, 58, 59
goal-line extended (GLE), 300
goals, about, 10–11, 44, 300
goals, setting, 189
goaltenders (goalies)
  angle goalies, 257
  in box lacrosse, 31, 36, 118
  clears controlled by, 138
  defined, 300
  equipment for, 22
  in field lacrosse, 31–32, 118
  goals scored by, 124
  penalties assessed on, 47, 48
  playing catch with, 94
  reflex goalies, 91, 257
  rules for checking, 48
  shooting drill guidelines for, 100
  stick head for, 19
  traits of, 14, 32, 36, 115–117
  warming up, 120
goaltending
  angle saves, 42, 121, 124
  anticipating shots, 123
  against breakaways, 122
  challenging the shooter, 120–122
  communicating with the defense, 117, 122–123
  drills, 120, 121–122, 124
  in field lacrosse, 42
  following the ball, 119–120
  keys for, 41–42
  protecting against fakes, 122
  ready stance for, 42, 118–119
  reflex saves, 42, 121, 123
  skills needed for, 115–117
  starting the offense, 42, 123–124, 257

goaltending *(continued)*
  staying centered, 119
  stick saves, 42, 120
  watching lacrosse, 256–257
going back door, 230
going one-on-one. *See* beating a defender
Grant, John, Jr. (player), 274
Greer, Zack (player), 274
grip
  for beginners, 66
  for cradling, 67
  for passing, 72
  for shooting, 66
  for stick handling, 66
  swapping hands after catching, 70
  for taking a check, 79
  top-arm hand for, 66
groin and abdomen stretches, 176
ground balls
  in box lacrosse, 133, 141
  defined, 132, 300
  drills, 134
  importance of, 132
  options after picking up, 74, 135
  situations resulting in, 133
  techniques for picking up, 133–135
  watching lacrosse, 256

### • H •

hamstring and quad stretches, 175–176
hand ball, 58, 59, 300
head coach's role, 52
heart, playing with, 105
helmets, 24
high play, 167
high school lacrosse, 44, 261, 263–264
high-sticking, 60
hockey, lacrosse compared to, 35, 249–251
holding, 60, 300
hole, defending, 104
home positions (women's lacrosse),
    142, 301
hooking, 60
hop-step for shooting, 93
hot buttons, knowing yours, 192
hot defenseman, 301
Huntley, Kevin (player), 275
hydration, 188

### • I •

Iannucci, Athan (player), 280
illegal body check, 60
illegal stick, 20, 47, 60
Indian pickup, 134
individual drills, 75, 82, 99
indoor lacrosse, 2. *See also* box lacrosse
injuries, 173, 258
*Inside Lacrosse* magazine, 307
Inside Lacrosse site, 308
inside spin, 82, 88
inside-fake move, 81
inside-slide move, 82, 88
Intercollegiate Women's Lacrosse Coaches
    Association, 308, 311
interference, 60
Internet resources
  lacrosse sites, 308–309
  magazine sites, 307
  organizations, 310–311
interval training, 180
invert formation, 146

### • J •

jump method, 129, 301
junior sticks, 25

### • K •

Kelusky, Tracey (player), 280
kidney or rib pads, 23
kids
  being a good teacher to, 202
  catching practice for beginners, 76
  coaching, 201–203
  college lacrosse, 44, 260–261, 265–267
  cradling for beginners, 67
  equipment for, 24–25
  fostering commitment, 203
  grip for beginners, 66
  ground balls' importance in, 132
  high school lacrosse, 44, 261, 263–264
  instilling confidence in, 202
  minor-level box lacrosse, 267–269
  patience with, 202
KSTC-TV, 260, 310

# • L •

*Lacrosse Magazine,* 307, 308
Langtry, Brian (player), 281
large cradle, 68, 69
LaxLessons.com, 308
LaxLinks.com, 308
LaxPower site, 308
LaxTips.com, 308
learning to play, reasons for, 290, 291, 292
leg stretches, 175
Leveille, Kevin (player), 275
Lindsay, Sean (player), 275
line (box lacrosse), 32
line changes, 52
Lodewick, Adam (defensive coordinator), 104, 150
long shots, 92–95, 98–99, 220
long stick, 301
long-stick midfielders, 30
long-term outcome goals, 189
loose ball. *See* ground balls
low play, 167

# • M •

magazines, 307
Major League Lacrosse (MLL)
  basics, 272–273
  defined, 301
  genesis of, 271, 272
  top players, 273–276
  Web site, 309
man-down. *See also* extra-man opportunities (EMOs)
  defense, 168–169, 170
  defined, 301
  drills, 170
  offense, 170
  success rate for, 47
Mann Cup, 295
man-oriented man-to-man defense, 234
man-short (box lacrosse), 301. *See also* extra-man opportunities (EMOs)
man-to-man defense
  as aggressive, 232, 236–237
  applying pressure, 236–237, 240
  in box lacrosse, 240
  bull-oriented, 233–234
  combination, 234
  communication in, 235
  defined, 232, 301
  against give-and-go play, 239–240
  initiating offense from, 235
  man-oriented, 234
  against motion offense, 239
  against odd-man break, 240
  against off-ball pick-and-roll, 238
  against player looking for a pass, 239
  rotations in box lacrosse, 238, 239
  sliding in, 151, 238, 304
  staying alert, 237
man-to-man offense, 219–220, 301. *See also* motion offense
man-up (field lacrosse). *See* extra-man opportunities (EMOs)
Marechek, Tom (player), 287
match penalty (box lacrosse), 301
McClay, Ryan (player), 275
medium cradle, 67, 68
Men's Collegiate Lacrosse Association, 309
mental preparation
  checklist for, 188–189
  emotional control, 192
  energizing yourself for a game, 193–194
  focusing on the game, 192–193
  positive self-talk for, 191–192
  pre-game routine for, 194
  pushing for mental toughness, 173
  relaxing, 189–190
  setting goals, 189
  staying in the zone, 172
  visualization for, 191
Merrill, Brodie (player), 275
middle play, 165
midfielders (field lacrosse)
  defined, 302
  in fast break, 227
  long-stick, 30
  overview, 29–30
  role of, 140
  traits of, 140
  two-way, 30
minor-level box lacrosse, 267–269
misconduct penalty, 302
MLL. *See* Major League Lacrosse
Montour, Ken (player), 281
Morris, Sean (player), 275

motion offense
  defined, 302
  give-and-go play, 224
  man-to-man, 221–226
  man-to-man defense against, 239
  moving without the ball, 222–224
  passing in, 221–222
  zone, in box lacrosse, 219
motorcycle (double over) grip, 129, 299
mouth guards, 24
movies featuring lacrosse, 296
moving with the ball
  bull dodge, 82
  after catching, 73
  dodging, 79–81
  inside-slide move, 82, 88
  outside-slide move, 82, 88
  protecting the ball in the stick, 78, 79
  skills needed for, 39
  spins, inside and outside, 82, 88
  taking a check, 68, 69, 78–79
moving without the ball. *See also* cuts
  cutting through the middle, 222–223
  effectively, 39
  faking, 81
  getting open for a pass, 74, 81, 223
  in motion offense, 222–224
  setting picks, 223–224
  watching lacrosse, 254
  in zone offense, 217
MSG Network, 261, 310
Murray, Bruce (player), 281

## • N •

National Collegiate Athletic Association
  (NCAA), 11, 260–261, 278
National Lacrosse League (NLL)
  30-second shot clock, 53, 305
  basics, 276–279
  broadcast games, 260
  defined, 302
  faceoffs in, 130
  franchise changes in, 279
  NCAA players in, 278
  offense-defense system in, 37
  stick-checking in, 41, 105

top players, 280–282
Web site, 309
wraparound checks in, 105, 151
neck and shoulder stretches, 177
Neporent, Liz *(Weight Training For Dummies)*, 185
net, 49, 57
neutral zone, 302
no-look pass, 302
non-releasable penalty, 302

## • O •

off-ball-side defending, 107–108
offense. *See also* set plays
  attacking in, 144–145
  balancing freedom and structure, 143
  in box lacrosse, 141
  drills, 146–148
  fast-break system, 208, 227–228
  in field lacrosse, 139–140, 142
  field vision for, 40
  initiating from man-to-man defense, 235
  man-down, 170
  man-to-man, 219–220, 225–226, 301
  man-up, 157–167
  mistakes in, 144
  motion, 219, 221–225, 302
  objectives of, 142
  pick-and-roll, 34, 35, 144, 302
  players, 37, 139–140
  screen, 303
  sets, 146
  simple and sound, 143
  slow-down system, 208–209
  stall, 304
  started by goaltender, 42, 123–124, 257
  team philosophy for, 142–145
  watching lacrosse, 254–255
  in women's lacrosse, 142, 228–230
  zone, 214–219, 306
offense-defense system, 37
offensive coach's role, 52
offensive players
  defensive players versus, 37
  keys for, 37–40
  roles of, 139–142

offensive skills. *See also* passing; shooting
  catching, 38, 69–70, 71
  coaching, 201
  cradling, 38, 66–69
  dodging, 79–81
  drills, 74–78, 83–87, 98–100, 146–148,
    183–184
  moving with the ball, 39, 73, 78–82, 88
  moving without the ball, 39, 74, 81
  overview, 13
  taking a check, 68, 69, 78–79
officials
  abuse of, 54
  in brawl situations, 56
  good, traits of, 54–55
  guidelines for, 56
  mini-games watched by, 55
  number of, 52
  responsibilities of, 52–53
  signals by, 57, 59
  types of, 55
offset heads, 20
Olympic debut of lacrosse, 295
1-2-2 formation, 213, 241
1-3-2 formation, 146, 212
1-4-1 formation, 212
1-4-1 set play, 162–163
one-handed cradle (field lacrosse), 67
1-on-0 drills, 75, 83
1-on-1 drills
  beating a defender, 86–87
  bump, 84
  charging defender, 85
  circle (protecting the ball in the stick), 84
  defending against stick handler, 110–111
  defending other offensive players,
    112–113
  equalize pressure, 85
  game, 87
  live half-field, 86–87
  man-in-the-middle, 85
  off the bench, 87
  offense from stationary start with a
    cross-field pass, 86
  offensive-move progression, 86
  taking a check, 84–85
1-on-2 circle drill, 84
one-on-one, going. *See* beating a defender

organizations, 310–311
out of bounds, 44
outcome goals, 189
outdoor lacrosse. *See* field lacrosse;
    women's lacrosse
outlet pass, 302
outside spin, 82, 88
outside-fake move, 81
outside-slide move, 82, 88
overhand pass, 72–73, 302
overhand shot, 95, 96, 302
over-speed training, 179
over-the-shoulder pass or shot, 74, 297

● *P* ●

passing
  basics of, 39
  behind-the-back, 74
  behind-the-back pass, 74, 297
  bounce passes, 74, 77
  catching before thinking about, 74
  clearing pass, 138
  dodging to create room for, 79–81
  grip for, 72
  importance of, 10
  keys to, 73–74, 75
  in man-up plays, 158, 160
  in motion offense, 221–222
  moving the stick forward, 72–73
  no-look pass, 302
  outlet pass, 302
  overhand pass, 72–73, 302
  after picking up a ground ball, 74, 135
  quick stick, 303
  sidearm pass, 304
  stance for, 70, 72
  stick fake, 304
  too much, avoiding, 144
  underhand pass, 305
  when taking a check, avoiding, 79
  wind up for, 76
  in zone offense, 217
passing drills
  distances for, 76
  faking passes and shots, 76
  individual passing, 75

passing drills *(continued)*
  keys to, 75
  partner passing, 76–77
  team passing, 77–78, 146–147
patience
  with kids, 202
  in man-up/power play, 157, 158
  in zone defense, 232
penalties. *See also* extra-man
    opportunities (EMOs)
  2-minute, 60–61
  5-minute, 61, 300
  10-minute, 61
  boarding, 61
  box lacrosse, 60–61
  butt-ending, 61
  charging, 61
  checking from behind, 60
  cross-checking, 47, 60, 299
  defined, 302
  delayed, 57, 299
  ejection of players, 59, 301
  in field lacrosse, 46–48
  fighting, 61
  free position shot, 47, 59, 300
  on goaltenders, 47, 48
  high-sticking, 60
  holding, 60, 300
  hooking, 60
  illegal body check, 60
  illegal stick, 20, 47, 60
  interference, 60
  match, 301
  maximum per player, 47
  misconduct, 302
  non-releasable, 302
  release of penalized players, 59
  slashing, 59, 304
  spearing, 61
  times for, 58, 60–61, 157
  too many players on the field, 61
  tripping, 59, 305
  unnecessary roughness, 60
  unsportsmanlike conduct, 60, 61
  warding off, 67, 305
  in women's lacrosse, 28
penalty area, 302
perimeter shots. *See* long shots
personal fouls (field lacrosse), 59–60

physical conditioning
  benefits of, 172–173
  eating and drinking, 188
  importance of, 15
  improving quickness and agility, 183–185
  running for, 178–183
  sleep for, 188
  stretching for, 173–177
  tips for, 171
  weights for, 185–187
physical contact. *See* checking
pick-and-roll
  in box lacrosse, 226
  cornerman's role in, 35
  defending against, 155
  defined, 302
  mistakes in defending, 150
  mistakes in executing, 144
  in motion offense, 224–225
  pick set by creaseman, 34
picks. *See also* pick-and-roll
  communicating about, 102
  defending against, 153–154
  defensive drill for, 111–112
  mistakes in, 144
  in motion offense, 223–224
  setting, 34, 223–224
  top pick play, 165
  up pick play, 165
Pietramala, Dave (player), 287
players
  in box lacrosse, 32–37
  defensive, 37, 40–41
  ejection of, 59, 301
  in field lacrosse, 27–32
  line (box lacrosse), 32
  line changes, 52
  maximum penalties per player, 47
  number for box lacrosse, 10, 52
  number for field lacrosse, 10, 27, 51
  number for women's lacrosse, 12, 27, 28, 43, 51
  offensive, 37–40
  selecting for team, 199–200
  ten greatest, 285–288
  top players, MLL, 273–276
  top players, NLL, 280–282
  in women's lacrosse, 28, 29

playing surface
  arc (women's lacrosse), 44
  best areas to shoot from, 95
  crease, 298
  faceoff X, 299
  field vision for, 40
  goal-line extended, 300
  layout for box lacrosse, 48–50
  layout for field lacrosse, 44–45
  neutral zone, 302
  penalty area, 302
  playing the proper side of the floor, 33
  restraining lines (box lacrosse), 49
  restraining lines (field lacrosse), 303
  sidelines, 304
  size for box lacrosse, 10, 48–49
  size for field lacrosse, 10, 44
  size for women's lacrosse, 12, 28, 44
  substitution box (field lacrosse), 46
  wings, 305
playing systems. See also style of play
  defensive, 231–232
  defined, 207
  factors for deciding on, 210–211
  fast-break offense, 208, 227–228
  keeping simple, 209–210
  man-to-man defense, 232, 233–240, 301
  offensive, 208–211
  slow-down offense, 208–209
  zone defense, 232, 240–244, 306
plunger method, 129, 303
plyometrics, 179
pocket
  for box lacrosse, 19
  creating, 20
  defined, 303
  evolution of, 18
  for field lacrosse, 19
  for shooters' sticks, 90
pointman (box lacrosse), 36, 141, 303
poke check, 105, 107, 303
Pollock, Sean (player), 281
position of readiness, 151
positioning
  ball-side, 108
  defensive, 104–105
  maintaining floor position, 155
  moving before the ball, 108

  off-ball-side, 107–108
  in zone offense, 217
positive self-talk, 191–192
possession. See also faceoffs; ground balls
  clears, 125, 137–138, 151
  draws (women's lacrosse), 28, 46,
    53, 127, 299
  importance of, 14
  rides, 125, 135–137, 303
  ways of gaining, 53, 125
  ways of losing, 54, 136
Powell, Casey (player), 136, 281, 288
Powell, Mikey (player), 288
power plays. See extra-man opportunities
    (EMOs)
pre-game routine, 194
preparation. See mental preparation;
    physical conditioning
pressuring the stick handler
  double-teaming, 243–244
  in man-to-man defense, 236, 237, 240
  overview, 150–151
professional lacrosse. See also watching
    lacrosse; specific leagues
  broadcast games, 260
  debut of, 295
  Major League Lacrosse, 271–276
  National Lacrosse League, 276–282
protecting the ball in the stick, 78, 79, 84
push method, 129, 303

# • Q •

quad and hamstring stretches, 175–176
Queener, Brett (player), 275
question-mark dodge, 81
quick stick, 303
quickness. See agility and quickness

# • R •

Rabil, Paul (player), 275
rake method, 129, 303
Ratcliff, Lewis (player), 281
ready stance, 42, 118–119
reflex goalies, 91, 257
reflex saves, 42, 121, 123
regular play, 167

relaxing, 78, 82, 189–190
resistance (weight) training, 179, 185–187
resources
  magazines, 307
  organizations, 310–311
  television networks, 260–261, 309–310
  Web sites, 308–309
respect, 292
restraining lines, 49, 303
rib or kidney pads, 23
rides, 125, 135–137, 140, 303
rip, defined, 303
Rogers Sportsnet, 260, 310
roll dodge, 80
roll with the rotation play, 163–164
rotations (box lacrosse), 238, 239
routine, pre-game, 194
rules. *See also* penalties; times
  3-second rule, 44, 229, 305
  5-second count, 45, 58, 59
  10-second count, 46
  30-second rule, 305
  crease violation, 44–45, 58, 59
  defensive clear-out, 45
  evolution of, 51
  game violations, 58, 59
  goal size, 10–11, 44
  illegal stick, 20, 47, 60
  net size, 49
  number of players, 10, 27, 28, 43, 51–52
  out of bounds, 44
  personal fouls, 59–60
  playing surface size, 10, 12, 28, 44, 48–49
  pocket width, 19
  stick head, 19
  stick length, 20
  stopping play, 53
  technical fouls, 60
running
  conditioning drills, 181–183
  correct form for, 179–180
  increasing speed, 179, 180
  interval training, 180
  long-distance, 178–179
  off-season and pre-season, 178–179
  in-season, 179–183
  stretching for speed, 177
  stride frequency, 179
running shoes, 24

• *S* •

Sanderson, Josh (player), 281
Schlosberg, Suzanne (*Weight Training
    For Dummies*), 185
Schwartzman, Jesse (player), 275
scoop pickup, 133–134
scoring. *See also* shooting
  in box lacrosse versus field lacrosse, 118
  goal disallowed signal, 57
  goal scored signal, 57
  by goaltenders, 124
  lacrosse as high scoring, 290
  pointers for, 142
  two-point goal, 305
scouting, importance of, 15
screens
  3-3 set with a screen, 162, 163
  communicating about, 102
  defending against, 154
  defined, 303
self-talk, positive, 191–192
set plays. *See also* pick-and-roll
  1-4-1, 162–163
  3-3 camouflage, 164, 166
  3-3 set with a screen, 162, 163
  advantages of, 225
  in box lacrosse, 165, 167, 219, 226
  crease pass and shoot, 161–162
  defined, 304
  down screen, 226
  give-and-go, 224, 300
  against man-short defense, 160–166
  in man-to-man offense, 220
  in motion offense, 224–225
  roll with the rotation, 163–164
  watching lacrosse, 254
  wide 2-2-2 set, 164, 166
  in women's lacrosse, 230
setting picks, 34, 223–224. *See also* picks
settled, defined, 303
Shaw TV, 260, 310
shin guards, 304
shoes, 24
shooters' sticks, 90
shooting. *See also* faking shots
  30-second rule, 305
  30-second shot clock, 53, 305

60-second shot clock, 46, 53
automatics, 94
basics of, 39
after beating a defender, 88
behind-the-back shot, 297
bombing, 92
on breakaways, 97
close-in shots, 96–97, 99–100
cocking the stick, 93
by cornermen, 34
dodging to create room for, 79–81
drills, 75, 97–100, 147
focus on good shot selection, 145
follow-through for, 94
form for, 91
getting the ball past the goalie, 90–91,
 92, 94, 97
grip for, 66
hop-step for, 93
keys to, 75
long shots, 92–95, 98–99, 220
in man-up plays, 159, 160, 161
missed shots, 44, 256
overhand shot, 95, 96, 302
pointers for, 142, 145
by pointman, 36
problems, resolving, 91–92
quick stick, 303
rip, defined, 303
shooters' sticks, 90
sidearm shot, 304
stick fake, 304
telegraphing your shot, 92
underhand shot, 305
wind up for, 70
in women's lacrosse, 229
against zone defense, 218
shooting percentage, 89
shooting strings, 304
shot clock
 30-second, 53, 305
 60-second, 46, 53
 violations, 58, 59
shoulder and neck stretches, 177
shoulder pads, 23
shuffle step, 103, 106
sidearm pass, 304
sidearm shot, 96, 304

sidelines, 304
signals by officials, 57, 59
six-on-five situation, 167
60-second shot clock, 46, 53
slashing, 105, 304
slashing penalty, 59, 304
sleep, pre-game, 188
sliding, 151, 238, 304
slough, 304
slow-down offense system, 209
small cradle, 67, 68
Smith, Alex (player), 129, 275
soft hands, 91
spearing, 61
specialty teams. *See also* extra-man
 opportunities (EMOs)
 defined, 304
 importance of, 157
 man-down defense, 168–169
 man-down drills, 170
 man-down offense, 170
 man-up defense, 167
 man-up offense, 157–167
 man-up set plays, 160–166
 overview, 14, 157
 six-on-five situation, 167
spectator's view. *See* watching lacrosse
speed, increasing, 177, 179, 180
sphere (women's lacrosse), 304
spins, inside and outside, 82, 88
split dodge, 80, 304
split field, 27
sprinting. *See* running
stack set, 230
stalling, 45, 46, 304
stance or body position. *See also*
 positioning
 for catching, 69
 defensive position of readiness, 151
 for faceoffs, 126, 128
 following the ball by goalies, 119–120
 for off-ball defense, 108
 for passing, 70, 72
 for picking up ground balls, 134
 ready stance of goalies, 42, 118–119
 for taking a check, 79
 in women's lacrosse defense, 244–245
staying in the zone, 172

Steenhuis, Mark (player), 281
stick fake, 92, 304
stick handling. *See also* passing; shooting
  catching, 38, 69–70, 71
  cradling, 38, 66–69
  drills, 74–78, 83–87
  great skills, described, 65
  grip for, 66
  importance of, 144
  in man-to-man offense, 220
  offense requiring, 13, 38
  practice needed for, 66
stick saves, 42, 120
stick-checking, 41, 104, 105, 304
sticks
  butt end, 66, 298
  for defense, 20
  evolution of, 18
  for faceoffs, 128
  handle, 18, 20
  illegal, 20, 47, 60
  lengths, 20, 25, 301
  for offensive players, 139
  offset heads, 20
  pocket, 18, 19, 20, 90, 303
  shooters', 90
  shooting strings, 304
  stick head, 19–20
  for women's lacrosse, 12, 18, 19, 20, 28
  for youth levels, 25
stopping play, 53
stretching
  abdomen and groin stretches, 176
  back stretches, 174
  guidelines for, 173–174
  hamstring and quad stretches, 175–176
  leg stretches, 175
  neck and shoulder stretches, 177
  for running speed, 177
  warming up before, 173
stride frequency, 179
strong-side offense, 213
style of play, 197–198, 207, 209. *See also*
    playing systems
substituting players, 46
Sweeney, Kyle (player), 275
swing play, 165
switching on defense, 153–154, 305

**• T •**

tag game, 85
taking a check. *See also* checking
  avoiding passing during, 79
  drills, 84–85
  grip for, 79
  large cradle for, 68, 69
  relaxing during, 78
  stance for, 79
Tavares, John (player), 281
team drills
  1-on-1 game, 87
  British bulldog game, 85
  offense, 146–148
  passing, 77–78, 146–147
  protecting the ball in the stick, 84
  tag game, 85
team members. *See* players
teamwork. *See* coaching; defense; offense
technical fouls, 60
telegraphing your shot, 92
television. *See* TV
tempo of lacrosse, 290
ten-minute penalties, 61
ten-second count, 46
Tewaaraton Award, 305
thinking
  defensive, 103–104
  finding intelligent players, 200
  by goaltenders, 119
third man in, 61
30-second rule, 305
30-second shot clock, 53, 305
Thompson, Mike (player), 282
Thomson, Merrick (player), 275
3-3 camouflage play, 164, 166
3-3 set with a screen, 162, 163
3-on-2 defensive drills, 156
3-on-3 offense drills (box lacrosse), 148
three-second rule, 44, 229, 305
Time Warner SportsNet, 260, 310
times
  2-minute penalties, 60–61
  3-second rule, 44, 229, 305
  5-minute penalties, 61, 300
  5-second count, 45, 58, 59
  10-minute penalties, 61

10-second count, 46
20-second count, 45, 58, 59
30-second rule, 305
30-second shot clock, 53, 305
60-second shot clock, 46, 53
  for box lacrosse periods, 49
  for faceoffs, 126
  for field lacrosse halves (women), 44
  for field lacrosse quarters (men), 44
  for penalties, 58, 60–61, 157
  for serving penalties, 46–47
too many players on the field, 61
top pick play, 165
top-arm hand, grip for, 66
Toth, Kaleb (player), 282
transition, 198, 240, 305
trap and scoop pickup, 134
tripping, 59, 305
TSN2, 260, 310
turnovers, 137, 144, 255–256, 305
TV
  networks, 260–261, 309–310
  shows featuring lacrosse, 296
  watching lacrosse on, 259–261
twenty-second count, 45, 58, 59
2-1-2 formation, 169, 241
2-2-2 formation, 146, 212
2-2-2 set play, 164, 166
2-3-1 formation, 212, 241
two-minute penalties, 60–61
2-on-0 drills, 76–77, 83–84, 100
2-on-1 drills, 111–112, 155, 182
2-on-2 screen on the ball drill, 148
two-point goal, 305
two-way midfielders, 30

## • *U* •

underhand pass or shot, 305
United States Intercollegiate Lacrosse
    Association, 309, 311
unity, team, 203–204
unnecessary roughness, 60
unsettled, defined, 305
unsportsmanlike conduct, 60
up pick play, 165
US Lacrosse organization, 309, 310
using the trailer, 230

## • *V* •

Vedder, Ethan (player), 116
Veltman, Daryl (player), 282
violation, defined, 305
visualization, 191

## • *W* •

wall ball, 134
Walters, Joe (player), 276
warding off, 67, 305
watching lacrosse
  community-type atmosphere, 253, 291, 292
  comparison with basketball, 250, 251–253
  comparison with hockey, 35, 249–251
  defense, 255–256
  end of a close game, 258–259
  excitement of, 289
  fan's perspective, 16
  finding information, 253
  game action, 257–258
  goaltending, 256–257
  offense, 254–255
  rules not important for, 253
  on TV, 259–261
Watson, Bob (player), 122
weather, 291
Web sites. *See* Internet resources
weight training, 179, 185–187
*Weight Training For Dummies* (Neporent
    and Schlosberg), 185
Westervelt, Drew (player), 282
wide 2-2-2 set, 164, 166
Wiles, Luke (player), 282
Williams, Shawn (player), 282
wind up, 70, 76, 102
wingers, 35
wings, 128, 135, 305
WMAR-TV, 261, 310
women's lacrosse. *See also* box lacrosse;
    field lacrosse
  3-second rule, 44, 229, 305
  attack positions, 29
  attack wings, 142, 297
  catching in, 70
  contact not allowed in, 10, 12, 28, 47

women's lacrosse *(continued)*
cradling as key to ball handling, 67
critical scoring area, 298
defense, 244–246
defensive positions, 29
draws in, 28, 46, 53, 127, 299
equipment for, 22
first game ever played, 11, 294
first NCAA game, 11
first U.S. game, 11
free position shot, 47, 59, 300
greatest players, 285
growing popularity of, 12
icon indicating information about, 5
men's lacrosse compared to, 28
number of players, 12, 27, 28, 43, 51
offense, 142, 228–230
penalties in, 28
playing surface size, 12, 28, 44
set plays, 230
sphere, 304
sticks for, 12, 18, 19, 20, 28
times for halves, 44
World Lacrosse Championship, 269
wraparound check, 105, 151, 305

**• X •**

Xbox LIVE, 260

**• Y •**

youth levels. *See* kids

**• Z •**

zone defense
1-2-2 formation, 241
2-1-2 formation, 241
2-3-1 formation, 241
advantages of, 214–215
in box lacrosse, 241, 242, 244
communication in, 242
defined, 232, 306
double-teaming, 243–244
as patient, 232
philosophy of, 241–243
weaknesses of, 216
zone for top performance, 172
zone offense, 216–219, 306
Zywicki, Jeff (player), 276, 282

## BUSINESS & PERSONAL FINANCE

978-0-470-24600-9

978-0-470-03832-1

**Also available:**
- ✔ Living Well in a Down Economy For Dummies 978-0-470-40117-0
- ✔ Managing For Dummies 978-0-7645-1771-6
- ✔ Marketing For Dummies 978-0-7645-5600-5

- ✔ Negotiating For Dummies 978-0-470-04522-0
- ✔ Small Business Marketing For Dummies 978-0-7645-7839-7
- ✔ Stock Investing For Dummies 978-0-470-40114-9

## EDUCATION, HISTORY & REFERENCE

978-0-7645-2498-1

978-0-470-46244-7

**Also available:**
- ✔ Algebra For Dummies 978-0-7645-5325-7
- ✔ Art History For Dummies 978-0-470-09910-0
- ✔ Chemistry For Dummies 978-0-7645-5430-8
- ✔ French For Dummies 978-0-7645-5193-2

- ✔ Math Word Problems For Dummies 978-0-470-14660-6
- ✔ Speed Reading For Dummies 978-0-470-45744-3
- ✔ Statistics For Dummies 978-0-7645-5423-0
- ✔ World History For Dummies 978-0-470-44654-6

## FOOD, HOME, & MUSIC

978-0-7645-9904-0

978-0-470-43111-5

**Also available:**
- ✔ 30-Minute Meals For Dummies 978-0-7645-2589-6
- ✔ Bartending For Dummies 978-0-470-05056-9
- ✔ Brain Games For Dummies 978-0-470-37378-1
- ✔ Gluten-Free Cooking For Dummies 978-0-470-17810-2

- ✔ Home Improvement All-in-One Desk Reference For Dummies 978-0-7645-5680-7
- ✔ Violin For Dummies 978-0-470-83838-9
- ✔ Wine For Dummies 978-0-470-04579-4

## GARDENING

978-0-470-58161-2

978-0-470-57705-9

**Also available:**
- Gardening Basics For Dummies 978-0-470-03749-2
- Organic Gardening For Dummies 978-0-7645-5320-2
- Sustainable Landscaping For Dummies 978-0-470-41149-0
- Vegetable Gardening For Dummies 978-0-470-49870-5

## GREEN/SUSTAINABLE

978-0-470-84098-6     978-0-470-17569-9

**Also available:**
- Alternative Energy For Dummies 978-0-470-43062-0
- Energy Efficient Homes For Dummies 978-0-470-37602-7
- Green Building & Remodeling For Dummies 978-0-470-17559-0
- Green Cleaning For Dummies 978-0-470-39106-8
- Green Your Home All-in-One For Dummies 978-0-470-40778-3

## HEALTH & SELF-HELP

978-0-471-77383-2     978-0-470-44539-6

**Also available:**
- Borderline Personality Disorder For Dummies 978-0-470-46653-7
- Breast Cancer For Dummies 978-0-7645-2482-0
- Cognitive Behavioural Therapy For Dummies 978-0-470-01838-5
- Depression For Dummies 978-0-7645-3900-8
- Diabetes For Dummies 978-0-7645-6820-6
- Healthy Aging For Dummies 978-0-470-14975-1
- Improving Your Memory For Dummies 978-0-7645-5435-3
- Neuro-linguistic Programming For Dummies 978-0-7645-7028-5
- Understanding Autism For Dummies 978-0-7645-2547-6

## HOBBIES & CRAFTS

978-0-470-28747-7     978-0-470-29112-2

**Also available:**
- Crochet Patterns For Dummies 97-0-470-04555-8
- Digital Scrapbooking For Dummies 978-0-7645-8419-0
- Home Decorating For Dummies 978-0-7645-4156-8
- Knitting Patterns For Dummies 978-0-470-04556-5
- Oil Painting For Dummies 978-0-470-18230-7
- Quilting For Dummies 978-0-7645-9799-2
- Sewing For Dummies 978-0-7645-6847-3
- Word Searches For Dummies 978-0-470-45366-7

## HOME & BUSINESS COMPUTER BASICS

978-0-470-49743-2    978-0-470-04059-1

**Also available:**
- Excel 2007 For Dummies 978-0-470-03737-9
- Office 2007 All-in-One Desk Reference For Dummies 978-0-471-78279-7
- Pay Per Click Search Engine Marketing For Dummies 978-0-471-75494-7

- PCs For Dummies 978-0-7645-8958-4
- Search Engine Marketing For Dummies 978-0-471-97998-2
- Web Analytics For Dummies 9780-470-09824-0

## INTERNET & DIGITAL MEDIA

978-0-470-44417-7    978-0-470-39062-7

**Also available:**
- Blogging For Dummies 978-0-471-77084-8
- MySpace For Dummies 978-0-470-09529-4

- The Internet For Dummies 978-0-470-12174-0
- Twitter For Dummies 978-0-470-47991-9
- YouTube For Dummies 978-0-470-14925-6

## MACINTOSH

978-0-470-27817-8    978-0-470-43541-0

**Also available:**
- iMac For Dummies 978-0-470-13386-6
- iPod Touch For Dummies 978-0-470-50530-4
- iPod & iTunes For Dummies 978-0-470-39062-7

- MacBook For Dummies 978-0-470-27816-1
- Macs For Seniors For Dummies 978-0-470-43779-7
- Switching to a Mac For Dummies 978-0-470-46661-2

## NETWORKING & SECURITY

978-0-470-53405-2    978-0-470-53791-6

**Also available:**
- Active Directory For Dummies 978-0-470-28720-0
- Firewalls For Dummies 978-0-7645-4048-6

- Identity Theft For Dummies 978-0-470-56521-6
- TCP/IP For Dummies 978-0-470-45060-4
- Wireless All-in-One For Dummies 978-0-470-49013-6

## PETS

978-0-764-58418-3    978-0-470-06805-2

**Also available:**
- Birds For Dummies
  978-0-7645-5139-0
- Boxers For Dummies
  978-0-7645-5285-4
- Cockatiels For Dummies
  978-0-7645-5311-0

- Ferrets For Dummies
  978-0-470-12723-0
- Golden Retrievers For Dummies
  978-0-7645-5267-0
- Horses For Dummies
  978-0-7645-9797-8
- Puppies For Dummies
  978-0-470-03717-1

## SPORTS & FITNESS

978-0-471-76871-5    978-0-470-83828-0

**Also available:**
- Exercise Balls For Dummies
  978-0-7645-5623-4
- Coaching Hockey For Dummies
  978-0-470-83685-9
- Coaching Volleyball For Dummies
  978-0-470-46469-4
- Fitness For Dummies
  978-0-7645-7851-9

- Mixed Martial Arts For Dummies
  978-0-470-39071-9
- Rugby For Dummies
  978-0-470-15327-7
- Ten Minute Tone-Ups For
  Dummies 978-0-7645-7207-4
- Wilderness Survival For Dummies
  978-0-470-45306-3
- Yoga with Weights For Dummies
  978-0-471-74937-0

## WEB DEVELOPMENT

978-0-470-38541-8    978-0-470-38535-7

**Also available:**
- Adobe Creative Suite 4 Web
  Premium All-in-One For Dummies
  978-0-470-41407-1
- CSS Web Design For Dummies
  978-0-7645-8425-1
- HTML, XHTML & CSS For Dummies
  978-0-470-23847-9

- Joomla! For Dummies
  978-0-470-43287-7
- Web Design For Dummies
  978-0-471-78117-2
- Wikis For Dummies
  978-0-470-04399-8